*Camus*

⚘

# Camus

## Love and Sexuality

Anthony Rizzuto

University Press of Florida

*Gainesville · Tallahassee · Tampa · Boca Raton*
*Pensacola · Orlando · Miami · Jacksonville*

03  02  01  00  99  98  6  5  4  3  2  1

*Library of Congress Cataloging-in-Publication Data*
Rizzuto, Anthony.
Camus: love and sexuality / Anthony Rizzuto.
p. cm.
Includes bibliographical references and index.
ISBN 0-8130-1589-8 (alk. paper)
1. Camus, Albert, 1913–1960—Criticism and interpretation.
2. Love in literature. 3. Sex in literature. I. Title.
PQ2605.A3734Z7343  1998
848'.91409—dc21  98-5411

The University Press of Florida is the scholarly publishing agency for the State
University System of Florida, comprised of Florida A & M University, Florida
Atlantic University, Florida International University, Florida State University,
University of Central Florida, University of Florida, University of North
Florida, University of South Florida, and University of West Florida.

University Press of Florida
15 Northwest 15th Street
Gainesville, FL 32611
http://nersp.nerdc.ufl.edu/~upf

This book is dedicated to my sons, Carlo and Tony

# Contents

# Acknowledgments

I owe more thanks than I can express to my friends and colleagues Frederick Brown, Carol Blum, Ruth Weinreb, Raymond Gay-Crosier, and English Showalter, Jr., who read the manuscript and gave me the benefit of their suggestions.

My thanks to the administrators at the State University of New York at Stony Brook, to past and present chairpersons of the Department of French and Italian whose generous travel grants allowed me to test my ideas at national and international conferences. Many thanks also to all the members of the *Société des Etudes Camusiennes* who encouraged my work and whose books and articles set the highest standards of scholarship.

I received invaluable aid from Debbie DeBellis, who, with Marie Sweatt, prepared the manuscript, and from Mark Shaiman, who prepared the bibliography. I thank them all.

Portions of this book, in different form, appeared in *Albert Camus: Les Extrèmes et l'équilibre, Actes du Colloque de Keele* (1994), *Modern Language Studies* (Winter 1983), and the *MIFLC Review 5* (1995). This material has been reprinted by permission.

In translating French quotations into English, I have been occasionally required to sacrifice stylistic considerations to ensure the most accurate possible rendering of the original text.

# Abbreviations

The sources from which I have quoted most frequently are abbreviated as follows:

| | |
|---|---|
| C1 | *Carnets*, vol. 1 |
| C2 | *Carnets*, vol. 2 |
| C3 | *Carnets*, vol. 3 |
| CAC3 | *Fragments d'un combat, Cahiers Albert Camus,* 3 |
| CAC4 | *Caligula version de 1941, suivi de La Poétique du premier Caligula, Cahiers Albert Camus,* 4 |
| CAC5 | *Albert Camus, oeuvre fermée, oeuvre ouverte? Cahiers Albert Camus,* 5 |
| CAC6 | *Albert Camus, éditorialiste à L'Express, Cahiers Albert Camus,* 6 |
| CG | *Correspondance: Albert Camus–Jean Grenier* |
| E | *Essais* |
| JV | *Journaux de voyages* |
| MH | *La Mort heureuse, Cahiers Albert Camus,* 1 |
| PC | *Le Premier Camus, Cahiers Albert Camus,* 2 |
| PH | *Le Premier homme, Cahiers Albert Camus,* 7 |
| TRN | *Théâtre, Récits, Nouvelles* |

# Introduction

The portrayal of intimate relations may reveal an author's view of the world's structure and how human character is constituted within that structure. When the author is Albert Camus, endowed with the energy of genius, questions of love and sexuality become especially pertinent, casting light on what we are and what we might become as products of instinct and culture. These questions, addressed in private notebooks, travel journals, and works of fiction and nonfiction that still have the capacity to move us, arise partly from Camus' analyses of the French and Algerian societies in which he lived, partly from his struggles with his own nature: how he perceived it, what he wanted it to be. Together they shaped his aesthetic achievements. *Nuptials, The Stranger,* and the short stories of *Exile and the Kingdom,* to give three examples, have their unique content, reflecting their author's unique temperament. Camus' works are also coherent in ways that allow readers access to the characters, societies, and landscapes that many of us recognize as ours. Pursuing the contours of his inner geography, Camus also maps our own.

Several of his characters, it is true, would prefer not to ask questions. Martha in *The Misunderstanding* dreams of torrid climates where the sun "kills questions" (*TRN,* 120), leaving behind sated bodies without an inner life, without a trace of soul; the priest in "The Renegade" thinks that it is possible to "settle love's accounts" (*TRN,* 1582) as if solving an arithmetic problem. In this they are following their author, who, at times, willingly turned away from society and from himself, only to return with even greater resolve.

In some of his early works, Camus too thought he could settle the question of love once and for all. He did so by dismissing the question. He would view love as an artifact, the moral and intellectual construct of a class or culture that unnecessarily complicated when it did not deliberately dilute the power of a sexual impulse. Love, unfortunately, was often keyed to theological concepts of eternal life, and Camus mocked "those who misrepresent it as an image of eternity" (*C2,* 75). Love was also too much a part of the social contract. The lover could summon the beloved into her body so that, with her consent, her character might suffuse her flesh, there to be enjoyed. As such she was no longer a mere body—which Camus would have preferred—but an embodiment. The beloved, initially veiled behind polite behavior and the clichés of public ceremony, falls in love and into her naked body and becomes vulnerable, exposed to a man as never before. Camus understood this and for a long time wanted no part of it. A woman, at best, would be not a person but a means, an instrument of sexual release. Whereas love might have something to do with the discovery of a woman and the subsequent knowledge of her character, something also to do with self-discovery and self-knowledge, a young Camus felt that there was fundamentally nothing to know or very little that could be known.

This obscure but tenacious conviction had much to do with Camus' mother. She was the most important woman in his life, a central character or implied presence in many of his works, the woman whom he loved "most in this world" (PH, 188). He knew her, or thought he did, and decided there was nothing else and no one else he needed to know. Love was about other persons, other subjects, who had their own delimiting perspectives, rights, and requirements. Sex instead was about depersonalized, erotic forces in nature, usually a maternal nature, and about synchronizing one's body with these powerful forces. Love was about character, reciprocity, potential joy and suffering with and through another person. Sex was about pleasure, innocence, and the absence of character.

"We must," Camus wrote, "experience love before experiencing ethics" (C2, 252). This simple command conveys a radical message. It was simple because Camus thought, rightly or wrongly, that he came from a North African culture that had long since put this command into practice. "I really believe," he informed his readers, "that virtue is a meaningless word in all Algeria" (E, 72), adding for emphasis that there was "nothing to hang an ethic on" (E, 74–75). Morality tended to have a leveling and normalizing influence on the potentially anarchic properties of intense, sexual experience, and the banal, average European preferred "ethics and tepid emotions" (C3, 78).

Had Camus written the word "sex" instead of "love," our response to his command would be somewhat less complicated. He would then be describing the physiological surge of erotic desire that, in and for itself, may know nothing of virtue or the obstructive laws of society. If morality has to make its presence felt at all, it must wait and then follow the dictates of sex—and not the other way around. He uses, however, the word "love" and prefaces it with an imperious "we must." Camus would disembed the experience of love from the topsoil of civilization, from morality, from those presumably nurturing notions of what love is or should be. Only then could love simplify and revitalize itself in the form of an individual's sexual exaltation enjoyed in a state of innocence. It would no longer be polluted by the prescriptions of law, the practice of virtue, the feelings of responsibility and guilt, or any other oppressive construct of a collective, moral system.

Camus, however, changed. He gradually came to the realization that perhaps his praise of sex masked a fundamental inability to love. Looking within himself without equivocation, he also discovered a sick and discontented civilization. Camus became convinced that Europe was dying for lack of love, "is convulsing" (C2, 92), as he vividly put it, and that love had to be returned to the center of cultural existence. He had in mind two world wars, the Holocaust, the political nihilisms of Nazism and communism that had become intellectually respectable among so many of his peers. What he ultimately had in mind was the nihilism and the emptiness he sensed within himself. Camus suspected that he too was diseased. That self-knowledge came slowly, and with it came revisions in his views of love and sexuality.

My goal is to trace Camus' evolution as a writer through those questions of love and sexuality that engaged him deeply throughout his life. That evolution did not follow a straight and steady line of development. Camus could turn back as many times as he moved forward. But even among the most disparate episodes and characters—Meursault's sexual relationship with Marie, Kaliayev's love scene with Dora, Jonas and his children, Don Juan, Patrice Mersault's macho swagger, Camus' lyrical odes to innocence, above all else Camus and his mother in *The First Man*, his unfinished novel—there are constant coordinates. Taken together, they argue Camus' sustained commitment to portray intimate relations so as to understand what he was and what we are as erotic beings and how individuals and societies may live or die by their views and practices of love.

## CHAPTER 1

# The Absence of Questions

Camus' characters, for the most part, have no biological future. In *The Plague*, Bernard Rieux is childless and Jean Tarrou unmarried, as are Meursault in *The Stranger*, Clamence in *The Fall*, Daru in "The Guest," and D'Arrast in "The Growing Stone."[1] Jan, also childless, is murdered by his mother and sister in *The Misunderstanding*. Dora, in *The Just Assassins*, devoting her life to the Russian Revolution and required to suppress private feelings, wonders if she is a woman. In the short story "The Adulterous Woman," the heroine Janine is childless and treats her husband, Marcel, like a child. These and other examples underscore the climate of desolate isolation so pervasive in Camus' fiction.

They also underscore Camus' concern as to whether he was indeed a novelist at all, at least the kind of novelist he wanted to become before his untimely death at the age of forty-six. Invoking Leo Tolstoy and "a liking for people" (*E*, 1132), Camus, already well along in his career, expressed the desire to create new and different characters who, instead of confronting the objective fact of death, preferred to confront the subjective compromises of everyday life. He achieved this ambition in several of the short stories in *Exile and the Kingdom* and, above all, in *The First Man*.

In the middle of his life and speaking as a professional writer, Camus asked himself two basic questions: "Was I wrong in accepting the simplest human tasks and duties, such as having children? In the end, does one have the right to have children, to assume the human condition?" (*C2*, 156). If we take these questions seriously—and I think we must if we are to understand Camus—then most of his characters assume a different human condition. They contemplate death and organize their energies so they can deal lucidly with death's finality. Given this heroic enterprise, the business of love, marriage, procreation, even work, activities of everyday life that were once a proper subject for fiction, might seem irrelevant or insufficiently dramatic.

That most of Camus' characters are unmarried or childless presents a paradox. Throughout his life and in varying degrees, Camus stressed the human body as a vehicle for shaping happiness. The body suppresses all hope of an afterlife because it offers conclusive evidence of death. Any civilization that organizes itself around such hope, on theological foundations, commits itself to deforming, perhaps even denying, the body's natural impulses and needs for the ostensible purpose of preparing each person for a future existence he or she cannot imagine. The rediscovery of one's body puts the pursuit of happiness almost entirely in an individual's own hands.

Camus, in his published works up to and including *The Myth of Sisyphus,* bent many of his efforts toward retrieving the human body from an unnatural body politic. In so doing, it was his firm conviction that both stood to gain. "The body," he argues, constitutes "culture's true direction" (*C1,* 90) for the essential reason that it demonstrates "our limits" (*C1,* 90). It is therefore incumbent upon individuals and societies to "bring intellect back to the body" (*C1,* 128), back to our mortal condition. Camus is unhappy in Paris (as opposed to Algiers) because "here the body no longer has any prestige" (*C1,* 205). He is unhappy with French theater: "The body on stage: all of contemporary French theater (except for Barrault) has neglected it" (*C1,* 237). This body, however, though released from theological and secular laws, hardly ever reproduces.

When Camus asked himself if he had the right to have children, to assume the human condition, and asked these questions in such a way as to make one proposition dependent on the other, he was experiencing the traditional dilemma of the artist trying to balance the pressing claims of his art and political commitments against the equally pressing claims of his family, a dilemma that Camus, divorced, remarried, and the father of twins, evidently felt personally. These two private questions, however, assume a much broader and more public significance in his works. They lead us beyond the conflict between personal freedom and familial duties into other, more radical situations where men in general, and not just artists, dream of sterility or purity or else a personal, sexual conduct that resolutely refuses to submit to any of the commandments of social legislation.

To examine this paradox of the human body condemned to death but incapable or unwilling to marry or reproduce, it is necessary to reread Camus' early writings such as *Wrong Side and Right Side* and *The Happy Death,* and most particularly his essays written between 1937 and 1939 and grouped together under the title *Nuptials.* It is in these essays, "Nuptials in Tipasa," "The Wind in Djémila," "Summer in Algiers," and "The Desert," that Camus establishes the priority of the human body over intellect, marriage, and work, establishes the proper relationships between the male body, sex, and love, and begins to examine the consequences of these new arrangements.

The opening line of the first essay, "Nuptials in Tipasa," reads: "In the Spring, Tipasa is inhabited by the gods" (*E, 55*). The gods are there, plural, pagan, and physical, and the essay describes the arrival of Camus, who quickly takes his place among them. Preparations or initiations are not required. He already belongs. The presence of gods in the essay's first line is only the initial step in directing readers away from familiar Judeo-Christian assumptions about human nature and morality toward stranger perspectives that come into focus as the essays progress.

Camus resembles the gods in their uncensored sensuality, but he differs from them in one important respect. The gods "speak in the sun and in the odor of absinth plants" (*E, 55*). Camus himself does not speak. He writes. The sensuality of the gods is direct and unmediated, their speech indissolubly joined to certain physical manifestations of life. Their speech is physical and therefore felt more immediately, more intensely. Camus' sensuality is also direct through lived experience but indirect through the written word. Men cannot compete with gods. They can only imitate them.

The essay, as Camus practices it here, acquires a special significance insofar as its discursive form is immune to the competing and contradicting voices of real or imagined characters. This absence of characters allows the lyrical essay, Camus' song, to shape itself successfully, with a minimum of distortion, around intensely lived moments. "It is enough for me to live with my whole body and to bear witness with my whole heart" (*E, 59*), Camus writes later in the same essay. The four essays of *Nuptials* belong, therefore, to the category of personal experience and personal testimony. The rhythmic repetition of "whole" hardly allows for doubt or tension. There will be no inner or interpersonal dialogues to create that psychological and moral dissonance that works of art may seek to resolve satisfactorily, if temporarily. When Camus states in his notebooks, "I have to write just as I have to swim, because my body demands it" (*C1, 25*), he is seeking, through his emphasis on the physiological, to eliminate as much as is humanly possible any aesthetic distance between himself and the work at hand, distance that would allow Camus' own intellect—and therefore the reader's—to intervene, question, and evaluate what is offered as a purely physiological and exalting exercise. Aesthetic distance enables reasoned reflection. It allows for questions. Camus' goal is not to ask questions but to affirm a certain number of indisputable truths, to craft a seamless coincidence of thought and action.

In two letters to Jean Grenier after the publication of *Nuptials*, Camus reacts negatively to this style of affirmation: "I will not write like that any more," he assures his teacher and mentor, "above all I will no longer try to conclude" (*CG*, 34). He continues: "I wrote the essays two years ago and I still believed at the time that I had to come up with conclusions" (*CG*, 35).[2] Camus apparently did not abandon this style without regret. Much later, looking back on the novels and plays he had written and lamenting the loss of creative power that would permit his art to conform to or in some absolute way mirror his own nature, he wrote in his preface to *Right Side and Wrong Side:* "The day when I can find a balance between what I am and what I say, that day perhaps . . . I will be able to build the work of art I dream of" (*E*, 12). What he desires is a synthesis between the artist and his art.[3]

There are no questions and no doubts in *Nuptials*. The essays are animated by joyful and compelling certainties. Gods speaking through the sun, powerfully and silently, become paradigms of Camus' goal: to make his art as indistinguishable from his body as are his body's graceful and athletic gestures, to cast his song in the mold of essays written in the first person singular that would celebrate the powers of his body. The artist's challenge in *Nuptials* is to make the silently written and silently read text an approximation of that divine absence of human sound because the polyphony of human voices would produce existential dissonance.[4] In the conclusion to "Nuptials in Tipasa" Camus writes in exaltation: "Sea, countryside, silence, perfumes of this earth, I filled myself with this scented life and I bit deeply into the already golden fruit of the world, overwhelmed at feeling its sweet and strong juice flowing over my lips. Now, neither I nor the world mattered, only the harmony and silence that between us gave birth to love" (*E*, 60).

With "I filled myself" anticipating Meursault's "I opened myself to the world's tender indifference" in *The Stranger* (*TRN*, 1211), Camus is reenacting the fall of man so as to reverse it. There is no woman and no fall. The solitary and sensual act of biting into golden fruit, the forbidden fruit or world ready to be ingested in carnal communion, does not translate into work, childbearing, or disease. It rejects those biblical afflictions that punish a now fallen human condition, those manifestations of a human body divided against itself, dual and forever duplicitous until its ultimate demise. It celebrates instead the human will for a unitary happiness and the aggressive human power to obtain it at any cost.

We are also told that a wordless harmony between Camus and nature engenders love. We realize then that the many lyrical and sensual descriptions of his activities—swimming, loving, walking, running, gathering flowers—are rituals preparing him for this union. Each physical exercise is one more piece of evidence of the body's rich capacity for pleasure. These activities are also rituals because they put him in contact with a nature that, in his view, exists outside historical time. Each physical gesture traced in human time mimes a timeless gesture in nature. Camus is explicit: "To clasp a female body is the same as holding close that strange joy that descends from the sky to the sea" (*E*, 58). He told us in the first sentence that the gods come to Tipasa in the spring. As a full participant, he must therefore synchronize his body with a deeply felt harmony that is only partly human and in fact requires the dissolution of human personality. As he put it: "Neither I nor the world mattered." And the reference to "a female body" is already a step toward celebrating a union of depersonalized masculine and feminine forces. This nature and this love are creative, rituals of the body performed and perfected outside of time, not procreative, performed within an imperfect human society and historical time.[5]

Stylistically, Camus is required to describe his body quite differently from one that is merely carnal, devoid of any divine spark. While swimming, he describes "my arms varnished by water rising out of the sea to turn gold in the sunlight" (*E*, 57). The water's "varnish "and the sun's "gold" transform an athletic body into a living statue, an object of aesthetic beauty that solves the problem of the inner versus the outer self. Later, returning to the shore, he admires his "soft blond hair" (*E*, 57). Camus may appear to be describing himself, but he was never blond. "Soft blond hair" incorporates "to turn gold." This color, as a linguistic and cultural code, sublimates the dark hair traditionally associated with a more animal nature. No episode in *The Stranger* better illustrates the difference between Meursault and Sintès, the sadistic pimp, than Meursault's reaction to his friend's body: "His forearms were very white beneath their black hair. They disgusted me a little" (*TRN*, 1160). Meursault also refuses Sintès' invitation to go to a bordello where one pays for sex, and Sintès is thus made to play Caliban to Meursault's Apollo. Camus describes Raoul's friend in *The Plague* in a similar fashion: "His long, skinny arms, covered with black hair, stuck out of his rolled up shirt sleeves" (*TRN*, 1339). The description of Jonas's wife, Louise, is also calculated to displease the reader: "Louise was . . . small, with very dark skin, hair, and eyes" (*TRN*, 1631). To move from "black hair" to "soft blond hair," therefore, is to move stereotypically up the scale of carnal being toward divine simplicity. Men (and Louise) may have black body hair. Angels are blond.

Although he never subscribed to any religion—Camus was at the very least an agnostic[6]—he nevertheless sensed the body's sacredness, its ability to respond to a timeless and immutable order. This sacredness is rooted as much in death as in life. The first two essays, "Nuptials in Tipasa" and "The Wind in Djémila," situate the reader on a seashore, midway between the ocean on one side and the ancient ruins of Djémila and Tipasa on the other. Camus writes: "The passage of many years has brought these ruins back to the home of their mother" (*E*, 56). This gradual reabsorption of civilization into "mother earth" becomes a key component of the body's destiny. The seashore's middle space between ocean and ruins becomes the human scene where Camus must balance the facts of life and death. Once he can delight in the body's capacity for pleasure and at the same time understand lucidly the body's annihilation, he can then describe "that loving understanding between earth and man released from the human" (*E*, 84). The second half of this bond, "man released from the human," constitutes an essential rite of passage away from the everyday world, personality, and contingency toward a sacred world defined by timelessness and anonymity.[7] "The world," Camus concludes, "always ends up conquering history" (*E*, 65). Only by understanding this plain fact, by incorporating it into the body's pursuit of happiness, can a man achieve this "loving understanding."

Throughout the four essays of *Nuptials* and particularly the third, "Summer in Algiers," Camus wants the reader to understand that his views of the sensual capacities and mortal limits of the body are shared with the Algerians of North Africa. "This race," he writes, "worships the body" (*E*, 74). This same race represents the contemporary rebirth of ancient Greece and its veneration of the body: "For the first time in two thousand years the body is displayed naked on the beaches. . . . The foot race of young men on the Mediterranean shores repeats the magnificent gestures of the athletes of Delos" (*E*, 69). Camus and the Algerians are apparently rejecting the Christian tradition, its religion of the soul at the expense of the body. In so doing, they are accepting the finality of death. Camus puts the matter squarely: "They wagered on flesh, but knew they had to lose" (*E*, 68).

This kinship that Camus feels with his birthplace and his fellow citizens, however, goes only so far. While he was expressing in *Nuptials* his solidarity with the Europeans of North Africa, he was also outlining the tragic plot of *The Stranger*.[8] Camus eventually so distanced himself from his heritage that he left North Africa for Europe. As a radical journalist in the first months of World War II, critical of the Algerian government and colonialism, he had to leave his country or face probable arrest.

In addition to this political necessity, the move to France satisfied Camus' artistic sensibilities, the need to address a wider audience for whom

North African beaches represented, at best, an exotic vacation—in other words, his ambition. In 1936 Camus explained to Jean Grenier: "I am not ambitious and . . . I am satisfied with very little" (*CG*, 27). As the second half of this sentence suggests, however, the subject here is money and the getting of it. Throughout his life, in his letters and private journals, Camus always insisted on his indifference to money. The ambition to write, to be read, and to become famous, however, required Camus to look beyond the borders of Algiers and of his body to address matters of intellect and the conditions of work. There is no contradiction or hypocrisy here if we accept Camus' repeated assertions, examined more fully in the next chapter, that his pride always prevented him from asking about prices, from making purchases, even from negotiating contracts with his publisher Gallimard. The essays of *Nuptials* are not explicit on the subjects of money and society. Camus, nevertheless, foreshadows his break with Algiers when he describes his friend Vincent: "My friend Vincent, who is a cooper and junior breast-stroke champion, has an even simpler view of things. He drinks when he's thirsty, if he desires a woman tries to have sex with her. . . . Then he always says: 'That feels better'" (*E*, 69). This important passage appears in a specific context. Camus is criticizing André Gide, who, in *Food of the Earth*, advised restraining one's desires so as to make those desires more intense. Camus dismisses such a practice as much too cerebral and calls Gide and his followers "those protestants of the flesh" (*E*, 68). Vincent is the carnal south's blunt answer to intellectual northern Europe. Camus, it is true, condemns Gide, but he is not entirely on the side of his friend. Vincent's physical pleasures, unlike Camus', are lacking in poetry, lacking the aesthetic and sacred dimensions that reverberate around Camus' physical activities at Tipasa or Djémila. They are prose. In fact, Vincent is relegated to a footnote. He has no place in the body of the essay.

Camus and Vincent certainly connect through their physical desire for women. In Camus' fond description, thirst and sex, two of the body's basic needs, are given equal weight. Like Vincent, Camus is an expert swimmer, and the season of spring releases in both men their athleticism and sexuality. In the opening pages of "Nuptials in Tipasa" Camus refers, for example, to "the great, free love of nature" (*E*, 56). Nature is therefore exempt from sexual morality, and Camus draws on all his resources as a writer to produce pages saturated in erotic imagery:

The first rocks that the sea sucks with the sound of kisses. (*E*, 55)
The embrace through which, lips to lips, sun and sea have been sighing for so long. (*E*, 57)

Together we go down to the port and man's treasures: the water's warmth and the tanned bodies of women. (*E*, 68)

These passages constitute an elemental hymn to the human body released from sin, chastity, or moderation, rediscovered after centuries of Christianity, and, as Camus amusingly puts it, "complicated clothing" (*E*, 69).[9]

Where Vincent is social and superficial, Camus celebrates a simplicity achieved through direct access to a timeless and anonymous nature. He extols the present moment precisely because the body, liberated from memory and hope, from ancestry and future generations, knows neither past nor future. "The body," he asserts in "The Desert," "is unaware of hope" (*E*, 80). In "The Wind in Djémila" he asks rhetorically: "What can words like the future, self-improvement, and jobs mean here?" (*E*, 63). Again in "The Desert," he calls the Italian painters of the Renaissance "novelists of the body.... They work in that magnificent and futile medium called the present moment" (*E*, 79). In the same essay he learns "that lesson which liberates us from hope and removes us from our history. Twin truths of the body and this present moment" (*E*, 82). By erasing hope and memory, the future and the past, Camus is erasing the inner life. Depth and complexity, psychology itself, are so many contaminants that smudge the body's sacred simplicity, a simplicity that extends to the following description of sexual intercourse: "The two bodies couple and make haste.... Magical night where love's hope is inseparable from rain, sky, and the earth's silence. True harmony of two beings externally joined and who have become indistinguishable through a shared indifference toward all that is not this one moment in the world" (*C1*, 96). Stylistically we are light years away from Vincent's prosaic "tries to have sex with." Camus renders in a convincing way that absolute focus of a sexual moment when lovers are intolerant of the slightest deviation from achieving the goal of overwhelming pleasure. But we are not really dealing with lovers, if a lover is attentive enough to arouse in the beloved a joy that crosses the body's physical boundaries to engage his or her subjective personality. Personalities here yield instead to loving bodies, who in turn blend anonymously with rain, sky, and earth. They are conjoined "externally."

Consequently, there is another complication that Camus rejects. It comes at the precise moment when his friend Vincent, after having slept with the woman, "would marry her if he loved her" (*E*, 69). To understand this complication, we need to remember that Camus' descriptions of the gods inhabiting Tipasa is a literary conceit. He does not believe in the gods.

Camus adopts this language because the sacredness of nature is derived in part from its sexual potency. He describes a bull copulating: "Swift as a bolt of lightning, a single, flashing dagger thrust, the bull's copulation is chaste. It is the copulation of a god. Not pleasure, but a searing flame and sacred annihilation" (C2, 326). It is a male animal, not a man, that achieves this sexual transcendence. Camus removes from the sexual act all references to fertility and insemination, going so far as to equate sex with murder and death. The divine bull, the ultimate, potent male, is sterile.

A sacred nature is a powerful nature. The sky and the earth exist to guarantee sexual plenitude. One wife would be a betrayal of that sexual power, children a betrayal of present pleasure for an uncertain future. In Camus' description of Vincent, the verbs "love" and "marry" function as a stylistic subversion of "desire" and "have sex with." To press this point, Camus goes on to describe a married man: "A thirty year old worker has already played his cards. He awaits the end with his wife and children. . . . Life follows the curve of our great passions, sudden, demanding, generous. It is not a life that is built but burned" (E, 72). Camus is referring to a worker who, like himself, comes from a working-class family. We sense his compassion, his ability to identify with this man's life, and we also observe his distance, his refusal to submit to the man's fate, not to die but to be effectively dead at age thirty, or "burned." Love, once consummated in marriage and children, is consumed.

Describing Belcourt, a working-class district in Algiers where he was brought up, Camus concludes: "I think we can feel a secret shame watching these men from Belcourt who work, defend their wives and children, and often without complaint. . . . There is not much love in the lives I am talking about. I should say that there is not much any more" (E, 76). There may be cruelty in Camus' description of love leading to marriage and children and in turn to the disappearance of love, which may have something to do with his "secret shame." These "men from Belcourt" also have jobs. They work not only out of economic necessity but as a consequence, apparently, of their fallen nature. Certainly Camus himself, who had turned down a job as a teacher and was recently separated from his first wife when he wrote these lines in 1939, understood that he no longer belonged to this social class or shared its unspoken assumptions about work and marriage and about a man and a woman's procreative duties.

These essays are collectively entitled *Nuptials*, but the marriages take place between man and nature. Sexuality here is limitless, and that absence of limits should pass into a man's life. Camus' evocation of extinguished lives in Belcourt, his shame notwithstanding, is an indictment of marriage and procreation, an indictment of what may be the only Judeo-Christian tradition remaining in this French, North African culture and in this lower class.

When Camus describes himself swimming in the Mediterranean, he refers to the "absence of any horizon" (*E, 57*). That absence abolishes a moral as well as a physical geography, which quickly translates into "the right to love without limits" (*E, 57*). Caligula, in the play's early version, makes a similar claim as he defines his absolute difference from everyone else, including present and future generations, on the question of love: "I return to history where those who fear loving too much have kept me a prisoner for so long" (*TRN, 1735*). To become the prisoner of history is to become trapped within a conditioned self limited as much by class and ethics as by genetic codes or some other form of biological destiny. "Loving too much" challenges any society in which sexual passion is checked and bound by prescribed codes of behavior.

Since Vincent is not as free as Camus, we realize how carefully Camus worded his "understanding" with nature. That understanding "gave birth to love." An intimate understanding with nature that gives birth to love is superior to a biological union with a woman that produces children.[10]

The body's limitless sexual potential can be enjoyed on the condition that bodies remain bodies and never achieve anything resembling a personality. This revolt against personality is consistent with the conviction Patrice Mersault expresses in *The Happy Death:* "As for me, I want to be that perfect actor. I could not care less about my personality and I have better things to do than to try and cultivate it" (*MH, 82*). The perfect actor invoked by Mersault functions almost as a platonic ideal to which he aspires, except that the actor, by definition, comes alive through fictive personalities.

Camus is proposing that the erotic hunger for "everything" be the carnal equivalent of a mystical yearning for "one thing." Vincent is merely an average Algerian.[11] Camus, speaking for himself, reinforces Mersault's views about the actor: "To make their gestures coincide with those of the ideal character they embody, to enter a predetermined pattern which they have brought to life with the rhythms of their own heartbeat" (*E, 60*). To realize this incarnation, a human personality, heavy with age and experience and with all the inner familial and cultural crosscurrents that compose an identity, must be simplified, if not entirely obliterated. It could then be easily transposed into fictitious characters who are both dead and complete.[12] This transition is from the real to the ideal, from the living to the already lived. "Here I am, a god among gods" (*E*, 62), Camus concludes triumphantly in "The Desert," the last of the four essays. His flesh, suffused with spirit, becomes divine. All inner disparities have been overcome.

That Camus should enjoy "the festivals of earth and beauty" (*E*, 86) would seem, at first glance, the opposite of spiritual experience except that Camus' language, in its insistence that the human personality represents the ultimate obstacle to a body's redemption, remains, for that reason, intensely spiritual: "What must be expressed here is man's initiation into the festivals of earth and beauty. For, at that very minute, like a neophyte shedding his last veils, he sheds before his god the loose change of his personality" (*E*, 86). Vincent is the only character in *Nuptials* who has a name and becomes therefore a footnote, dropped by the sheer weight of prosaic personality from the rhapsodic lyricism of the essay. If we assume that personality or character is inseparable from the conditioning factors of family and social life, we are not surprised that Camus' erotic lyricism should remain free from names and from psychology. This freedom is particularly evident in his references to women:

> And so I think . . . that my whole horror of death lies in my jealousy for life. I am jealous of those who will live and for whom flowers and desires for women will retain their meaning of flesh and blood. (*E*, 64)
>
> In these flowers as in these women there was a generous opulence, and I did not see that desiring these differed all that much from lusting after those. (*E*, 84)

This fusion of flowers and women contributes to the depersonalization of women, who in turn become brilliant elements of an erotic landscape. The equation of flowers and women is a recurring feature of Camus' writing in *Nuptials*, in other published works, and in his journals. Other examples include the following:

> This splendor of the world, these women and these flowers. (*E*, 84)
>
> Each year the flowering season of girls on the beaches. They have but one season. The year after, they are replaced by other flower-like faces. (*C1*, 226)
>
> Marie came over as we agreed. I really wanted her because she had on a beautiful red and white striped dress and leather sandals. You could make out the outline of her firm breasts and her tan made her face look like a flower. (*TRN*, 1150)

Meursault's description of Marie and her flowerlike face in *The Stranger* is, in and of itself, an uncomplicated, erotic response to a woman. It makes her presence vivid, and it motivates Meursault's arousal. In conjunction with the passages just quoted, however, a pattern emerges in which floral beauty becomes a principal factor in a man's sexual response to a woman. She becomes both beautiful and passive. It might therefore appear logical to accuse Camus of superficiality in his attitude toward women if not outright complacency in stressing their floral passivity. Some feminist critiques on this and other points have already been published, and many more will no doubt follow.[13] These critiques do have some basis in fact, although there is little feminists can say against Camus that he had not already said against himself in *The Fall*. If women are flowers, then they exist to be collected. Camus' goal, however, in almost all instances in which these metaphors are proffered, is to increase the intensity of sexual sensation in both partners. The floral images of women are not ornamental. They are essential to his purpose.

We can study three passages from "Summer in Algiers," *The Happy Death,* and "Love of Life," observing how briefly a woman's presence is felt before she is transformed into an impersonal, sexual force. In the first, Camus describes a woman dancing:

> I remember . . . a magnificent, tall girl who had danced the entire afternoon. She was wearing a jasmin necklace on her tight, blue dress, which was wet with sweat all the way down her back. . . . When she passed by the tables she left behind a scent of flowers and flesh. . . . By evening I could not see her body anymore . . . but blots of white jasmin and black hair revolved around each other against the sky. . . . It is to such evenings that I owe my idea of innocence. I am learning not to separate these beings charged with violence from the sky where their desires revolve. (*E,* 71)

Camus' detailed description of this woman's carnality—flesh, floral perfumes, and sweat intermingling—are developed so that the reader will be surprised, if not shocked, when Camus equates her and all the other dancers with "innocence." The dancers are innocent in part because their guard is down. They are what they are. Camus' gaze also extends beyond them, his descriptions moving to a higher level. The turning point occurs when Camus no longer sees the woman's body. He dissolves it entirely to place in the foreground the impersonal forces of desire now revolving or dancing on their own, liberated from profane flesh, released from identity.[14] Camus is able to transform the dancer because she disappears completely as a subjective presence. The innocence or simplicity of nature requires that disappearance. When Camus claims that he can see no difference between desiring women or flowers, he adds: "The same pure heart sufficed" (*E*, 84). The narrator himself, once his heart is pure, disappears as a subject along with the object of his attention. The emphasis on flesh and blood, on the plural profusion of flowers, desires, and women, becomes the prerequisite for the adjective "pure," which, because it traditionally applies to the spirit or soul, would strike us as astonishing and out of place if Camus did not make it clear that purity is the result of anonymity. A landscape inhabited by the gods leaves little room for human beings, Camus and women included, who wish to retain their human features and imperfections. Gods do not have personalities.

As long as Camus is writing a personal essay and is carried along freely by his erotic impulses, his praise of inexpressive women has no immediate social or psycholgical consequences. In a novel, however, private lyricism gives way to public and interpersonal drama. Camus tried to manage this transposition without compromising his views of love and sexuality in a novel he never published, *The Happy Death*. Its principal character, Patrice Mersault, attempts to relate to women in the same way Camus relates to nature. He describes his lover Marthe: "He sat next to her and, leaning over her parted lips, searched for the signs of her animal divinity" (*MH*, 61). What little character Marthe has disappears altogether. Her open mouth, speechless and inexpressive, is robbed of its communicative function, its ability through language to direct a woman's subjective point of view toward a man's point of view. Instead, it facilitates a man's access to an impersonal, divine force that only the "animal" in her can vouchsafe. Were she a person, she would be willfully active and demand to be interpreted by the man who presumably loves her. As an animal divinity, however, she becomes the passive bearer of "signs" that function through her and lead the man beyond her. For Mersault, she must be both there and not there. Another girlfriend, Lucienne, also becomes transparent: "He looked at Lucienne's full lips and, behind her, at the earth's smile" (*MH*, 204). Camus once again focuses on a woman's mouth so as to focus on the kiss, a point of erotic contact between a man and a woman but not primarily so. The essential point of contact is between man and nature. The attention Mersault pays to Lucienne's lips also allows him to avoid the woman's eyes through which her character might express itself and impede her required descent into animality. If Mersault gives the impression, at times, that he prefers unintelligent women, it is because intelligence, like personality, would obstruct access to divine simplicity. Mersault is perfectly frank: "Mersault noticed Lucienne's silence and the closed expression of her face. He thought that she was probably not very bright and was delighted. There is something divine in soulless beauty and Mersault knew how to respond to it" (*MH*, 144). Lucienne's face is "closed" and "silent," and Mersault rejoices in its inability to speak or to look upon someone meaningfully in the sense of either finding meaning or bestowing it. Mersault gains immeasurably by this absence and decides that female beauty minus soul is essential to a man's spiritual quest.[15]

Camus' most exaggerated, if not grotesque, version of this necessary union between a woman's carnal reality and her inner emptiness appears in the opening pages of "Love of Life" from *Right Side and Wrong Side,* a collection of essays preceding *Nuptials.* Camus is visiting a cafe in Palma and describes a female entertainer. The description covers two full pages, and I will quote some highlights:

> It was a small, very low room. . . . Miraculously fitted into this small space was an orchestra, a bar . . . and the customers squeezed in so tightly shoulder to shoulder they could hardly breathe. Only men. . . . Not one was conscious. All of them were screaming. . . . An ageless dwarf was telling me the story of his life.
>
> Cymbals suddenly crashed and a woman leaped . . . onto the dance floor. . . . I was stunned. The face of a young girl, but sculpted out of a mountain of flesh. . . . The sexual excitement in the room knew no bounds. . . . The room seemed to be crushed.
>
> Standing in the center, sticky with sweat, she lifted up her massive torso. . . . Like an impure goddess rising up from the waves, with her dumb, low forehead and hollow eyes . . . she was like the ignoble and exalting image of life, with all the despair of her empty eyes and the thick sweat of her belly. (*E,* 42)

This complex description is more class conscious than the descriptions of women and places in either *Nuptials* or *The Happy Death.* The cafe belongs to the working class, and its patrons bring to their pleasures a raucous vitality that Camus enjoys and shares. He is still a tourist and an outsider, however, as well as a writer who must function within the scene to participate and outside the scene to describe it. That he is "stunned" by the enormous woman, well-known to everyone else, argues his own strangeness as well as hers. Camus' description compresses the crowded men and the woman's massive flesh into a cramped space. The reference to the "dwarf" is amusing. He is, of course, a dwarf, but he is also dwarfed by the sheer weight of everyone around him. This compression leads to a series of explosions: the patrons "scream," a cymbal "crashes," Camus is "stunned," the room is "crushed." Sexual excitation knows "no bounds."

The ultimate explosion is the woman herself. Her physical nature bursts all norms, her mountainous flesh carrying a prepubescent face. She is both formed and unformed, sexual in her body and sexless in her face. Combining a swollen and powerful physical presence with stupidity, she represents a grotesque and epic exaggeration of Lucienne's stupidity and her "full lips." This entertainer becomes Venus, but a lower-class Venus or "impure goddess." Most important, her eyes are dead. It is their very transparency that, more than any other aspect of her person, allows Camus to identify and recognize her animal divinity. While everyone else is sexually aroused, Camus, while participating in this somewhat aestheticized orgy—the woman sings and dances—looks beyond the collective frenzy to identify a sexuality without human form or identity.

In the same essay Camus offers a revealing aesthetic judgment: "It is with the appearance of smiles and an expressive look in the eyes that the decadence of Greek sculpture and the dispersion of Italian art begin" (*E*, 44). The appearance of the human violates aesthetic perfection. A variation of this same judgment will appear in "The Desert," where Camus evaluates the Italian Renaissance: "They do not paint a smile or a fleeting expression of modesty, regret, or expectation, but a face with its bone structure and its blood's warmth" (*E*, 80). This aesthetically rendered impersonality that Camus admires in the dancer, Mersault's lovers, and the female entertainer reappears on the sacred canvas of sexual nature. The anonymous body does not release an immortal soul; instead, it guarantees a body's boundless pleasure. The following description of a woman's face is a powerful illustration of Camus' sense of the carnal and mystical forces unleashed in a sexual act: "A pale and resplendent face where kisses had removed its makeup and even its expression. Her face was naked" (*C1*, 159). We may accept makeup as a social convention, an act of conformity, a means enabling women to assume a public face. Camus' goal in this act of love, however, is not to remove a "mask" to attain the woman's hidden character about to be revealed to her lover. The explicit goal is to erase her "expression," to remove both her public and private identities, to attain an absolute, not just carnal, nudity.

To simplify and sanctify the body in *Nuptials,* Camus offers comparisons with paintings. It is as if he knew that a written text, his own text, which renders meaning sequentially and therefore through human time, needed these references to painted bodies fixed in an eternally present moment on a flat and silent surface. To call the great Italian painters "novelists of the body" makes no sense as logic but perfect sense as an ideal to which Camus aspires: to flatten and sanctify the body by denying the dualism of the external versus the inner self and by denying or disregarding the procreative process. "All the girls I knew," Camus informed Jean Grenier after a return visit to Algiers, "have become fat mothers" (*CG,* 144). The girls became pregnant and gained weight, filling space within themselves and outside themselves. They "became." For workers in Algiers, women conceive and become historically situated in a human curve composed of a past, a present, and a future. Camus, in contrast, invokes pagan deities in the very first line of *Nuptials* because they are divine, timeless, and self-begotten.

If the reader, however, accepts the notion of gods in the spring as a literary code through which a man's body becomes omnipotent, can we not say the same of Camus' many descriptions of nature as mother? How is this mother different from all other mothers, in particular the "fat mothers" of Algiers? Camus is surely aware, as is the reader, that he is using an image of mother earth that had long since, even by the late 1930s, become a hopeless cliché. That cliché, however, is only a point of departure. The erotic power of Camus' descriptions invites the reader to respond to his images of mother earth literally. The cliché explodes by the sheer force of his sexually explicit language: "The Carob trees are covering all of Algeria with the scent of love. In the evening, after the rain, the entire earth, its womb moistened with almond-scented seed, rests after having yielded all summer to the sun" (*E,* 76). If Camus is a witness to nature's intercourse, he is also witness to a mother's intercourse. As he translates what he sees into his essays, what roles does he play? He is a writer, and he has told us that he is a man. He concludes the passage just quoted: "This scent consecrates the nuptials of man and earth and raises in us the only manly love we can enjoy in this world: generous and mortal" (*E,* 76). This consummation of love between earth and sun, between a man and mother earth, produces two marriages and one incestuous union. Once Camus moves in the direction of a sanctified sexuality that is carnal, unrestricted, and omnipotent, the logic of that journey requires that he celebrate incest, that ultimate transgression in almost all ethical, human societies.

Incest, the union of a son with a maternal nature, is a central and controlling theme in *Nuptials,* so much so that Camus, in one of the defining moments of the book, misreads a sentence scrawled on a wall in Florence: "Alberto fa l'amore con la mia sorella" (*E,* 85). It means "Albert has sex with my sister." Camus reads his own name, "Alberto," and, free-associating, rewrites the sentence in his own mind to reach this conclusion: "I am no longer surprised that Italy is the land of incest . . . of incest openly admitted" (*E,* 85). Camus knew some Italian, and anyone who understands Italian even slightly knows that the sentence does not refer to an incestuous relationship. What Camus imagined that he read was "Albert makes love to his sister," as opposed to "my sister" or "our sister." Camus did not read the objective text and read instead his subjective heart. He became, in spite of himself, psychological.

Camus' claims of manhood, reiterated throughout the four essays, requires that his female conquests be plural and depersonalized while his relationships to the earth be personified and unique, a union of earth and sky, mother and father, mother and son. If the sexuality of Camus' working-class friends produces children, then his omnipotent and transcendent sexuality is sterile. His notion of purity, which required the animal and divine anonymity of women, extends also to his definition of masculinity: "It is not always easy to be a man, even less a man who is pure. But being pure means rediscovering that land of the soul where the world's kinship enters your very senses, where the blood's pulse mingles with the violent throbbings of the sun" (*E,* 75). Pure mankind rests on this recognition of familial kinship, not with society and other individuals but with nature. This underlying kinship that Camus perceives may well transform each woman into a flower, a product of nature, a beautiful image of the incestuous mother but an approximate image only: pleasurable, imperfect, easily discarded, quickly forgotten. And what is erotic here may be a man's body but it is a body that, according to the passage just quoted, takes its sexual cues from the sun, image of a divine father.

Camus wrote in *Nuptials* four of the most erotic essays in the French language, but it is an eroticism that, for all its youthful vitality and uncensored sexuality, is ultimately grounded in purity and sterility. The cliché of "mother earth" is revitalized by Camus, who makes this image and the theme of incest that attends it a controlling force of his writings. That same cliché, moreover, simultaneously affirms and contradicts Camus' own desire to escape psychology. In his attempt to achieve parity with the gods, to attain purity, to be creative, he subverts the human body's capacity to be procreative and assume, in his own words, its "human condition." What finally needs to be stressed, however, is that incest here is a theme, not an act. As Camus, exasperated with reductive identifications of an author with his characters, writes in his essay "The Enigma": "It is possible of course simply to write about incest" (*E*, 863).

It is true that mother and earth occupy the imaginative center of these essays and that women appear as mere flowers, the products of nature, able to reflect but never to compete with that maternal power. If Camus the son, however, is imaginatively contained within the body of the mother, the figure of the mother is in turn contained within the body of the essay.[16] This mutual containment is again realized in "The Desert," during a visit to a church named Santissima Annunziata:

> I was reading inscriptions on the tombstones and the ex-votos. This one had been a kind father and faithful husband; that one was a shrewd merchant as well as the best of husbands. . . . Over there a young girl was the hope of her whole family. . . . But none of that really affected me. Almost all of them, according to the inscriptions, had resigned themselves to death, and why not since they accepted their other duties. Today, children had run into the cloister and were playing leap-frog on the tombs that wanted to perpetuate their virtues. Night then fell, I had sat down on the ground, leaning against a column. A priest smiled at me as he passed by. In the church an organ was playing softly. . . . Alone with my back against the column, I was like someone grabbed by the throat and who shouts his faith. . . . Everything in me protested against so much resignation. . . . I said no with all my strength.
>
> I wanted to define . . . a truth which I felt at the very center of my revolt . . . a truth that extended from the small, late roses of the cloister . . . to the women on that Sunday morning in Florence, their breasts free beneath their thin dresses and their lips moist. . . . This truth might seem a blasphemy to some. (*E*, 83–84)

Appearing near the end of *Nuptials*, Camus' description compares this house consecrated to the Virgin Mother with "the home of their mother" (*E*, 56) in the first essay, that maternal tomb to which all civilizations return. This long description of a living church balances the brief reference to the house of death because it embodies a social ethic for the living based on commandments and therefore on limits. Unlike the "mother-tomb" for which Camus can offer no adjective, much less an extended description, the Christian house is populated: there are the dead, the children, a priest, the sound of organ music, Camus himself as tourist and stranger. This house is a sacred space, but Camus emphasizes its sociability.

Judging from the inscriptions on the tombs, the principal commandment concerns the family. The children appear or rather "invade" the church as if to overthrow it or at least to transform its grim seriousness, its excessive devotion to social meaning. They accomplish this by their childish games, the joy of nonutilitarian and meaningless play. There is potential anarchy in their energy, and Camus' relationship to them is complex. The dead form a group underground; the children play aboveground; and Camus is alone. The dead seek to instill in these unsuspecting children a sense of familial duty to "perpetuate their virtues." Social duties for Camus, however, are synonymous with being "resigned to death," to die before one is dead, like the working-class men of Belcourt who are emotionally dead at age thirty. In Camus' satire, familial duties and virtues are inscribed on tombs made of stone and not on living bodies. Everything in this church, including the fact that it is architecture, a structured and moral space, is opposed to the ocean's "absence of any horizon" in "Nuptials in Tipasa" (*E,* 57) and its amoral equivalent, "to love without bounds" (*E,* 57).

Unlike the gods, who come and go with the seasons, who are cyclical, this church and this God are permanent, and their power extends from this life to that afterlife which Meursault, like Camus, also will reject. Certainly Camus is inside this church, but he inhabits it as a potentially subversive visitor. His vision does not extend upward but outward, toward what he calls "a truth that extended from the small, late roses of the cloister . . . to the women on that Sunday morning." Everything in this inclusive vision is within reach, and Camus replaces prescriptive ethics and the vertical pull of the afterlife with the physical imperatives of this life.

While working on a first draft of this description, Camus had written in his journal: "If I had to write a book on morality, it would be 100 pages long and 99 would be blank. On the last page I would write: 'I only know of one commandment—love'" (*E,* 1363). Church and society would apparently fill in the other ninety-nine pages with other questions, other answers, and other duties. For Camus, there are no questions. "For everything else," he says, referring to both the blank pages and the inscribed tombs, "I said *no*" (*E,* 1363).

It is surely no coincidence that this church is named the "Annunciation," that moment of conception when God becomes a man.[17] Camus has been tracing his own private journey from man to god—a god with a small g, a mortal god. Their paths intersect in a maternal church. Would it be blasphemy to suggest that neither Christ nor Camus had a father and that in this long passage Camus is perhaps more than a tourist?[18] Camus himself is willing to "blaspheme." In using that word he is appropriating a theological vocabulary which the church—and society—might well use against him and will in fact use against Meursault, also a man without a father and who Camus will refer to as "the only Christ we deserve" (*TRN*, 1929).

This entire episode is a first draft of Meursault's confrontation with the chaplain in *The Stranger*. Here the priest smiles at Camus, unaware of the visitor's revolt, and accepts his presence. In revolt against restricted love and familial duties, Camus is a man "grabbed by the throat and who shouts his faith." He is attacked at the throat, the source of his communicative voice and his art. His outburst against the social notions of love and useful procreation, however, is silent, a drama taking place within himself, resolutely personal and private. His revolt is actually quite tolerant and respectful, without being any the less absolute. The priest smiles, and no one hears Camus' scream. The chaplain in *The Stranger*, in contrast, appears uninvited, asks too many questions, and Meursault now takes him by the throat and screams a revolt that everyone hears. To obtain poetic as well as legal justice, Meursault wants his scream balanced on the day of his execution by "cries of hate" (*TRN*, 1212).

The chaplain did his job well, forcing Meursault, who, up to this point, also had been tolerant, if not respectful, of all those personal opinions and social practices that meant little or nothing to him, to give voice to and understand clearly his own alien and subversive nature. But *The Stranger*, unlike *Nuptials*, is tragically conceived.[19]

By entering the church of the Santissima Annunziata Camus enters once again an idealized, preexisting structure. Though he is a stranger, he moves about freely and, in contrast to "Alberto fa l'amore con la mia sorella," understands perfectly well everything he reads. The essays of *Nuptials* are in part organized around such preexisting structures into which Camus enters to take the measure of all things living, to note carefully where he agrees and where he rebels. There are, for example, the actors who synchronize "their gestures and the gestures of the ideal character in a predetermined pattern" (*E*, 60); Camus also describes "a man's initiation into the festivals of earth and beauty" (*E*, 86); finally, all civilizations enter "the home of their mother" (*E*, 56).

Camus the son thus can present himself to the reader as alive and sexually potent within another idealized structure, a nonhistorical and creative maternal nature, his radical response to the mother church and the secular society that organizes its sexual ethics within that church. He achieves omnipotence through symbiosis with an all-powerful mother, an incestuous union, certainly, but one without tragic effect. The reason it is not tragic is that, in the final analysis, incest is itself contained within the written word. It is written down, not acted out, and it reveals itself outside the boundaries of society. No one is involved. The text, after all, is Camus' creation, and it is he, through his own personal, existential effort, who sets limits to that maternal omnipotence. It represents a civilized, humanistic, and liberating alternative to tragically conceived works such as *Caligula, The Stranger, The Misunderstanding,* and *The Plague.* After *Nuptials,* Camus will dramatize social conflicts in which men and women from different social classes become lovers, husbands and wives, sons and mothers. Incest will cease to be an innocent song and become instead an emotional and deadly tyranny. After *Nuptials,* Camus will ask questions.

## CHAPTER 2

# Class, Love, and Sexuality

"Everything," Camus confessed, looking back on his life, "comes from my congenital inability to be bourgeois and a contented bourgeois. The slightest sign of stability in my life terrifies me" (*C3*, 150). Although Camus was employed as a writer and editor at Gallimard and was celebrated as a licensed sensibility, the matter of social class both for himself and the characters in his books remained to be determined. He needed to decide what characters he would present, where in society he would place them, and how he would portray their intimate relations. He needed also to decide how he could situate his male characters in society without any appreciable loss of access to nature, to the universal and timeless. A successful writer, a justifiably proud product of French education and upward mobility, Camus nevertheless remained socially displaced. As late as 1952 he could write: "I am a man without a country" (*C3*, 44). He had long since left Algeria, and he felt out of place in France and in the French middle class.

The inclusive "everything" in the passage quoted above offers the opportunity to extend Camus' confession to questions of love and sexuality. Hardly has the word "bourgeois" appeared on the page when Camus writes, as if by a kind of verbal automatism, "stability." In social and in intimate terms the word could signify conformism as well as emotional atrophy. Caligula himself recoils from that threat: "Loving someone means growing old together. I am not made for that kind of love" (*TRN*, 105). Love, marriage, and fidelity, as social conventions and as concepts of stability preempted by the middle class, would be contributing factors in the mind or the heart's demise.

There is a brief passage in *The Stranger* that illustrates, in a manner similar to Caligula's self-assessment and Camus' confession, the relationship between a man's sexuality and his reaction to conventional assumptions about love and fidelity. Meursault is walking through the streets of Algiers with Marie, whom he has just agreed to marry: "We went for a walk and crossed the main streets to the other side of town. The women were beautiful and I asked Marie if she'd noticed. She said yes and that she understood me. For a while we didn't say anything more" (*TRN*, 1156–57).

The silence following this brief exchange amplifies what both characters have said and gives the reader time to reflect on its importance. Meursault and Marie are unofficially engaged, and their relationship has reached a complex stage. Meursault's reference to the beautiful women in Algiers and what he means by that reference may appear somewhat oblique to the reader but is perfectly clear to Marie. He has no intention of honoring the prescribed vows of marital fidelity. Just before this walk, Marie had remarked that marriage was "a serious matter" (*TRN*, 1156), and Meursault's quick response was a blunt, monosyllabic "no" (*TRN*, 1156). A similar exchange takes place in *Caligula:*

> Mucius: But I love my wife.
> Caligula: Of course you do, my friend, of course you do. But it's so common! (*TRN*, 42)

In contrast, a fisherman in *State of Siege* explains why he married: "I married because that's what you do if you're a man" (*TRN*, 234). What makes this man's pride acceptable to Camus is that the speaker is not of the middle class and that he is explaining his marriage to a totalitarian interrogator. Otherwise, Caligula's contempt for marriage and for all that is common echoes Camus' own personal observation: "I refused to be common" (*C2*, 178).

Camus also called marriage "a pretext for betrayal and lies" (*C1*, 106). One devastating experience that no doubt contributed to this condemnation was his marriage to his first wife, Simone Hié, which he analyzed at the end of his life: "The first woman I loved and to whom I was faithful escaped from me through drugs, through betrayal. Many things in my life were perhaps caused by this, out of vanity, for fear of suffering again. . . . But I in turn escaped from everyone else since and, in a certain sense, I wanted everyone to escape from me" (*C3*, 279).[1] Camus looks into himself and it becomes evident that Meursault's "no" to fidelity is still reverberating years later in this summation. As for Marie, we can decide for ourselves whether her ability to "understand" and accept Meursault is owing to some seductive power in him or to some defect in her. Clearly one of a woman's roles is to understand. Marie does have one moment of lucidity, when she realizes that she may one day hate Meursault for the very same reasons that she presently loves him. For the moment, given the many times she smiles, giggles, or laughs, she seems primarily a woman desperate to please.[2] In this respect, I disagree with Patrick McCarthy's assessment of Marie as a free spirit.[3] She is free to the extent that, breaking with conventional assumptions about appropriate mourning made explicit during Meursault's trial and contributing to his condemnation, she is willing to have sex with him the day after his mother's funeral.[4]

We do note Marie's rapid progress from intercourse to marriage—and it is she who proposes and not the man—and her proposal argues a conventional mind trying to deal with Meursault's unconventional spirit. The transition from sex to love and then to marriage and family represents a gradual entry into a society that is basically nonpermissive. Unfocused sexual energy has anarchic possibilities, and society would harness that energy for productive and reproductive purposes. Camus' Don Juan from *The Myth of Sisyphus*, echoing Meursault, rejects this middle-class ethic: "The regret for desire wasted in sexual enjoyment, that justification for impotence, is alien to him" (*E*, 153). Although every society values sexual potency, its only means of survival, Camus brands the conservative sexual customs of marriage and family as impotent, the better to make Don Juan's revolt absolute and irreversible. The noun "impotence," in its literal sense, is not logical here. What Camus has in mind are men willing to accept sexual limitations, their unmanly submission to the dictates of culture.

Meursault's oblique warning that he will not submit his sexual impulses to the restrictive institution of marriage and its theoretical assumptions of sexual fidelity should come as no surprise to readers familiar with Camus' works written before and immediately following *The Stranger*, in particular *The Happy Death, Nuptials,* and *The Myth of Sisyphus*. One of Camus' goals in *Nuptials* was to remove from erotic desire all notions of hierarchy and taboos, what society, and in particular middle-class society, would deem acceptable or unacceptable sexual behavior. Camus' announcement in *The Myth of Sisyphus*, "I've lost all sense of hierarchy" (*E*, 140), summarizes a view evident throughout his earlier works. Another goal was to jettison all notions of religious or secular utility (sex as procreation), above all, to return sexuality to its primordial purity, set apart from morality, guilt, and the very notion of personality. However deeply we respond to the lyrical and sheer erotic power of *Nuptials*, we need also to be aware of its radical message. Magnificent images and privileged, poetic moments are meant to be extended over an entire lifetime and become, therefore, not only a description of a man's proper place in nature but a prescription for a man's authentic sexual life in society.

Certainly no social marriage could compete with Camus' epic images of sun and earth. He laments: "What most distinguishes man from beast is imagination. Our sexuality therefore can never truly be natural, in other words blind" (*C2*, 94). Blind sexuality would apparently put us in touch

with an unmediated, primordial truth, whereas imagination would intro-
duce into the sexual act alien or fictive considerations such as love, a play-
ful mind, social purpose, even subjectivity. That lucid attention Camus can
bring to the powerful sexual forces he responds to in nature requires a
compensatory blindness to those individuals, women in particular, who
may temporarily embody them. He does not want sex to be a partial or
approximate experience. He wishes it to be a total if not totalizing experience.[5]

When Marie asks Meursault whether he would accept a marriage proposal from any other woman to whom he was similarly attached, he responds without a trace of irony: "Naturally" (*TRN*, 1156). The adverb
does not apply to marriage but to the succession of desirable women. Re-
luctantly agreeing to marry may even be part of the seduction. Marie is
perhaps dimly aware that her views of love, conventional though they may
be, are somehow related to personality, that love may well be a force pressing us toward the perfection or completion of personality insofar as one
person is now two. Camus, however, writes: "I call life and love what
leaves me empty" (*C1*, 229). He wishes to counter the notion of love as
enriching or modifying character in some definable way, as fostering some
measurable change or insights into ourselves and others. Love, as Camus
uses the word, allows a man to transcend existential limits, allows an inner
"void" to come into being, itself a kind of negative, religious permanence
not bound by time. "Empty" removes the experience of love from the social scene, from any sense of human consequence, procreative or economic,
where such experience might result in a personal or collective enrichment.
It would be useful in this context of the inner void to read Camus' description of sunlight during a voyage to Greece: "The light at eleven o'clock falls
with all its weight, rebounds, shatters into a thousand white and flaming
swords. The light digs into the eyes, makes them tear, enters the body with
painful speed, empties it, opens it in a kind of completely physical rape, at
the same time makes it clean" (*C3*, 156).[6] Camus renders in an extraordi-
narily powerful way the presence of light that is violently physical and
results in rape. "Rape," however, is deeroticized by the verb "clean" and
carries no pejorative connotations. It obliterates the violated person as a
thinking or feeling being, and Camus describes himself impersonally. There
are no personal subject or object pronouns. It is precisely the absence of
consent or cooperation that transforms the experience of violent sex and
sunlight into an experience of grace that is inseparable from the experience
of overwhelming power. Light shatters only to reconstitute itself as a sexually potent, irresistible, and therefore divine force. Camus is writing as a

subject but minimally. The person does not really matter. Similarly, although at a much lower level of intensity, Meursault exclaims to the priest in prison: "What did it matter that Marie this very day might be giving her lips to another Meursault?" (*TRN,* 1211). This outburst may well be egotistical in that Meursault cannot imagine Marie's new lover by any other name but his own. It is also the opposite, an expression of plain indifference, of detached and impersonal sex. The man's identity does not matter. In the succession of human experiences, nothing carries over.

The radical impact of these passages from *The Happy Death, Nuptials,* or the notebooks is only implicit. Camus does not provide any theory of sex, however much such a theory might be gleaned from his descriptions or the dramatic confrontations of his fictional characters. Nor is *The Stranger* explicit, at least not in the first half.[7] We must wait for *The Myth of Sisyphus* and its chapter on Don Juan for Camus to provide the intellectual framework to explain—and justify—his views on sexuality, its relationship to class, and its overall place in society.

Camus' command in *The Myth of Sisyphus,* "consume everything, be consumed" (*E,* 139), similar to his praise of "emptiness" or to the experience of "rape," derives from his conviction that the world in which we live either has no inherent, objective meaning or at least no meaning that we might apprehend given the imperfection of our faculties, reason included, our inadequate human constitution. This conviction, what Camus calls "absurd thought," leads not, as we might expect, to modesty, to a scaling down of what is now humanly possible, but instead to a celebration of a world in which anything is possible. Objective meaning limits, whereas meaninglessness opens up limitless possibilities. Don Juan, to whom Camus devotes an entire chapter, has his place in this new order because he replaces the notion of the quality of sexual experience—linked to social hierarchy, legislation, and moral judgments—with a doctrine of sexual quantity. Quality and quantity are not necessarily antithetical. One may or may not condition the other. Quantity, for Camus, basically represents the abolition of inner restraint and external constraints. There is no objective reason why anything or anyone should check the force of a now unleashed sexual impulse, as long as a young body is equal to the task and the mind is free of all prejudice and illusions. Given this system of values, a man's worth is to be measured, in large part, by his libidinal performance.

Several years later, Camus, thinking against himself, will make two observations: "Unbridled sex leads to a philosophy of a world without meaning" (*C2,* 55) and "With Sade systematic eroticism is one of the directions of absurd thought" (*C2,* 111). "Nuptials in Tipasa" argued for a sexuality that was "without bounds." Camus now turns his attention to the question of sexual anarchy. Originally, limitless sex derived logically from an inherently meaningless world. Camus is now reversing the terms and considering the possibility that promiscuity may be purposeful and not merely reactive, that it seeks to destroy meanings that may already exist in life. In the second observation, we see that the root cause of Camus' eventual condemnation of the Marquis de Sade in *The Rebel* is contained in the word "systematic." It describes erotic relationships anesthetized by excessive intellectualization or reduced to unthinking and unfeeling automatic responses.

For now, a young Camus is proposing Don Juan as a model of the modern, liberated lover. His relationship with women is summed up as follows: "He loves them with an equal passion and each time with his entire being" (*E*, 152). Such a statement would not be possible if Camus at this time was "systematic" or if he believed in anything resembling a past, a future, or an inner life. Present pleasure is neither enriched nor diminished by intellectual theories, past experience, or future anticipation. Psychologically, yesterday's Don Juan is synchronized with today's, so much so that "equal passion" and "his entire being" are easily realized, unencumbered by doubt or mind.

Don Juan's ardent, total, but temporary investment of his self in a woman, consistent with *The Myth of Sisyphus*'s theme of a perpetually alert male lucidity, prevents his erotic focus from hardening into a predictable system or collapsing into mere biological automatism. That self-awareness, however, also coexists with an extreme simplification of erotic language regarding women. Camus refers, for example, to "that same sentence he uses with all women" (*E*, 153). This verbal efficiency may well strike the contemporary reader as condescending, cynical, and sexist.[8] It is all these things, but such judgments are beside the point. The anonymity of women, all of them aroused and seduced in precisely the same manner and by the exact same combination of words that have proven their efficacy, also corresponds to the anonymity of the male seducer who repeats that same sentence, unwilling to modify one syllable. The situation is reversed when Camus' male characters speak to other men. Clamence in *The Fall*, for example, once he has taken up residence in a bar in Amsterdam, brags how he is able to adjust his speech to his listener, picking up every possible nuance in the other's conversation and physical mannerisms, calling upon all his intellectual and psychological resources to keep his listener in his seductive grasp. Clamence's listeners are always men.

Ultimately, it is the undifferentiated but intense equality of each sexual experience that leads Camus to praise "all those deaths and all those rebirths" (*E*, 155). Each encounter is total. It then dies completely so it can be reborn, signifying that there is no sense of experience as a cumulative process, above all no marriage or fidelity, insofar as these reflect social commandments. Such views help to explain the cynical attitude toward love and marriage so evident in young heroes such as Patrice Mersault, who states in *The Happy Death:*

> I feel like marrying, killing myself, or taking out a subscription to *L'Illustration*. You know, a desperate gesture. (*MH*, 68)
> Come on now, we don't fall in love at our age. It's later, when you're old and impotent that you can fall in love. (*MH*, 62)

Such statements, however much they may translate the macho swagger of a young, Mediterranean male, merely drift on the surface of Camus' meaning, like superficial reflections of a more powerful and more disturbing source of light. These remarks by a fictional character correspond closely to views Camus himself expressed in his notebooks and in his preface to *Right Side and Wrong Side:*

> A man who sought the meaning of life where one usually finds it (marriage, job, etc.) and who suddenly realizes, while reading a fashion magazine, how much he is a stranger to his own life. (*C1*, 61)
> To be worth something or not. . . . To create or not to create. In the first instance, everything is justified. Everything, no exceptions. In the second instance, life is a total absurdity. All that's left is the most aesthetic suicide: marriage and a 40 hour work week or a revolver. (*C1*, 89)
> So called bourgeois happiness bores me and frightens me. (*E*, 8)

Camus, still thinking along similar lines, sums up his maternal grandfather's life in *The First Man:* "He died prematurely, worn out by the sun and hard work, and perhaps by marriage" (*PH*, 82). Also in the same novel we read this satirical description of his uncle Joséphin: "He . . . married a piano teacher who was not really ugly and who, with her furniture, gave him at least a few years of bourgeois happiness. It is true that Joséphin ended up keeping the furniture and not the wife" (*PH*, 114). There seems to be little difference between middle-class happiness and inert furniture. It also seems that both the uncle and Camus, whose first mother-in-law was an ophthalmologist, married up in class but ended with little or nothing to show for their erotic and social ambitions except perhaps furniture.

Jean Sarocchi is clearly on the mark when he states that Camus viewed marriage and middle-class property and propriety as "an image of death."[9]

As Alan Clayton also points out, marriage is "too confining" and there-fore, in Camus' opinion, "an injustice,"[10] a denial of the body's unlimited capacity for pleasure. It is not only a question of marriage but also of work. Camus' variation on Hamlet's soliloquy was "to create or not to create," not "to work or not to work." Creativity is the opposite of the "forty hour work week." Jacques Cormery in *The First Man* describes his summer job in terms that are consistent with everything Camus wrote about meaning-less work: "Selling and buying, everything turned on these mediocre and petty activities" (*PH*, 246), referring further on, in even stronger language, to "his curse, the curse of stupid work" (*PH*, 248). Patrice Mersault is obsessed with money but only because it represents "free time."[11] He kills and robs for it so he never has to work for it. The central point is that, for Camus, creativity is to work what desire is to marriage. One of the impor-tant dividing lines between them is the social enslavement brought about by money, and Camus is consistent on this point:

> The unthinking respect they give to that other world (the world of money). (*C1*, 16)
> There is so much that is sordid and miserable in the conditions of a working man and in a civilization based on men working. . . . I must devote myself to my liberation—where money is concerned. . . . With luck, there is one chance in ten in escaping the most sordid and mis-erable of conditions: that of a man who works. (*C1*, 106–7)
> I am indifferent to money. (*C2*, 27)
> His dealings with money. Due in part to being poor (he bought noth-ing for himself), and also in part to his pride: he never bargained. (*PH*, 318)

Expressed at regular intervals over the years, Camus' disdain for money was a determining factor in his choice of careers, and he wanted writing to be somehow disengaged from capitalism. Referring to his published works, Camus states categorically: "I expect no financial gain from them" (*C2*, 34).[12] In his notes for *The First Man* Camus sketches this autobiographical portrait of Jacques Cormery: "Ambition made him laugh. He did not want to have, he did not want to own, he wanted to be" (*C3*, 148). "Having," even if we include wife and children as well as money, diminishes "being." And if, by force of circumstance, one does "have," then possessions must be kept to a minimum, lest we become, to use one of Camus' favorite adjectives, powerless or impotent. In the novel, still a propos of Jacques, we read: "Preparing himself . . . to being capable some day of receiving money without ever having asked for it and without ever submitting to it" (*PH*, 255).

Camus understood that his services as a writer in a capitalist system required that he be paid. Never asking for money, however, eliminates the fundamental practice of negotiation and reciprocity. There is also the matter of never submitting, of never becoming submissive, not so much to a legitimate authority as to an illegitimate power.[13] Negotiations regarding class, money, or sex become a synonym for unmanliness. We learn from Herbert R. Lottman's biography that Camus deposited his Nobel Prize check and promptly forgot its existence.[14] His publisher Gallimard, rather than pay Camus directly, had to put all royalties into a direct deposit account, and Camus never knew the exact sum.[15] This arrangement allowed all parties to engage in monetary exchanges without ever appearing to do so.

A key episode in *The First Man* that illuminates Camus' negative attitude toward money involves the stolen two-franc piece. The young Jacques lies and tells his harsh, disciplinarian grandmother that the coin slid down the communal toilet hole in the hallway outside the apartment. "Nothing," Camus writes, preparing the reader for what is to come, "could keep the toilet's stench from overflowing as far as the stairs" (*PH*, 87). The skeptical grandmother decides to "stick her hand into the excrement" (*PH*, 87) to check out the story, but the money is hidden in the child's pocket. His reaction to his grandmother's gesture is shock, intense nausea, and overwhelming shame. Money, thereafter, would always be "filthy lucre" for Camus.[16]

Camus' concern for cleanliness, to be cleansed, ultimately to be pure, extends in a direct line to the questions of love and sexuality and their relationship to social status. When Camus describes love as "self-abnegation and . . . dying to the world" (*C2*, 310), he is describing a monastic, spiritual experience that transcends the purely social and existential dimensions of human passion. In stark contrast, Caligula, in the play's first version, refers to the sexual act as "a matter of mucous membranes" (*E*, 55); Patrice Mersault, more inclusive, evokes "the exalting and sordid power of love" (*MH*, 60); describing the early settlers in Algiers forced to live in communal tents, Camus depicts "the filthy promiscuity in those enormous tents" (*PH*, 175); while working on *The Fall*, Camus confesses with an almost puritanical intensity: "I'm a dog too. I've sniffed and I've fornicated" (*C3*, 55); a ship's cook says to D'Arrast in "The Growing Stone": "Buying and selling, eh! What filth!" (*TRN*, 1669). In the final analysis,

Don Juan's use of "the same sentence," simultaneously banal and magical, to seduce all women is tantamount to getting money "without ever having asked for it." Don Juan's repeated sentence denies both the possibilities of language and the complexities of emotions. Clamence in *The Fall* reformulates Don Juan's seductive cliché by defining masculine charm as "a way of getting the answer yes without asking a specific question" (*TRN*, 1504). In each and every instance cited thus far, negotiations, economic or sexual, are scrupulously avoided.

Money and filth become integral features of an unredeemed love that fails to achieve transcendence. Recalling the day his mother informed him that he was now grown up and that he would henceforth receive "useful gifts" (*C1*, 109), Camus complains: "Even today I can't help feeling a secret annoyance whenever I receive gifts like that. And I really understood that it was love that was expressing itself but why does love sometimes use such a pathetic language?" (*C1*, 109–10). Love's proper language, one that is nonutilitarian and antisocial, will be one of Camus' central preoccupations. Sex and women need to be factored into this language of love, and if Meursault responds negatively to Marie's view of marriage it is because she depends on conventional social and linguistic codes. In fact, it would be best not to speak at all and let love speak, as we saw in *Nuptials,* the language of flowers.

If Don Juan asserts the primacy of "that same sentence he uses with all women" it is because, in spite of its cynical tone, it best approaches incantation, one that would provide both lovers with instant gratification. It would be the closest thing to silence. Here, for example, is Camus' violent reaction to businessmen he is forced to associate with on his boat trip to America: "They know all about business. . . . Rotten bastards corrupted by greed and impotence. Fortunately, there is the company of women. They are the truth of the earth" (*JV*, 27). Women are not to be associated with these middle-class men. They and the mute truths they represent exist against men, who are corrupted and made powerless by greed. Women and earth embody silence. As early as *The Happy Death*, Camus tried to place women outside social conventions and practices, outside middle-class politics and economy. To this end, Mersault praises "the magnificent uselessness of a woman's face" (*MH*, 52), and in a variant to the manuscript he develops the image further: "Feminine luster, crystal through which passes all the beauty and uselessness of this world"(*MH*, 214). This image, similar to the woman's "truth of the earth" in the travel journal, recognizes neither the woman's biological fertility, her place in society, nor her capacity to love. Women are temporary sexual companions. They may represent the earth, but they are never property. Camus accepts no other contract with them. In her purest state, a woman is a depersonalized but vibrant "crystal" whose transparency allows a man privileged and unimpeded access to nature. "Crystal," at first glance, appears to contradict the woman's "animal divinity" evoked in the same novel, but they are basically antonymic variations of Camus' single purpose: to remove women as much as possible from the responsibilities and conditions of social existence. Even Camus' reference to his own children, quoted in the first chapter,[17] while weighing the writer's responsibility to his art alongside what he owes his family, brings up the embarrassing question of savings and insurance, of putting money aside, "the modest future I am preparing for them" (C2, 156). Given Camus' wealth, "modest" is surely an attempt to downplay a socially prescribed convention that even so unconventional a father had to endure.

An episode that perhaps exemplifies most eloquently a convergence of the questions of class and love and marks Camus' development as a writer appears in the short story "The Growing Stone." The title refers to a miraculous stone that reconstitutes itself each time the community chips away pieces for its use. Camus is looking into the spiritual foundations of human society that might bypass organized religion. In this passage a ship's cook meets the story's hero, D'Arrast, an engineer of aristocratic ancestry:

> "But you're a noble. . . ."
>
> "No, I'm not. But my grandfather was. . . . There are no more nobles in my country."
>
> "Ah!" the Negro said, laughing. "I understand; everyone's a nobleman."
>
> "No, you don't understand. There are neither noblemen nor commoners. . . ."
>
> "No one works; no one suffers?"
>
> "Yes, millions of people."
>
> "Well then, they're the commoners."
>
> "In that sense, yes, but their masters are policemen or merchants. . . ."
>
> "Humph! Buying and selling, eh! What filth! And with the police, dogs give orders. . . . And you, do you sell?"
>
> "Hardly ever. I construct bridges, roads. . . ."
>
> "That's good! . . . Listen, I like what I'm hearing. And let me tell you something. Perhaps someday you will love." (*TRN*, 1669–70)

The meeting of D'Arrast and the cook brings together two classes, two cultures that have little to do with the middle class. The easy use in French of the intimate "tu" also breaks down social barriers. The upper-class man and the lower-class man discover they have much in common because both live outside the ruling class. It is D'Arrast, however, who is examined. As the stranger in the black man's country, it is he who must pass the test. D'Arrast, the cook learns, and in spite of the qualifying "hardly ever," neither buys nor sells. His profession is to build roads and bridges. It is, however, an ambiguous profession. Since D'Arrast is working either for the French government or a French corporation, his presence could be viewed as a colonialist one. Unlike Clamence, who is D'Arrast's contemporary in Camus' fiction and who "never crosses a bridge" in Amsterdam, a city of bridges, D'Arrast is opening roads and bridges to other people. Hearing his answers, the cook is pleased, offers to cook his special dish of black beans, which D'Arrast graciously accepts, and validates him as the story's hero. His final statement is the most important: "Perhaps someday you will love." While "perhaps" balances D'Arrast's "hardly" it is clear that D'Arrast does have the capacity to love. He is uncommonly free from economics and its tendency to view persons as commodities. It is, moreover, love that Camus is talking about and not just making love. This feature, more than any other, distinguishes "The Growing Stone" and almost all the stories in *Exile and the Kingdom* from Camus' early works.

In contrast, the essays in *Nuptials,* as well as the characters Mersault, Meursault, and Don Juan, none of them concerned with love, are offered to the reader as sexually vital and viable alternatives to a middle-class and devitalizing ideology. We note, for example, how Patrice Mersault describes his acquaintance Noël: "Noël . . . believes in a wife, children, and patriarchal truth within a heavy and concrete life" (*MH,* 140).[18] Unlike the feminine "crystal," Noël's life is opaque, "heavy" with responsibilities. Mersault has this existential burden on his mind when he says to Dr. Bernard: "You and I are the only men in this country who live alone. I'm not referring to your wife and friends. I know they're only temporary episodes" (*MH,* 182).

Mersault's satirical description of Noël as a man who accepts "patriarchal truth" points to a sexual life that we might call precultural, free of excessively rigid definitions of gender. Mersault's tripartite summation of Noël, "wife-children-patriarchal truth," transforms women into mothers and leads ultimately to a procreating father now bound to his wife and responsible for his family. Mersault's rejection of this triumvirate is total, and he even relegates Bernard's wife to the status of an "episode," a mere pretext. Although he does not subordinate women to the stereotyped conventions inherent in patriarchy, they still disappear as willful subjects. This general dislimning of women is somewhat arrested in *The Happy Death*. Mersault marries. As he informs Bernard, however, a wife is a mere chapter in a narration over which the male hero/author exercises absolute control. This narration is divorced from any notion of social responsibility and therefore the opposite of Noël's patriarchy. Camus himself was a fatherless child.[19] If the son is to be the voice of the father, then Camus never had that model to imitate and later transform. He never enjoyed (or suffered) that willful predecessor.

We cannot assume, however, that the relationship between Camus and his male characters is seamless, one indistinguishable from the other. In *Nuptials*, Camus undoubtedly speaks in his own voice. In *The Happy Death* and *The Stranger*, however, autobiographical and confessional elements, though powerful and essential to the meaning of the narratives, are challenged by other characters demanding to be heard, even though they speak in a minor key. Camus is both projecting his image and competing against it, examining it, taking stock. In *The Myth of Sisyphus*, Camus once again reaffirms himself as a unitary consciousness. Don Juan exists in opposition to patriarchy, bourgeois marriage, and the bourgeois family, and his life proceeds from female conquest to female conquest. There is no morality, if by morality we mean, at the very least, private deeds visible in the public domain and subject to interpretation, evaluation, and judgment.

Camus' opposition to marriage and family has biographical roots. He was not of the middle class. He was a poor boy from Algeria. Through his steadily increasing fame and wealth, however, Camus became keenly aware that he was moving inexorably into the middle class, with its strict sense not only of financial but of sexual economy. Don Juan is the antidote. He is an aristocrat. Camus too will be an aristocrat, if not by birth then through the merit conferred by sexual achievement. That achievement brings into focus Camus' attempt to legitimize his views of love and sexuality, at least in part, by elevating certain sexual characteristics of the Algerian lower class to aristocratic status, bypassing the middle class altogether. While such an attempt may ignore the sociological reality of family life among the poor in Algiers, the attempt neverthless is there.

Camus refers, for example, to their "sensual wealth" (*E*, 67). That natural wealth, conjoined to their impoverished economic straits, transforms the lower class into "an island in society" (*C1*, 16). That magical isolation represents a positive version of Oran's isolating disease in *The Plague* because it avoids not a viral but a social contamination. That proletarian island in turn becomes a laboratory for a reinvented aristocracy that Camus thought necessary for society's survival and would examine in greater detail in "The Growing Stone":

> The people are the only source of aristocracy. Between them there's nothing. That nothing . . . is the middle class. (C3, 106)
> Every society is based on aristocracy. Because true aristocracy means setting the highest standards for oneself and without those standards societies die. (C3, 135)
> This world . . . is searching for its aristocrats. (C3, 148)[20]
> The people and aristocracy . . . are the two sources of every civilization. (E, 1084)

When Camus also states that poverty is an economic condition whose principal virtue is "generosity" (C2, 62), he makes an imaginative connection in his early works between a money-free and value-free aristocracy and a redefined and socially unencumbered sexuality. Don Juan is explicit. When a priest accuses him of not comprehending charity and love, he responds: "I only know tenderness and generosity which are the male forms of those female virtues" (C1, 215). Are the church and middle class, by this declension, feminine? This affirmation of a virile sexuality against feminine love expels not only the social and conformist components of that love but, keeping "charity" in mind, all altruistic components of procreative love that would give birth to another life.

Generosity is the opposite of charity because it is spontaneous. It is authentic because it is free of institutional rules and restrictions, a personal not a social gesture. Camus writes in *Myth:* "The only generous form of love is one that knows itself to be short-lived and exceptional" (E, 155). If it were not unique and passing, love would be caught in the web of enduring human relations, in situations that require couples to work their union through the endurance of time. For the epigraph to his first version of *Caligula* Camus chose a quotation from Suetonius: "We must be either frugal or Caesar." The choice is to be in society or above it, careful with money and passions or generous. Generosity, in turn, requires an imperial indifference to consequences. Camus removed the epigraph from subsequent versions of the play, but it reappears in modified form in *The First Man.* Jacques is affectionately teasing his mentor and good friend Malan:

> "You are, let's say, frugal. . . . It's a serious flaw that I generally dislike. . . . You are instinctively unable to believe one can have disinterested feelings. . . . What if I were to tell you that if you just said the word I would immediately give you everything I have. . . ."

"Oh, I know. You're generous. . . ."

"Just say the word, right now, everything I have is yours. . . . Honest, everything I have is yours." (*PH*, 37–38)

Cormey's offer is not charity because it is not institutional. This man-to-man relationship is based on "disinterested feelings," free from self-interest and financial interest. Cormery is staging his own impulsive generosity, a performance all the more radical when we take into account that he is married and has a young child.

Middle-class financial and sexual economy with its emphasis on marriage, children, and money, on clearly defined and socially prescribed sexual roles, and, above all, on self-control will be replaced by energy, munificence, and immediate gratification over the time-consuming and restrictive requirements of collective society. In Cormery's offer to Malan, two key words are "immediately" and "right now." Cultural and sexual economy must give way to Don Juan's motto of "consume everything" and "be consumed" (*E*, 139). Don Juan does not live his sexual life in prescribed doses. He spends it and saves nothing.

Camus, therefore, must have understood that his idealization of the Algerian proletariat, relegated to his private notebooks, would not stand up to public scrutiny. Their "natural" aristocracy differs radically from Don Juan's. They fall in love, marry, have children. They work to make and, whenever possible, save money.

Camus wrote *The Myth of Sisyphus* not only to explain his program for a revitalized life but also to justify it. He stresses that the human body is the ultimate vehicle for shaping and legitimizing happiness because the body, once it is removed from the traditional and censorius body politic, is fundamentally "innocent."[21] He does not understand innocence to mean the absence of experience. He refers rather to a state of mind and a sexual life unaffected by experience. "Love can only be preserved," he writes, "for reasons external to love. Moral reasons, for example" (*C2*, 124). Camus, at this point in his life, viewed love as a purely social construct. Love purged of all "external" attributes now reappears in the authentic form of a purified sexuality. Camus explains: "My love has no value for me unless it is innocent and without an object" (*C1*, 73). "Without an object" explains "innocent" because it views the sexual partner not as a delimiting personality but as one more occasion or episode in the ongoing, self-centered discourse of happiness. "Innocence" is a recurring litany everywhere in the early writings, and Camus, describing the absurd man in *The Myth of Sisyphus*, sums up its centrality: "They want him to recognize his guilt. He feels innocent" (*E*, 137). Camus had already claimed that there was no objective truth. "Feels," therefore, puts the question of innocence where it belongs, in individual, subjective perception, but a perception so absolutely subjective as to be impervious to interpretation or negotiation. There is no social contract.

We could, if we wish, agree with Roger Quilliot, who feels that Camus and Don Juan develop their sexual strategies in order to get back in touch with "a sincere desire."[22] There is no doubt that Camus' view of sex as a "game" supports such a view. "Game" too is synonymous with sincerity and innocence because there are simple rules understood and freely accepted in advance by everyone involved. Don Juan, for example, accepts "all the rules of the game" (E, 156).[23] Similarly, in his notebooks, Camus writes: "A man who takes pleasure in games is always happy in the company of women. Women are a good audience" (C1, 102). As "audience" makes clear, sexuality for Camus shares attributes of innocence found both in theater and in sports because all of them are staged spectacles. The script is known in advance.

Quilliot's reference to "a sincere desire" is, I think, an honorable attempt to bring Camus a little closer to the cultural mainstream that may accept sex as play, as a matter of mental and physical hygiene, a necessary antidote to middle-class, nonpermissiveness and its traditional ethic of hard work. Camus' intellectual stance, however, is far too radical to be thus diluted. By grounding his thought in the notion of our absolute innocence, Camus places himself in opposition to the Judeo-Christian tradition, at least that part of the tradition which equates sexuality with the fall of man, with his guilt. In *Nuptials* Camus attempted to reinvent pagan Greece on the shores of North Africa. Camus' early writings up to and including the chapter on Don Juan are powerfully seductive and subversive because they propose an image of human sexuality that is prelapsarian, before the fall. Class and class divisions, work, guilt, and self-denial were the driving forces of a tragic society. It was tragic to the extent that external, social constraints on male and female sexuality cheated human beings of their potential for an uncensored sexual happiness. Meursault, after all, is condemned to death for three reasons: he killed the Arab, he did not cry at his mother's funeral, and he had sex with a woman the day after his mother's burial. For Camus, there is only one tragedy, and that is a body's demise, after which there is nothing.

At the end of the chapter, Camus places Don Juan, now grown old, in a monastery. We can appreciate Camus' irony since monasteries are devoted to chastity, but we need not be too shocked. Given Camus' scheme of things at this point in his life, he is merely offering the church as the appropriate sanctuary for Don Juan's old age, his spent life, and his now impotent body.

By placing Don Juan in a monastery Camus is also restating the conclusions he developed for the Santissima Annunziata episode in *Nuptials*. Cloister or monastery, Don Juan and Camus occupy a sacred space constructed beyond the pale and devoted to sexual abstinence.[24] Camus' final remarks about Don Juan repeat the conclusions of *Nuptials*: "Sexual pleasure . . . ends up as asceticism" (*E*, 157).[25] This asceticism or stripping away represents a nakedness that is much more than the absence of clothes or money. It is the absence of ego. This purification of self is therefore best preserved by a theological vocabulary and theological architecture. These sacred spaces are marginal, tangential to the social scene, but they are also spiritually essential and thus appropriate for the Camusian lover who is seeking a transcendent sexuality. They are the authenticating spaces of an inner nakedness and an anonymous sexuality.

In Greece, responding to the light and landscape of a country he considered an ancestral home, Camus writes: "The light is sacred. . . . The clear water is less cold but the air especially has become transparent and the mountains . . . unveil themselves with a strange purity. . . . Chaste, sober pleasure strong as joy itself, as the very air one breathes" (*C3*, 172). The experience of pleasure in this description is not followed by chastity in two distinct and consecutive steps as in *Nuptials* and *Sisyphus*. They are inseparable. The mountains represent Camus' religious corporeality. They are pure because they are absolutely, physically there. The human body and a convent are also jointly celebrated during this same journey, each one reflecting and reinforcing the other: "A body's strength and joy. Repose of the soul and heart. In the distance a convent sleeps, that strong and naked house where silence contemplates" (*C3*, 233). Camus was more than a tourist when he wrote these lines. Attacked and shunned by the political left after the publication of *The Rebel*, he was unable to write for years and was seeking inner renewal. Once again Camus was deeply moved by the landscapes of his youth and the carnal and mystical yearnings they embodied. Camus responded deeply to the undistracted, purely physical presence of the convent, powerful even in its sleep, especially in its dreamless sleep, where, contrary to its theological purpose, the soul and the heart are sufficiently absent so that another absence—"silence"—can do its work and contemplate. Once again, there is no direct object pronoun, no reference external to itself. We have silence contemplating either something unnamed or else nothing, a spiritual exercise sufficient unto itself.

What this convent means to Camus sexually and spiritually and how it is closely related to his "cloister" and Don Juan's "monastery" become even clearer when we compare it to another "home" Camus described years earlier: "When one is lucky enough to live in the world of intelligence, what madness to want to hear screams and enter the terrifying house of passion" (C2, 327). The contrast is between a convent and a home, the sacred and the profane, and between a sexuality rendered mute once it is cleansed of speech and personality and those "screams" of passion that represent the sound and fury of human psychology, where emotions are very much awake, active, and confrontational. This "house of passion" resembles the inn of *The Misunderstanding* where Jan, in a horrible reversal of biology, is murdered by his mother and sister. It resembles the city of Cadix in *State of Siege*, whose citizens are murdered. It is the home, above all, of an intolerable human nature. No event devastated Camus more than the civil war in his homeland Algeria, and he described the war between Arabs and French as a "house of passion," a Greek tragedy: "They belong to the same tragic family and now its members slaughter each other in the middle of the night, without recognizing each other, groping, in blind conflict" (*CAC6*, 158). In contrast, the convent in Greece, Don Juan's monastery, Camus' cloister in the Santissima Annunziata, incarnate and celebrate simple, sexually fulfilled bodies filled with silence.

This silence, and the concrete forms it takes in *Nuptials* and the Don Juan chapter in *Sisyphus,* can be traced directly to Camus' mother. "What was her silence saying," Camus asks himself in his private journal, "what was that mute and smiling mouth crying out" (C3, 191).[26] Sibylline, it is through her mouth, not her person, that mysteries are conveyed. Every woman, in one way or another, will be measured against her and found wanting. The same urgent questions Camus asked about his mother, he had Mersault ask about Lucienne. Kissing her he feels "the unbridled will to seize on those living lips the ultimate meaning of this inhuman world, sleeping like a silence within her mouth. . . . He bit deeply into her lips and, for a few moments, drank in that warm indifference which enraptured him as if he were embracing the world in his arms" (*MH*, 145). In *Nuptials* Camus himself bit voraciously into the "golden fruit" of the world to become one with it. Mersault bites into Lucienne and breaks her down to drink her in. He expects her silent mouth to release not something within her to which he is being given privileged access but the secrets of nature of which she herself is ignorant. Camus' mother was somewhat retarded, with a vocabulary of about four hundred words, hard of hearing, often strangely indifferent to her children and surroundings. She was not, according to Camus, of this world. He describes himself as a child "full of despairing love for his mother, and for something deep within her that did not belong or no longer belonged to the world and the triviality of passing days" (*PH*, 159). The more Camus describes her, the more transparent and timeless she becomes. She belongs to no social class. If she is an enigma to her son, it is not because of a secret or unfathomable inner life of which she seemed to have none. It is because of her mute mouth, her patient suffering, and her resilient body. Camus surely had his mother in mind when he wrote: "Flesh, poor, miserable, dirty, fallen, humiliated flesh. Sacred flesh" (*C3*, 263). The profusion of negative adjectives achieves a reverse incarnation, not the spirit made flesh but the flesh made spirit. This miraculous transformation sums up eloquently, but without solving, the questions of love and sexuality in Camus' early works as he bypasses society and seeks transcendence downward, in and through the human body, his own and the bodies of women, and all of them resolutely removed, like his mother, from society and the "triviality of passing days."

Camus' ambition was to place at the center of his work "the admirable silence of a mother" (*E*, 13) and to find a love or justice "that would balance that silence" (*E*, 13). Writing his preface for *Right Side and Wrong Side*, Camus was projecting into the future. He had partially achieved his ambition, though not exactly as he formulates it in his preface. The cloister and the monastery for Camus in *Nuptials* and for Don Juan in *The Myth of Sisyphus* appear at the conclusion of a man's sexual adventures, not coincidentally, not even all that ironically, but as a necessary conclusion to what all along was a spiritual as well as carnal quest. Camus' mother sometimes visited her son in the south of France, and Camus, reflecting on *The First Man*, his novel in progress, noted: "When his mother lived in a room for a while, she never left a single trace, except, sometimes, a handkerchief" (*C3*, 29). His mother, transforming everything into her own image, transforms the room into a sacred space, as devoid of personality and as naked as the Greek convent Camus admired.

Camus wanted to find a love that would balance his mother's silence. But thus far he had been reversing the terms, with silence coming after love. He had concluded in "Nuptials in Tipasa": "My relaxed body enjoyed the inner silence that comes from satisfied love" (*E*, 59). Similarly, by putting Don Juan in a monastery, Camus again imagines a silence that balances a life of satisfied love.

Even though sexual conquests and monasteries seem to follow each other in chronological order, Camus is ultimately describing orgasms and silences unfolding within a male body that is its own sacred sanctuary. It is a body encompassing both east and west, dawn and sunset, lovers present and lovers gone, or, as Don Juan puts it, "all those deaths and all those rebirths." Camus, however, as his preface demonstrates, would sooner or later have to write works that would make silence not the end result of sex but the point of departure for love, that would dramatize the social scene and not just the inner scene. He would write narratives in which everyone is a subject, not just mothers and sons. The contract with nature and the satire of class will gradually become a renewed contract with society.

## CHAPTER 3

# Men, Women, and Social Contracts

Reevaluating his relationship to society required Camus first to reevaluate his notion of manhood. Questions about manhood engaged Camus deeply in almost all his published works and, judging from his notebooks, also in his private life. His initial responses, formulated within the narrow precincts of male characters portrayed as living in willful isolation, are most often negative. They reject manhood in its more common forms of a limited biological and social identity. Families "where male and female relations would be established," have no meaning for them.[1] More generally, if social encounters are irrelevant or perhaps even dangerous, then isolation is salvation. "Man weakens man's strength," Patrice Mersault states categorically, "the world leaves it intact" (*MH*, 132). Camus paraphrases his fictional character in "Nuptials in Tipasa." He takes his place in nature and concludes: "Everything here leaves me whole, I give up nothing of myself" (*E*, 58). The world—or nature—is safe, and both Camus and Mersault interpret most social dealings with men and women as useless and sometimes fatal liaisons.

Camus' ongoing and radical redefinitions of his own person coexist with assumptions about manhood—derived largely from his Algerian youth—that are simple, occasionally simplistic, but always beyond discussion. He affirms in "Serving Man" that to be a man meant that you kept your word, that you demanded respect for your family and yourself as long as you did not take unfair advantage of your physical or mental powers (*E*, 1544–46). Céleste tells the jurors in *The Stranger* that Meursault is "a man" and assumes that they automatically understand what he means (*TRN*, 1191); Sintès also calls Meursault a man (*TRN*, 1148) attempting to foster a strong bond; Cottard does the same for Rieux (*TRN*, 1377); Balducci in "The Guest" tells Daru: "You were born in this country; you're a man" (*TRN*, 1616), male gender reproducing, as far as he is concerned, the clear and unambiguous contours of a geographical place; and in "The Silent Men" Yvars thinks to himself after a failed strike: "They were men, enough said" (*TRN*, 1606).[2] These examples are a kind of shorthand, idioms that both Camus and his male characters use to take moral and psychological shortcuts, to get through quickly and efficiently whatever social business is at hand.

These characters have clear convictions about manliness. These convictions sometimes have fragile foundations. We read in *The Happy Death*: "The crease in his pants had disappeared and with it that glow and confidence a normal man exudes" (*MH*, 68); and the relationship between external appearance and virility is underlined again: "He had lost that wonderful self-assurance provided by a well-made suit or the steering wheel of a car" (*MH*, 100). The young Camusian male is making an investment in external and superficial props. Their very superficiality, however, also argues their magical power to reflect and support unambiguously a man's virility.

As we read further in Camus, we pick up more information about what constitutes manliness. To be a man is to be "egoistic" (*E*, 26), and a man's unique duty in life, according to Patrice Mersault, "is only to be happy" (*MH*, 202). Male egotism and the pursuit of happiness do not demonstrate the same shorthand efficiency of the common, everyday clichés already noted. They are more problematic because egotism and happiness, unlike suits and cars, may require lengthy negotiations with other people, may even threaten collisions with other kinds of shorthand, with other lives and egos, particularly those of women. "What counts is being a man" (*E*, 26), Camus had stated early in his career. Many years later, however, Clamence will admit in *The Fall*: "We are 'almost' in all things" (*TRN*, 1480). These statements constitute the two stages of an important evolution in Camus' thought about individual manhood and its relationship to society. Contrasting definitions of manhood clash throughout Camus' novels and plays: Meursault versus the prosecuting attorney, Caligula versus Cherea, Rieux versus Tarrou, Stepan against Kaliayev, Camus ultimately against Camus, intense battles in which, if we take Camus' meditations on suicide and murder seriously, both the meanings of life and life itself are at stake.

Throughout Camus' works, from the earliest essays of *Right Side and Wrong Side* to *The First Man*, we encounter reassuring affirmations about uncomplicated manhood. They are uttered by Camus himself and also by Yvars, Balducci, Sintès, Céleste, Don Juan, and others, by characters who have neither the ability nor the inclination, much less the passion or need for self-discovery, to ask any troubling questions. Their affirmations function as the literary equivalent of a scientific control, a neutral base from which Camus will explore the more obscure regions of human personality.

Camus' questions about manhood are evident in his frequent use of the words "sterility" and "fertility." These antonymic terms, sometimes used literally, at other times figuratively, also raise the question of the role of women in society. Their relationship to women brings into focus two contradictory requirements in Camus' nature: to withdraw into narcissistic isolation, to step outside time and history, to transcend heterosexual reproduction, to avoid the emotion of love that might in some way diminish male identity and male authority, or to revitalize in himself and in others the notion of manhood linked in some essential way to a pluralistic, procreative, and creative society. Camus comes to understand that he depends very much on his idea of what men and women are. For example, Caligula says to his mistress Caesonia shortly before his assassination: "There are two kinds of happiness and I've chosen the murderous kind. And I am truly happy. There was a time when I thought I had reached the limits of pain. Oh no, one could go still further. At the outer limits of pain lies a sterile and magnificent happiness" (*TRN*, 105). In *The Myth of Sisyphus* Camus addresses the reader directly: "I want to speak solely . . . of a world where human thought, like our lives, has no future. Everything that makes a man work and get involved utilizes hope. The only idea, therefore, that is not a lie is a sterile idea. In this absurd world, the worth of a notion or a life is measured by its sterility" (*E*, 151). The following comments on totalitarianism are from a speech entitled "Witness for Freedom": "Wanting to dominate a person means wanting that person to be sterile, silent, or dead" (*E*, 401). Finally, the nameless priest in the short story "The Renegade" worships the totalitarian rule of a savage tribe: "It is they who are the masters! They reign over their sterile homes, over their black slaves" (*TRN*, 1583).

The word "sterility" appears each time, but it is no longer the same man who is writing. Camus contradicts himself. Caligula expresses the desire to live a life beyond pleasure and pain, and that tactic is part of a larger strategy called "becoming a man" (*TRN*, 26). His basic assumption, shared by Mersault, who murders Zagreus, and by Meursault, who murders the Arab, is that violence is conclusive proof of manhood. The virtue of violence is in its direct, physiological simplicity. It offers a way of invading other beings to avoid invasion oneself, whether in the form of an individual opponent or society itself. Clamence in *The Fall* puts it plainly and vividly: "Haven't you noticed that our society is organized for this kind of liquidation? You've heard about . . . those minuscule fish in the rivers of Brazil that attack the careless swimmer by the thousands, clean him up . . . and leave behind an immaculate skeleton? . . . Do you want to live right? . . . O.K. We'll clean you up. Here's a job, a family, organized leisure. And the tiny teeth bite into your flesh, right down to the bone" (*TRN*, 1479). This passage is based on a fundamental assumption that more is less, the more social a man the less authentic his manhood. The goal, therefore, is to remain "intact," as Mersault put it, to avoid invasion, and, more pertinently, to evade compromising language and negotiations, all the social complications that attend human relationships. A man guarantees his future by denying any future, individually or collectively, to others.

In the passage quoted from *Sisyphus,* Camus concludes that the proper life requires that we divorce ourselves from the future and hope—specifically that future we call the afterlife—so as to live solely in an urgent and self-centered present. A true or "sterile" man, divorced from the future, willingly suffers this temporal amputation in order to attain a higher form of life.

In his speech, however, Camus examines how totalitarian rule corrupts even our most elementary, biological existence. That corruption in turn receives its most violent expression in the renegade priest's self-abasement before his masters who inhabit "sterile homes." In each of these four passages Camus leads us toward a central issue, one that binds his life and work, the desire to transcend the human condition, particularly as embodied in its collective forms, what he calls "man released from the human" (*C1,* 75). This deliverance will be definitive once a man can overcome his emotions, suppress his biological nature, the willingness or need to procreate, and suppress the future, whether that future takes the form of the afterlife or the one prepared here and now through marriage and children.

A brief look at Camus' youth in the 1930s shows a person deeply divided on the issue of manhood and social contracts. Whether as a soccer player, director of a regional theater, journalist, member of the Communist Party, one of several authors collaborating on the play *Rebellion in the Asturias,* or a married man, Camus was living according to the time-honored prescription of participation. His self-fulfillment, his sense of himself as a man, was largely measured by what he could offer others and what these friends, colleagues, and lovers could in turn offer him. This ability to engage in social and intellectual as well as moral conversation informs the many political causes Camus supported and political gestures he performed throughout his life. Eventually it came to define his sense of the artist's place in society. To the members of the Swedish Academy who had awarded him the Nobel Prize, Camus affirmed: "The artist will nourish his art and his individuality only by asserting his resemblance to all persons. He creates his identity in that perpetual journey between others and himself" (*E,* 1072). In an interview that same year in which he contradicted two of the passages I quoted earlier,[3] Camus summed up his achievements: "As for me, the source of my hope has always been the word, the idea of fertility" (*E*, 1899). By "fertility" Camus is referring not only to procreation, society's commitment to its survival, the physical continuity of life, but also to its figurative meaning of creativity, all acts that would enhance the potential of each human life.

The word "always," however, is excessive. If everyday life put the young Camus in contact with a community and with dialogue, his novels, always pressing toward monologue, organized themselves against human beings. Camus recognized this temptation when he confessed: "If I had enough strength and patience, I know . . . I could willfully annihilate everything in my life" (*C1*, 82). Writing in his travel journal on the way to America, Camus confronted his nihilistic penchants even more explicitly: "I have always been torn between my appetite for people, the vanity of human activity and my desire to resemble these oceans of oblivion, these immeasurable silences that are like death's hypnotic enchantment. I have a law within me which is the sea and everything that resembles it" (*JV*, 52). Camus maps his divided nature and seeks an inner balance. Stylistically, however, there is no contest. Living beings, vanity, and action, those apparently ludicrous manifestations of our existence and collective agitations, seem feeble compared to the "oceans of oblivion" and death's "enchantment." That inner sea and compelling rule of life (or anti-life) that Camus observes within himself always threatens to carry both him and his male characters beyond the social forms and moral constraints of culture. Camus' art or politics or everyday gestures, therefore, did not grow out of a commitment to "fertility" alone. His achievements, as the above passage suggests, were as much against his divided nature as inspired by it. We can therefore measure the full force of Camus' dilemma when he admits to himself: "I have no desire whatsoever to be a genius, since I'm having enough trouble just being a man" (*C2*, 172). This private utterance is made public through Rieux in *The Plague* who, in opposition to Tarrou's ambition to become a saint, comments: "Being a man is what interests me" (*TRN*, 1427).[4]

Camus' style, as we saw in *Nuptials*, is intensely lyrical whenever sex is enjoyed outside society. In nature, no one can interrupt, compromise, or in any way evaluate his erotic songs. On vacation in Cordes, Camus writes: "Silence and beauty. . . . Around Cordes the sky, soft, airy, luminous and cloudy at the same time, rests on the perfect circle of its hills. At night, Venus, fat as a peach, sits upon the western hill with mad haste. She hesitates a moment on the crest, then quickly disappears. . . . Now the stars swarm and the milky way becomes cream" (*C3*, 203). Unlike the hypnotic seas of oblivion and death he observed on his way to the United States, Camus is now witnessing a universal orgasm. The difference, however, is minimal only in the sense that these opposing forces are depersonalized forces in the cosmos and that Camus is each time begging the question of civilization. He is ready to view and transcribe the world's sexual release and plenitude because his primary relationship is with nature.

As the willing recipient of a cosmic message or scene he appears passive. Unlike Meursault, however, who accused the sun of murdering the Arab, no feelings of danger are mobilized by this passivity because nature, organized around Venus and the night, is feminine. Once this generative force of nature begins to manifest itself in society, however, and integrate itself into the human scene, a tragic tension is immediately felt. A good example is Camus' evaluation of Roger Martin du Gard's novels: "With three thousand newborn babies every hour, and just as many deaths, an overwhelming force sweeps the individual away in the neverending flood of generation, drowns him in the insatiable ocean of our mortality" (*E*, 1151). There is no enchantment in this description. The tragic finitude that Camus perceives in the world, a generative force that obliterates an individual's identity before dissolving his life, that feeds death instead of opposing or balancing it, corresponds to a profound, nihilistic penchant within himself. The anguish that Camus sees recorded in Martin du Gard's works and evidently in his own is attributable to the inescapable fact that the human body guarantees the death of the life it breeds, that death is constituted in the very flesh reproducing itself, an atheistic version, so to speak, of original sin. For many years Camus wrote works that explore another, secret anguish, and characters such as Mersault, Caligula, Meursault, and even Tarrou will give their consent not merely to the fact of death but also to that part of them that wants to die. In this they echo their author: "There is always a part of man," Camus wrote privately, "that rejects love. It's the part that *wants* to die" (*C2*, 318). Because Camus underlined "wants," it becomes clear that death is more than an objective fact and that such a wish or ambition is not presented as the painful outcry of an irrational mood. On the contrary, if Camus argues intellectually against suicide in *The Myth of Sisyphus* and against murder in *The Rebel* it is because he had argued intellectually, or so he assumed, in their favor. When Caligula explains that "loving is the opposite of living" (*TRN*, 28), he is doing more than directing our attention to a subjective and negotiable point of view. He is outlining a program for the correct life. In works contemporary with this play, such as *The Happy Death, Nuptials, The Stranger*, and *The Myth of Sisyphus*, Camus creates a set of circumstances that conform, in varying degrees, to that program.

That program appears to rest on a fundamental contradiction: to refuse to love, Camus wrote, is to want to die, but to love, according to Caligula, is to die. The contradiction is resolved, at least in part, when death is understood not only in its literal sense of the body's demise but also, in a positive sense, as the demise of a limited, social, and inauthentic existence. Love and love's duties, by this declension, become a force for social entrapment or, in Clamence's vivid metaphor, the "piranha." Caligula's opposition between living and loving also represents the opposition between the physiological demands of the body and all restrictive social laws. Camus had stated in "The Desert": "Nothing could be more vain than to die for love. Instead we must live" (*E*, 82). Don Juan asserts: "There are those who are made for living and those who are made for loving" (*E*, 101). Patrice Mersault informs Catherine: "I would risk having you fall in love with me and that would prevent me from being happy" (*MH*, 155). In each instance the experience of life is disconnected from the experience of love. The less love, the more life. Conversely, whereas sex is a necessary expression of virility, love is not.[5] As a purely social artifact or pose, love would break the circuit of unfocused desire, male egotism, and the male pursuit of happiness. Catherine is a woman in love, but Mersault will accept her only as an occasion of pleasure. Don Juan's distinction between those who live and those who love divides society into two distinct classes: an aristocracy that is above love and plebeian lovers who, like Vincent in *Nuptials*,[6] end up marrying and begetting children. For Don Juan—and for Camus at this particular point—love is carnal and there is no knowledge.

The correct and proper life is not lived according to social prescriptions or theological sacraments but according to an objective truth about our mortality. That truth transcends our individual longings and agitations and requires our consent, if not our submission. This yielding to a transcendent objectivity helps to explain why so many of Camus' heroes can be both rebellious in relation to society and passive in relation to nature.

When Camus wrote in 1946, "We're being suffocated by people who think they are absolutely right" (*E*, 332), he had apparently forgotten that Meursault, his "Christ" as he called him,[7] had shouted at the priest in 1940: "I had been right, I was still right, I was always right" (*TRN*, 1210). It is undoubtedly a matter of balance in this particular instance, Meursault's knowledge of death balancing the priest's belief in the afterlife, and Meursault is justifying himself to a man who has his own unshakable convictions. The young Camus also does not wish to negotiate his personal experiences with the reader, which would somehow imply that he does not possess the entire truth. He wishes to obey a universal and therefore irresistible truth.

This climate of absolutism derives from the conviction, expressed by Camus, Caligula, Mersault, Meursault, and Don Juan, that loving is the opposite of living, that life itself, in its interpersonal manifestations, is a brief flaw in death. Camus concludes: "Death is there, the only reality" (*E*, 140). The bluntness of "there" is placed in the sentence to stifle any further discussion. In the notebooks, too, we read: "Death alone is true knowledge" (*C2*, 65). To suppress our contradictory emotions and the interpersonal requirements of love is logically to incorporate into ourselves this "only" reality, to yield to the inner tides of death, to paraphrase Camus, and to become ourselves part of the "hypnotic" force of death. It is a matter of philosophical consent. Caligula, who perceived this truth and stopped loving, is transformed from a virtuous leader into a murderous emperor. In *The Misunderstanding*, both mother and sister discard their apparently superficial identities of givers of life and affection to become the murderers of their son and brother, Jan, who had already met them halfway by deserting his wife. Camus transforms himself in "The Wind in Djémila" into a "stone among stones" (*E*, 62). With the possible exception of *Caligula*, which may have some real application to the phenomenon of totalitarian rule, these works are not political in the sense of demonstrating one or another political thesis. The force of death dictates the terms of our lives. Politics, prescribing human relationships and developing social contracts based on relative matters of liberty, justice, and love, hence guaranteeing citizens of the polis their group survival, is therefore superficial and retrograde. Love places us in front of persons, in front of their individual and delimiting perspectives as well as their partial, negotiable judgments of our intrinsic value or lack thereof. But death, whether it takes the form of a totalizing idea or emotion, of suicide or murder, embodies a permanent judgment that admits of no appeal.

When Caligula strangles Caesonia we realize that all the victims in the play had to lead to her, his final victim. His mistress and an older woman, she calls Caligula a child and plays mother to his murderous whims. She must die violently—Caligula crushes her throat with his forearm—not naturally, so that he may willfully cancel his biological identity and his past. His outcry, "Hate alone makes us intelligent" (*TRN*, 55), may appear to contradict his desire to live life beyond emotions, but the two views are basically complementary. A destructive emotion opens us up to a destructive, transcendental force. Hatred is mobilized to serve an objective fact— Caesonia herself uses the expression "objective hatred" (*TRN*, 64)—and

Caligula truly believes he is an intellectual murderer. We do have emotions, but hatred possesses the virtue of facilitating the mind's task of grasping an impersonal truth. The renegade will carry Caligula's point of view to its most extreme, psychological conclusion. If love is an opening through which we reveal ourselves to each other, then hatred is monolithic: "Only the reign of malice," he concludes, "was seamless" (*TRN*, 1589). What he is describing and worshiping is totalitarian rule and a seamless, totalitarian self.

In what we might call the politics of sterility the goal is to remove oneself from process and contradiction, to die or to resemble death in life. Camus' exclamation in the 1939 essay "The Minotaur," "To be nothing!" (*E*, 830), summarizes through that clash and synthesis of antonyms the refusal of many of Camus' male characters to assume a generational place in society. In Camus' assessment of Martin du Gard, the body itself is a traitor that plants the kernel of death in its own generative seed. That the death of Meursault and Jan also coincides with a tragic reunion with their mothers does not invalidate this premise. These young and fatherless men do not visualize themselves as proceeding outward from their mothers into life, of going forth into society. They have instead radically reversed the process, what Caligula calls "changing the order of things" (*TRN*, 27). This powerful and incestuous impulse pulling the son back toward the mother exerted its influence even in Camus' last novel, *The First Man,* which describes a child's uneasy liberation from a socially and psychologically impoverished milieu.

These mothers or maternal figures are also victimized, but they at least have the dignity of being essential mediums for these strange rites of nonpassage from life into death, impersonality, or sterility. Other women, such as Marie in *The Stranger* or Maria in *The Misunderstanding,* are left in the wings, empty-handed representatives of a future never to be because their husbands or husbands-to-be are moving backward to their origins or point zero. When Camus jots down, "Renounce that servitude called feminine attraction" (*C1*, 227), he makes the woman a principal enemy of death, "the only reality." Women pose no problem as long as they merely satisfy a man's sexual appetites or, at the other extreme, become passive conduits for a man's possession of nature. They cannot, however, cross the line into organized society. Marie crossed it when she proposed marriage. This view of women is evident in the misogynist attitudes of Patrice Mersault, Meursault, even Jan, and also Caligula, particularly in the first version of the play in which his homosexuality is prominent. Women seem useless to their purpose, which is to deny that procreation and biology—

for men—is destiny. Ivan Karamazov (from Fyodor Dostoyevsky's novel *Brothers Karamazov*) was Camus' hero in these early years,[8] and Camus explains in *The Rebel* that Ivan "chooses to attack procreation" (*E*, 469).

It is that choice, and it is not a matter of mere noncompliance but of an aggressive attack, that guarantees deliverance from the human condition and from all social and biological definitions of manhood. Camus, in various ways and in varying degrees, is trying to answer a fundamental question he had put to himself in 1932: "When will I have the courage not to be a man anymore?" (*PC*, 185). Not to be a man is to refuse everything that is given in life and constructed within society in return for an identity one creates entirely for oneself. This refusal leads Camus to deny women any real status in his works. They are too much part of the social contract, their sexuality too much keyed to reproduction and to the reciprocal impulses of love and intimacy. They cannot gain purchase into a man's private contract with himself.

Camus' denial, however, conflicted directly with his own often overwhelming sexual urges. The conflict was not with sexuality itself but with sex's potential to transform itself into love. Patrice Mersault laments because he is "aware of our misfortune that love and desire express themselves the same way" (*MH*, 54). Most of Camus' male characters are required to maintain that crucial distinction.

Don Juan, a central figure in *The Myth of Sisyphus,* interests Camus because he offers a resolution to this conflict between love and sex. He represents "the brilliant and wealthy seducer" and embodies a "physical nihilism" that leads him to commit in the realm of love "the same crime as Caligula in the realm of universal happiness."[9] There is one major difference, however. Don Juan never harms his lovers. He seduces a woman, but only once, and then moves on. He loves, Camus writes, "each time with his entire being" (*E*, 152). Don Juan's commitment of his entire person to the erotic act seems, at first glance, to resemble the passionate attention a lover might give to an irreplaceable beloved. "Each time," however, transforms that commitment into a succession of intensely pleasurable seductions. "His entire being" also underlines the absence of all that is interpersonal in the experience of love where the woman is solicited, where, as the philosopher Roger Scruton points out, her character as well as her body is fully engaged.[10] There are, in other words, many seductions but no love scenes; fusion, but no union.

Don Juan's total and totalizing presence displaces the woman as a person in her own right, transforming her, as "each time" clearly suggests, into one more occasion of pleasure. To linger would risk becoming vulnerable.

Camus is well aware of how the Don Juan male, or any other sexual athlete, must appear to the women he seduces: "How unbearable for women," he wrote in his notebook, "that tenderness without love that men offer them" (*C1*, 57).[11] These unhappy women are not speaking the same language as the Camusian male. For him, the woman is a means, not an end. She has been instrumentalized, an important and all-consuming stopover, but still a stopover on a man's journey to somewhere else. Camus' male characters are aliens to love, and Camus, in his description of a sleeping Mersault in *The Happy Death,* is willing to be literal: "He seemed to be a solitary god . . . cast asleep into a strange world" (*MH*, 57). A man's language of physical desire can therefore never synchronize with the language of a woman in love. Camus notes: "It is not love that she represents, but another chance for life" (*C1*, 201). That chance, however, never involves conception, the beginning of another life. The moral hyphen joining Camus' male characters and Don Juan is the trait in Ivan Karamazov that never ceased to obsess Camus, the "attack against procreation." But how can this particular form of nihilism coexist with those chapters in *Sisyphus* and in other works that exhort the reader to live life fully?

As we saw in *Nuptials,* if the woman is never fully engaged as a person in the sexual act, neither is the man. Camus' consistent linguistic shift from "love" to "life" illustrates the shift toward a depersonalized force of love in the world at large in turn wedded to the force of death. "To be nothing," that exalting cry in "The Minotaur," appears regularly in Camus' works, right through *The First Man.*[12] "Don Juan," Camus tells us in *Sisyphus,* "has chosen to be nothing" (*E*, 155). This observation may appear out of place in a book whose principal argument is against suicide. Don Juan, however, is not suicidal in the literal sense. He wishes very much to live and to live intensely ("to be"), and his life will be all the more intense if it is never complicated by personality, love, and the human business of everyday life ("nothing"). He becomes a transcendental equation, embodying a tense and precarious equilibrium between being and nothingness. Janine, the heroine of "The Adulterous Woman," leaving her husband's bed and all that it represents of the sexual compromises and failures that are eroding her marriage, joins bodily and mystically with the cosmic forces of life and death that she discovers in the world and experiences within herself: "Each time Janine opened herself a little more to the night. She took deep breaths, she forgot the cold, the weight of others, the long anguish of living and dying. . . . The night's black water began to fill Janine, submerged the cold, rose little by little from the hidden core of her being and overflowed in endless waves up to her mouth full of moans" (*TRN*, 1574–75). This erotic union with the night brings to fruition an earlier perception in the story. As Janine looks at the desert from a rampart, Camus directs our attention to a point in the distance far beyond civilization, to the beginning of life: "Over there where the first river impregnates . . . the forest" (TRN, 1570). Janine's primordial experience is therefore similar to Meursault's: "For the first time I opened myself to the tender indifference of the world" (TRN, 1211). Indifference also anesthetizes consciousness. Neither experience is truly personal because identity has been erased. Janine flees her husband, Marcel, a middle-class merchant who is weighed down by his pathetic, narrow-minded humanity and by the things he sells from his heavy suitcase. She, too, is heavy, burdened by overweight middle age. She is also heavy with the moral and sexual discontents of her married life.

Janine does share with her husband an almost paralyzing fear of death, but, unlike her husband, she acts on her fear. She does so by calling forth death in her own body, the same body Camus describes throughout the story as pregnant. But she carries no child, only the possibility of her own redemption. She escapes her burdens for another burden—but this one lightly carried—of the cosmic sky: "The entire sky stretched out over her, fallen back on the cold earth" (TRN, 1575). Her ambiguous comment to Marcel when he wakes up from his sleep to hear her crying at his side makes more sense if we read each word literally: "It's nothing, dear . . . it's nothing" (TRN, 1575). She is fully alive as well as dead in the sense that she, like Meursault, had the exceptional capacity to strip herself of all subjectivity, to abandon personhood so as to become fully integrated with an overwhelming, cosmic power. As such, her experience is incommunicable. Janine represents one stage of an ongoing struggle in Camus, the conflict between self-discovery and self-obliteration, perhaps the one defining feature in each of the six stories in Exile and the Kingdom as well as The Fall. She, along with Mersault, Caligula, Meursault, the nameless renegade, even Rieux, who refuses to identify himself as a subjective voice while writing his chronicle of The Plague, are characters who wish to shed their character. In doing so, they elude at all times the fundamental problem of social contracts. Janine is unique in that this is the first time Camus has granted a woman an opportunity that he previously reserved exclusively for men.[13]

The Myth of Sisyphus remains, nevertheless, Camus' first social contract because the issues he addresses differ from the essentially self-regarding goals of his previous heroes. Without being a treatise offering specific political proposals, it is, as most critics have pointed out, a response to Nazism, an affirmation of political activism. The Myth of Sisyphus does not present a new Camus. Those familiar with his politically active life and his journalism have no trouble recognizing the author of this essay. What sets it apart is a shift in emphasis. Because of an impending war and because Camus had already conducted literary experiments to see, in his own words, if he had the courage and the patience to follow his own "active" nihilism to the end, the focus begins to move away from the male, inviolate self toward a more sustained consideration of a human community. But can there be a nihilist politics? What forms can a social contract take when it is based on "sterility" and political activism?

Whether he discusses philosophers, conquerors, actors, or artists, Camus discusses them in the plural, and the word that best articulates his feeling, both in *Sisyphus* and in the postwar editorials of his newspaper *Combat,* is "fraternity."[14] In contrast to his previous novels and plays, the emphasis is on collective groups, on multiple—though still restricted—human relationships. Camus writes: "Tense faces, threatened fraternity, that strong and chaste friendship of male brotherhood" (*E,* 167). Camus' dialogues with other men as a journalist and as a theater director in Algeria are revived and strengthened by his experience in the Resistance. We read in *Combat:* "For four years we were never alone. We experienced the years of fraternity" (*E,* 257); "We will never forget the great virile fraternity of those years" (*E,* 257–58); "I would like . . . to speak with . . . the fraternity and clear discernment that we owe our comrades in arms" (*E,* 263); "I speak in the name of a fraternity of combat" (*E,* 264); "We will help [our country] with a fraternal hand and a manly language" (*E,* 302).

The only reference that contradicts these resounding affirmations appeared years earlier in *The Happy Death.* Mersault calls up in his mind the image of Zagreus: "He saw again . . . the face of Zagreus in all its bloody fraternity" (*MH,* 199). Mersault murdered Zagreus for his money, and "fraternity" reminds him that the older and infirm Zagreus had cooperated with his young killer, that this consent made his death as much a suicide as a murder. As Jean Sarocchi points out, Zagreus plays father to a new Mersault now liberated from poverty and its social restrictions.[15] To dramatize this rebirth the deed is described as a sexual act, a consummation: "He accepted this green sky and this earth moist with love with the same tremor of passion and desire as the day he had murdered Zagreus" (*MH,* 186), and again: "He understood that by killing him he had consummated a marriage that joined them forever" (*MH,* 201). These erotic images of sex and marriage, more powerful, more durable than the marriage vows of lovers, serve to sacramentalize murder. They make the partners involved players in a cosmic drama. They also describe Mersault's new life. Speaking in the third person, as the author of himself, Mersault is now able to attribute to himself the same fecundating powers he attributed to his victim: "He had given birth . . . to this new self" (*MH*, 123).

By the 1940s, however, Camus had moved away from this one-on-one male and murderous bond. From the solitude of his prewar heroes to his portrait of a community of men, Camus moved from a world organized around one self seeking deliverance from the human condition to engender a new and unconditioned identity toward a society historically organized around a male group rooted in contemporary political events. Camus writes: "I have chosen history. There comes a time when you must choose between action and contemplation" (*C1*, 65). He concludes by offering the same phrase that punctuates each turning point in his own life and in the lives of his male characters: "It's called becoming a man" (*C1*, 65). That Camus "chose" history, that he thought he even had a choice, speaks volumes about his differences with Jean-Paul Sartre, for whom there was only history. Camus, however, was always politically active. He decides in the passage just quoted to shift the emphasis from a contemplative and self-absorbed life toward a life devoted to political commitment. This new emphasis governs his redefinition of what it means to be a man. Once isolated, he now belongs. Becoming a man, linked to the notion of fraternity, represents a new stage in Camus' work. It contrasts sharply, at least at first glance, "not to be a man anymore" or its variant, to be a contemplative man coupling with nature outside society's iron gates.

If Camus invests many of his ideas and feelings in fraternity, it is because this male association, in contrast to the erotic bonds between Mersault and Zagreus and between men and women, satisfies the indispensable condition of chastity, a "chaste friendship." Consequently, Camus still does not grant women any true measure of political existence. Their figurative absence in the realm of love becomes a literal absence in the political fraternity. We note this absence because Camus himself points to it and makes it a distinguishing feature of *The Myth of Sisyphus*, his first social contract. Don Juan becomes the essential complement to an exclusively male activism. If Camus were to accept women as more than objects of satisfaction, the fraternity he invokes as paradigm of a new political era would assuredly disintegrate. It is male associations that allow Camus to validate his contract with society or, more accurately, a new society projected into the future, while surrendering the minimum of the male self's domain. Raymond Gay-Crosier sums it up: "For Don Juan, fidelity to one woman represents an intolerable bond. Loyalty towards one's friends, on the other hand, is genuine."[16] Camus, author of *The Stranger*, has discovered other strangers.

Between 1942 and 1944, at the height of his fraternal fervor, Camus recorded in his notebooks numerous derogatory remarks about women, examples of misogynist contempt:

> Sexuality has been given to man to lead him away from his true path. It is his opium. With it everything sleeps. Without it, everything comes back to life. But at the same time chastity destroys the species. (*C1*, 49)
> Sexuality leads nowhere. It's not immoral, but it's unproductive. One can give in to it for whatever time one doesn't wish to be productive. But chastity alone is necessary for personal progress. (*C2*, 51)

Gay-Crosier calls these passages "outbursts" that Camus scribbled in his notebook during moments of extreme anger or depression.[17] This term, with its connotation of superficiality, transforms these statements and others like them into little more than products of insensitive moods. I think instead that they go to the very heart of the matter and that they bring into clear view an important component of Camus' nihilism which is rooted in part in the social and psychological incommensurability of men and women.

What, in fact, is the matter? What is a man's "true path" and why does sexuality, equated with passive sleep, deflect him from it? What is it about sex that is "unproductive" and what makes chastity "productive"?

To begin to answer these questions it would be useful to look first at Jean Tarrou in *The Plague*. Camus presents him to the reader as "a friend to all pleasures without being their slave" (*TRN*, 1235). Like a contemporary Montaigne, Tarrou is able to consent to his body's pleasures while keeping his mental distance. Clamence, before his breakdown, will make a similar claim in *The Fall* but with an unparalled arrogance: "Flesh, matter, in short the physical which baffles or discourages so many men in love . . . brought me, without enslaving me, so many constant joys" (*TRN*, 1490). To be pleasure's friend and not its slave is to hold oneself forcefully at an equal distance between indifference and promiscuity. Such a friendship keeps the intellect and will intact. Tarrou wants very much not to be vulnerable. To be married, like his friend Rieux, would be unthinkable; to write, like Joseph Grand, the same love letter over and over in his mind to the wife who left him would be equally unthinkable. Tarrou is free. It becomes increasingly apparent, however, that his reserve, his distance from his body's needs, conceals a secret horror. He knows that the same body he so carefully keeps in check ultimately wins in death. Camus' description of Tarrou's death, therefore, follows his demise in agonizing, physical detail. The following phrase is of particular interest: "All Rieux could see now was an inert mask" (*TRN*, 1457). In spite of Rieux's exhortations to "fight," Camus describes the body's inert triumph over an active but ultimately helpless will. Tarrou and his body are no longer mere friends. They have become one in death, and Tarrou's subjugation is total.

At about the same time he was writing *The Plague* and describing Tarrou's sexual self-control, Camus noted in his diary: "My immoderate appetite for pleasure" (*C2*, 340). *Sisyphus* was nothing if not a carpe diem, a manual for the pursuit of pleasure in a godless world condemned to death. Even before the publication of his essay, however, Camus was deeply concerned by the correlation he was beginning to perceive between pleasure and personal dissolution, that a man could become pleasure's slave and not, like Tarrou, its friend. For more than two decades he periodically returned to this concern in his notebooks.

> Pleasure divides us from ourselves just as Pascal's "diversions" divide us from God. (*C1*, 26)
>
> Many men who exalt the senses only do so because they are its slaves. The absolute necessity, therefore, of having experienced chastity. (*C1*, 193)
>
> As long as man has not dominated sexual pleasure he has dominated nothing. And he almost never dominates it. (*C2*, 266)
>
> Sexual liberty has at least brought us this, that chastity and a superior will power are now possible. . . . Intellectual freedom is now almost complete, self-control almost always possible. (*C3*, 41)
>
> Demolish systematically all habits from the most trifling to most lofty. Tobacco, food, sex . . . and *creativity itself*. Asceticism not over desire which must be kept intact but over its satisfaction. (*C3*, 221)

These passages veer between optimism and pessimism concerning a man's ability to control his erotic appetites. Camus also raises questions of personal freedom and psychological integrity. Both, in his view, are based fundamentally on the exercise of willpower. Both are threatened when the pursuit of happiness and "the quantity of joys," as Camus proposed in *Sisyphus* (*E*, 153), degenerate into mere automatic responses. These concerns are certainly not uncommon, shared as they are by most thinking people. In Camus, however, libidinal impulses acquire a particular intensity, hurtling always toward the extreme. One example is Clamence's physical and moral exhaustion when he confesses, "Not taking what you don't desire is the most difficult thing in the world" (*TRN*, 1508). The body's physical gestures are divorced from both will and desire, resulting in a kind of sexual robotics. The situation became extreme enough for Camus to fear the total loss of his personal liberty: "Sex, strange, stranger, solitary, that always decides on its own to keep pressing further on, that you cannot resist and must blindly obey, that, after years of violent passion and just before many more years of sensual madness, suddenly stops and falls silent, that prospers in routines, becomes impatient with novelty and surrenders its independence only when one agrees to gratify it completely. What person, with any self-respect, would ever consent from the bottom of his heart to such tyranny? Chastity, oh liberty!" (*C3,* 79–80). Much of the vocabulary in this significant passage is that of insanity and subjugation, the loss of mind, will, and self-control. All of *The Myth of Sisyphus* is dedicated to conquest, the unimpeded exercise of a man's will in an absurd world without objective rules or social law. Camus now portrays himself as the conquered. He feels degraded by sex, not exalted as in *Nuptials.* Sex, described in those four essays as an embodied mystical experience, has now become a humiliated body whose sexual organ lies beyond a man's will. Camus was no doubt referring to this unresolved ambiguity of the body when he stated, "Hell is life with this body" (*C1,* 51). Most important, Camus feels that he has become the passive woman to his own male, erotic impulses. As he repeatedly invokes chastity, his moral pendulum swings in ever-widening circles in search of that elusive center called manhood.

No such torment shadows Camus' description of Don Juan. No sooner has this lover seduced a woman than his desires surge in the presence of another. It is not at all a matter of youthful and zestful escapades. Don Juan is not Cherubino. Camus' sense of his own sexuality and manhood, as I pointed out in Chapter 2, is inseparable from his acute sense of his own native nobility. He will not be common. Don Juan, moreover, seduced to conquer. Conquest in turn transformed each sexual encounter into an opportunity to perform and stage the spectacle of male superiority and female submission. That equality that Camus explicitly grants other men in friendship and in political fraternity does not extend to women in matters of love and sexuality. What is particularly relevant in Camus' reference to Pascal, that "diversions" divide man from God just as pleasure divides us from ourselves, is the implicit concern with the ability to engage in sexual pleasure and remain both aristocratically aloof and psychologically intact. If action of any kind fractures our being, then interaction is dangerous and erotic interaction particularly so. Camus' reference to an unnamed colleague is revelatory: "That mouth scoured by the filthy erosion of pleasure" (*C2,* 266). That Camus should refer to the eroding (as opposed to the constructing) power of pleasure tells us that he had at times a quantitative view of human nature, believing that the experience of pleasure can diminish a man's finite fund of energy and will, a contemporary take on Oscar Wilde's *Dorian Gray* and Honoré de Balzac's *The Wild Ass's Skin*. Chastity, in contrast, could perhaps shore up a too easily expendable personality. "The question," Camus wrote, "is to live lucidly in a world where dispersion is the rule. . . . The real problem . . . is the problem of psychological unity" (*C2,* 19).

Camus had originally praised the ability of the erotic act to render people "empty," and the rallying cry in *Sisyphus* was "consume everything and be consumed." Now Camus invokes chastity, and he does so for several reasons: to prove a man's ability to conquer himself and be his own man, to demonstrate that, in a world without law, an identifiable human nature, or divine transcendance, a man could, by sheer will, become the chaste opposite of his promiscuous self, above all to stanch any further psychological hemorrhaging.[18] The goal, ultimately, is to recapture a threatened wholeness and enjoy a seamless unity of consciousness.

Chastity also serves a more practical purpose. Pleasure may take time, but so does art. Camus was profoundly worried that he was betraying his art and the artist in himself. He was not a little discomfited by a remark of Gustave Flaubert, an author he admired greatly, which he quoted in his private journal: "Success with women is generally a sign of mediocrity" (*C2,* 24). He writes about Jacques Cormery in *The First Man,* in effect about himself: "J. can indulge in women—but what if they take up all his time" (*PH,* 280); "Jacques has four women at the same time and therefore leads an *empty* life" (*PH,* 285). What were for Don Juan a succession of erotic moments fueled by inexhaustible energy has become for Jacques, as it does for Clamence in *The Fall,* simultaneous erotic liaisons, a complicated multiplication table of women that clashes ironically with the underlined adjective "empty." Jacques worries about time. So does Camus, whose notebooks are regularly punctuated with desperate time schedules and promises to keep:

> *One month* of self-denial in every respect.
> Sexual Chastity.
> Intellectual Chastity—forbid your desires to wander, your thoughts to be dispersed. . . .
> Work on a fixed schedule, without fail . . . (moral asceticism, too).
> One sign of weakness and everything founders. (*C1,* 193)
> Work at least to perfect both silence and creation. (*C1,* 202)
> Four months of ascetic and solitary life. The will, the mind will become stronger. But the heart? (*C2,* 77)

Disciplined work until April. (*C2*, 305)

Before writing a novel. . . . Attempt at daily concentration, intellectual asceticism, extreme focus. (*C3*, 272)

These exhortations rehearse again a tradition in which art, like God, is better served by chastity than by sex. The dispersive impulses of desire driving us into the world would be captured instead and concentrated in a room, at a desk, on a blank page, ultimately within oneself.[19] Camus praises Roger Martin du Gard, who was "faithful . . . to an ascetic vocation" (*E*, 1135); Joseph Grand in *The Plague*, writing endless variations of his novel's first sentence, leads a life that is "quasi ascetic" (*TRN*, 1254); the creative act, Camus asserts in *Sisyphus*, "constitutes an asceticism" (*E*, 156); he praises Tolstoy, who, observing his wife, notes: "I love her less than my novel" (*C3*, 83). This quote is a variation of what Camus had already revealed about his own investment in art: "My work . . . has enslaved me. And if I pursue it, it is because . . . I value it over everything else, even liberty, even wisdom or true fertility and, yes, even friendship" (*C3*, 76). Art is an "enslavement," and Don Juan's pursuit of women contrasts sharply with the artist's "pursuit" of his art. "True" or procreative fertility competes with its creative counterpart, but sexuality in an earlier quote was labeled "unproductive."[20] The contrast Camus is attempting to draw is the traditional opposition between the material products of the flesh and the productions of the spirit. They share a similar vocabulary demonstrating thereby the interchangeable dynamics of sex and aesthetics.

As a young man visiting Vicenza, admiring and yielding to the silent beauty of the Italian countryside, Camus felt a libidinal surge within himself and wrote: "I populated the universe with beings like myself" (*E*, 38). In a similar vein, Caligula, insisting that he is an artist who writes not on a mere page but through the superior medium of human flesh and human lives, exclaims: "I feel rising within me vast numbers of beings" (*TRN*, 26). He can then conclude: "I don't need art. I live" (*TRN*, 98), breaking down entirely the notion of aesthetic distance between artist and artistic product. Camus asserts in *The Myth of Sisyphus*: "Every healthy human being tends to reproduce himself" (*E*, 152). Both the author and his characters are usurping a divine prerogative, the ability to create life and reproduce oneself without a woman, out of one's own self-fecundating powers.

This vocabulary of fertility passes back and forth between sex and aesthetic practice. Camus advances the claim in *Sisyphus* that a work of art represents "the triumph of the carnal" (*E*, 176). Although words are the abstract representations of things, Camus is referring to the novel as an externalized embodiment through characters of inner ideas and feelings, a socially licensed form of the divine surge Camus experienced in Vicenza, dramatized in the tragic destiny of Caligula, and proposed in *Sisyphus*. Literary conception often borrows its vocabulary from the procreative act, and Camus describes the joys of literary creation: "I encounter them at the moment of conception, at the very second when the subject reveals itself to me.... Then there's the actual work, that is to say a long labor" (*E*, 9). Art is carnal because what Camus in this same passage calls the coupling of "imagination" with "intelligence" (*E*, 9) results in a physical as well as cultural creation that owes little to flesh. Making, an independent achievement, is better than the cooperative and dependent process of generating.

Camus was, among many other things, politically active, a family man with a wife and twin children, sexually promiscuous, and a creative artist. Many of the entries in his private notebooks are attempts, often desperate, to establish a balance between these commitments. Women were at the center of his life both as sexual conquests and carriers of divine "signs." They were, at the same time, utterly alien to his existence as fully realized persons. Camus eventually came to understand this paradox. He writes about women and their relationship to political and creative forms of action: "Except for love, women are boring. They know nothing. You must live with one and do nothing. Or sleep with all of them and do" (*C1*, 58). Living with one identifiable woman, presumably a reference to marriage and the moral attention required by fidelity, results in silence but the wrong kind of silence. It is the silence of unrealized potential, of aborted revolt, and of unmanly submission. "To do," in turn, as a generalized reference to all human endeavor, depends on "sleeping with all of them," those undifferentiated sexual encounters practiced by Don Juan.

There is, however, a contradiction that Camus does not resolve or even confront. Other notebook entries commented that multiple sexual encounters threatened to rob the artist of precious time. It now appears that the value of promiscuity is that the lover need not pay the ongoing attention that one woman apparently requires, hence liberating him. We could also add that if "to do" depends on "sleeping with all of them," it is because this form of sexuality is without personal consequence. Neither Don Juan nor his women are sexual to the extent that their physical engagement does not provide for the possibilities of either moral loyalty or physical conception. The thought that sex may have social or generative consequences seems never to have occurred to Don Juan. What Camus professes instead is "a life devoted to short-lived joys" (*E*, 157). Sisyphus himself, pushing his rock, is engaged in a series of acts that are "unrelated" (*E*, 198). The ideal life is "the present and the succession of present moments" (*E,* 145). Having sex with women is therefore inconsequential. Physical conception, as opposed to artistic conception, risks transforming "succession" into a sequence in which a human act, such as the act of love, has consequences, is involved in causality, introducing responsibilities and a social ethic. Don Juan's goal is to score vast numbers of female conquests. "For those who seek quantities of joy," Camus wrote in *The Myth of Sisyphus,* "efficacy alone matters" (*E,* 153). If so, then fidelity and children would be the height of inefficiency.

Don Juan's sexual energies are sterile because, in the final analysis, they are directed back to himself. One reason why Don Juan, fraternal politics, and an absurdist aesthetic coexist in *Sisyphus* is that, in different ways, they exclude women. Since women, at the very least, represent and guarantee biological continuity, love and politics must both be made inconsequential.

Camus makes this claim: "Aware that I cannot separate myself from my time, I have decided to become intimately united with it" (*E,* 165). But when this politician unites with history, like Don Juan with the female body, they engender nothing. The sterility of the isolated man in *The Happy Death, Caligula, The Misunderstanding,* and *The Stranger* has evolved into a politics of sterility. *The Myth of Sisyphus* was written before the end of the war. Although Camus insists on his commitment to history, it becomes increasingly clear that he is in effect espousing a cataclysm in history, the advent of Nazism. He does not suggest in *Sisyphus* that there is anything beyond this particular and, from all appearances, definitive apocalypse. Camus had already written in *Right Side and Wrong Side:* "At a certain stage of deprivation, nothing more leads to nothing more" (*E,* 28), a variant of "to be nothing." Whether political or biological, fraternal or solitary, asceticism is the logical consequence of a womanless universe or a society of depersonalized women because, like a metaphysical or aesthetic birth control, it was always there.

*Sisyphus* carries forward motifs of Camus' previous work because it reconciles the two terms of an antithesis: the need to satisfy overwhelming sexual urges and to stop life. It reconciles promiscuity with sterility. This theme of sterile sexuality is one of Camus' contributions to the monastic vow of chastity he had described in his thesis for the Diplôme d'Etudes Supérieures: "If Marcion preaches sexual abstinence it is because the God of the Old Testament said: 'Be fruitful and multiply.' What resonates in this proud refusal to obey is a completely modern sensibility" (*E,* 1257).

This scholarly and apparently objective student essay coincides with the misogynist passages of the notebooks. This "completely modern sensibility" is the politics of sterility, and it reveals itself first in Camus' solitary heroes and then again, but in a different light, in Don Juan and the community of men in *The Myth of Sisyphus* and in the editorials of *Combat*. Certainly male friendship allows for a flow of human emotions and for reciprocal relationships lacking in the previous works. I refer particularly to the friendships of Rieux, Tarrou, Grand, and Rambert in *The Plague* and also Camus' moving tribute to his friend René Leynaud, a Catholic resistant murdered by the Gestapo. And yet Camus returns periodically to the ascetic, making it a necessary if not always realizable condition of his art and private life. Up to the publication of *Sisyphus*, we are dealing with men, isolated or in groups, whom nothing influences and who influence nothing.

In his editorials after the war, however, Camus expresses the conviction that the fraternity of men he had discovered in the Resistance and who had survived the Götterdämmerung could be extended into peacetime and become the vehicle for social revolution. It was a propitious time to build a future because the Nazis had been defeated and Europe had to arrange its rebirth.

The ideal in *Sisyphus* was to be a man "without a future" (*E*, 151), and Camus was referring specifically to the afterlife. He also was expressing the conviction, developed in his assessment of Roger Martin du Gard, that each child's birth merely serves to swell the floodtide of our collective death. But now we read: "Life can have no value without giving thought to the future, without the promise of ripeness and progress" (*E*, 331). Nature's "ripeness" posed no problem for Camus. It was cyclical; it disappeared and returned. A word, however, like "progress," denoting a linear and cumulative development that was anathema to the author of *Sisyphus*, now finds favor with the postwar editorialist of *Combat*. Camus was skeptical of social law and recognized few, if any, moral laws in nature. The survival of France, nevertheless, required an ethic and a new social contract. In 1944 Camus wrote to the literary critic Guy Dumur: "No truth can have any value for me unless it is attained through human beings; I do not believe in solitude" (*E*, 1671). This statement argues for a profound change in Camus. Previously, the one and only truth—death—had been comprehended, as in *Caligula*, in opposition to others who, unlike the play's patrician protagonist, were vulgar enough to want to live.[21] The phrase "through human beings" is important because it replaces the mystical and solitary body of *Nuptials* with a body politic. It blocks a man's trajectory toward total freedom against or beyond humanity, and will develop into the doctrine of "limits" in *The Rebel*.

Most relevant to our subject is whether "human beings" includes women who might mediate a man's contract with society and who would themselves become active agents in formulating the terms of that contract. Camus was discovering that society too has its roots in love and sexuality and that, as Donald Lazere points out, "private love is necessary to energize social commitment."[22] Will "future" and "progress" remain abstract concepts? Will they have their origins, as Camus claimed at the Swedish Academy, in "fertility"? Will fertility be restricted to the aesthetic and creative process, the procreative relegated to self-reproduction or the occasional rhetorical flourish, as in this description of the liberation of Paris: "This fearful birth is that of a revolution" (*E, 256*).

What we can ascertain is that during the postwar years, when Camus in his editorials was offering the male fraternity as an appropriate vehicle for the political reconstruction of France, he was simultaneously questioning it while composing *The Plague*. Insofar as the plague represents the fight against Nazism or, in more general terms, against any totalitarian regime, it depicts in documentary fashion a tragic destiny suffered by a victimized people and the triumph of a cadre of male resistants. Once the plague takes up residence in the human heart, however, a point Camus makes clear throughout the novel, particularly in his portrait of Tarrou, who guides us through that moral terrain, it becomes a choice, a destiny willed. Of its many manifestations the one of interest here is the separation of men and women. Later, the allegorical figure of the plague in *State of Siege* will admit: "I begin by separating men from women" (*TRN, 228*). That separation is a fact of war and was a fact in Camus' personal life. During the Occupation he was separated from his wife, Francine, she in Algeria, he in France. This question of separation also represents Camus' first sustained reevaluation of virtually every important work he wrote.

Except for the mother, there is an almost total absence of female characters in *The Plague*, particularly wives. Describing the Bowery during his only visit to New York, Camus had noted with amusement: "It's the most sinister neighborhood in the city, the one where you don't see a single woman" (*E, 1833*).[23] The fraternity of Rieux, Grand, Rambert, Paneloux, and Tarrou, all celibate through choice or circumstance, like the plague, has created its particular desert. Rieux's wife, sent to a sanitarium outside the city, is replaced by Rieux's mother, Madame Rieux replaced by Madame Rieux. A wife is replaced by a mother, and there are no other women left. The plague is both the historical cause and the psychological result of an unnatural and, in this instance, eventually permanent separation. The wife dies. The sterility in Oran, traced over the plague of sterility in the

Oedipus legend, is the sine qua non of exiled wives and celibate husbands and of sons reunited with their mothers. That sterility is also Camus' condemnation of virtually every misogynist view he had expressed in his notebooks, his fiction, and *The Myth of Sisyphus.*

Women in Camus' works will be gradually admitted into the polis. The transcendent sexuality of *Nuptials* and the self-regarding sexuality of Mersault, Meursault, and Don Juan will yield to a broader-based social contract. Where Camus once viewed society, in particular middle-class society, as inimical to a sexuality that he felt needed to be liberated from morality and politics, he now is beginning to understand that society's energies, too, draw deeply from the intimate relationships of its men and women. An important passage from the notebooks dated 1944 marks a step in Camus' evolving attitudes toward women, love, and sexuality: "Men who love all women are men moving closer to abstraction. They're moving beyond this world, appearances notwithstanding. For they are avoiding the particular, the individual case. The man who would flee all ideas and all abstraction, the truly desperate one, is the man involved with one woman. Through persistence in that unique face that cannot satisfy everything" (C2, 126). Camus is rereading Camus and taking a critical look at Don Juan. This lover celebrated the body and its erotic desires that were renewed in the presence of each desirable woman. Love concentrated in one beloved through time was tantamount to folly, an unnatural denial of a man's inexhaustible capacity for pleasure. In this passage, multiplicity is equated with superficiality, a synonym for abstraction. Both Rieux and Rambert have wives. The chapter on love in *The Plague,* Camus' extended meditation on men and women who are separated, as well as the episodes devoted to Rambert's exhaustive efforts to escape Oran and rejoin his lover in France, are eloquent, deeply felt, and among the most moving Camus ever wrote. And yet women are still absent.

Camus' expressive range, nevertheless, is widening considerably as he rethinks what constitutes manhood and intensifies his critique, from *The Just Assassins* to *The Rebel,* of fraternity and the politics of sterility. Dora exclaims: "What a repulsive taste fraternity has sometimes" (*TRN,* 387), and it is a woman, the central character of *The Just Assassins,* who pronounces sentence. In *The Rebel,* after examining the totalitarian mentality of political terrorists, Camus concludes: "They glut their foul hunger for fraternity" (*E,* 649). Referring in the same essay to Lenin's secret network of agents, Camus labels them "the secret society of monks . . . of the revolution" (*E,* 631). He quotes approvingly Dostoyevsky's description of young political extremists as a "proletariat of graduates" (*E,* 632).

Surely the most important summation is this one from "Defense of *The Rebel*": "Nineteenth century ideology . . . abandoned Goethe's dream to unite, with Faust and Helen, contemporary revolt with classic beauty, and to give them a son Euphorion! Our modern Faust then wanted to have Euphorion without Helen, in a kind of sullen and arrogant delight. But all he could give birth to was a laboratory monster instead of a wondrous child. In order to exist and create, he could not do without Helen" (*E*, 1711). This passage compares the procreated child with the creation of a political Frankenstein. In spite of its somewhat high-flown and hyperbolic imagery, Camus is still illustrating what was for him a new truth, a woman's essential presence in any future social contract. In his essay "René Char" Camus also indicates how much he has changed when he praises his friend's poetry: "And here, by virtue of a discreet and bountiful art, the woman exists" (*E*, 1165). *The First Man* begins with a mother about to give birth. Publishing *Exile and the Kingdom*, Camus, for the first time in his entire career, dedicated a book to a woman, his wife, Francine. Quentin Anderson expresses the view that each new couple may create a "new nation."[24] "To exist and create," in opposition to the slogan of the young Camus, "to be nothing," seriously erodes the vow of solitary sterility "not to be a man anymore" and the politics of sterility, "to be a man" but only among other men. Camus rejects the political church dedicated to an abstract utopia invented by men alone out of their self-fecundating powers. Unlike Patrice Mersault, Caligula, and the terrorists of *The Rebel*, Camus no longer believes that a man could be born of a man.

*The Myth of Sisyphus* had praised sterility and denied process and change. The absurdist writer required "un coeur sec" (*E*, 165), figuratively a "closed heart," literally a "dry heart." What this means in part is that a newborn child may be wet and dirty, which is exactly how Camus describes it in *The First Man*, but that the artist and his artistic products, subtracted from flesh, are dry and clean. In *The Rebel*, Camus' second social contract, we are given to understand that revolt "is love and fertility or it is nothing" (*E*, 704).

Creativity always retains its high prestige. Camus will continue to borrow from the vocabulary of fertility to describe the creative process. To explain how much he owes his teacher and mentor Jean Grenier, he offers the following definition of "teacher": "Spirit engenders spirit . . . over generations" (*E*, 1160). In a satirical and also affectionate way Camus describes the apartment of the painter Jonas: "The rooms were filled with paintings and children" (*TRN*, 1635), the artist fertile in his body and in his art. Jonas understands intuitively the isomorphism that exists between creation and procreation: "He would think about his painting with that tenderness and warmth that he had never felt except for his children" (*TRN*, 1649). Jonas fails to sort out his commitments to his art, his family, and his public, but that is a human failure. In opposition to his early works, Camus is trying to restore the notion of generation and generations, to restore chronology and therefore biography—that Grenier preceded Camus—to outline, as he claimed he was doing to the members of the Swedish Academy, a politics and an aesthetic of fertility.

We can therefore understand why the central episode of *The Plague* is the death of a child. The death of children reverses the forward course of procreation and chronology. In the context of the plague as evil willed, this sterility occurs when wives are replaced by mothers and husbands become only sons again. The banding together of sons in a confraternity leaves no room for women and children and cancels the future.

Camus' wife gave birth to twins in 1945, and I would suggest that the detailed description of the boy's death was written by a man who, except for his tuberculosis, had never before felt so vulnerable, who felt through someone else's body the risks we take when we live our lives with and through others. There are no children in Camus' works up to *The Plague*, only childlike men insisting on their innocence and convinced that death was the "only reality." Camus began to pay closer attention to the child because it represents a fundamental part of that "fertility" he claimed was an essential source of his inspiration. In *The Just Assassins* the terrorist Kaliayev refuses to kill the children in the grand duke's coach and is opposed by Stepan, the doctrinaire revolutionary.[25] Clamence the lawyer mocks widows and orphans but indirectly expresses his longing to be a husband and father. One of the torments of the Algerian war to which Camus constantly returned was the assassination of children. In "The Adulterous Woman" Janine wants to have a child. Yvars in *The Silent Men* is a father. Camus describes his own childhood in *The First Man*, and Jonas attempts to reconcile his art with his children: "Sending them away, he felt that they filled his heart's space completely, without reservations. Deprived of their presence, he felt only emptiness and loneliness. He loved them as much as his art because they were the only things in this world just as alive" (*TRN*, 1647). Jonas has reason to speak of his heart's unrestricted "space" because he finds himself in a small apartment, an enclosed and almost claustrophobic domestic space where meals are prepared and eaten, beds and love made, visitors welcomed, where his children play, his wife works, and he produces his art. He has, in other words, a home.

Camus' flight from the human required that women and children remain marginal in his literary and imaginative universe, for they were proof
of life's stubborn and low-class will to live. Death was the only truth, and
death was sterile. Camus changed. He writes in "Return to Tipasa": "It is
a misfortune not to love. All of us today are dying from that misfortune"
(*E,* 873). That change is also signaled in a note he wrote during the Occupation: "Our Europe . . . is convulsing and that is why it will die if peace
does not signify a return to beauty and to love's rightful place" (*C2,* 92).
That convulsion is dramatized in *The Plague,* where the separation of lovers and the absence of love are symptoms of a moral as well as physical
disease. It is explained in *The Rebel,* where Camus traces the bloody history of European and Russian nihilism. It is also fixed once and for all in
*The Fall,* Camus' most self-denunciatory work.

This novel is ostensibly the confession of a lawyer who lives under the
assumed name of Jean-Baptiste Clamence. As such, he poses a fundamental
problem of perception and self-perception. Other people may appear to us
as unified persons whose gestures and deeds are governed by inner disposi-
tions that are more predictable, more easily identifiable to outsiders than to
themselves. This is not so for Clamence. He is supremely aware of his own
unified being, which he presents to his reader-listener as a perfect coincidence of mind, body, and experience. He is not self-conscious. "I was," he
tells us, "in complete harmony with life" (*TRN,* 1489). Going one important step further, he assumes a divine prerogative: "I never had to learn
how to live" (*TRN,* 1489). There are no rites of passage through which the
multiple and imperfect meanings we find or put in life develop through
time. A woman's suicide, however, does divide his life as it divides the
novel, just as the Arab's death divides *The Stranger.* Meursault seemed to
have no problem dismissing the victim from his mind. Clamence tries to
dismiss the woman but cannot. The essential question for our subject is
why this death had to be a woman's death.

She herself has no identity, which balances Clamence's invented one.
Clamence is not his real name. She lost her life, "took it," as we say,
whereas Clamence, fearing the loss of inner coherence, renames himself in
order to recapture it.[26] Her death does not immediately make Clamence
self-conscious and therefore self-divided, a man required by circumstance
to think against himself. A subsequent episode involving laughter marks
this first step. It deserves to be quoted at length: "I had reached the Pont des
Arts, deserted at that hour. . . . Facing the Vert-Galant, I dominated the
island. I felt rising within me a vast feeling of power and—how shall I
express this—of completion which made my heart swell. I straightened up

and was going to light a cigarette, the cigarette of satisfaction when, just then, laughter burst out behind me. Surprised, I suddenly turned around: no one was there" (*TRN*, 1495). The "cigarette of satisfaction," a cultural cliché, usually denotes a postcoital moment, but the deeds that Clamence had listed for this particular day do not include sex. He mentions instead a successful law case, acts of charity, and brilliant conversation. The entire episode is nonetheless sexual because all of the events listed are explicitly linked by Clamence to his own exhilarating feelings of godlike power and domination. The verb "rising" appears twice in the original French, and "I felt rising within me" recalls Caligula's "I felt rising within me countless beings."[27] Clamence's exercise of power throughout the novel manifests itself consistently and most tellingly in his sexual exploits. The link between the laughter he hears behind his back and the unidentified woman is made more explicit still when Clamence describes the laughter "as if it were going downstream" (*TRN*, 1495). The dying woman's cry for help after leaping into the Seine also "went downstream" (*TRN*, 1511). Hearing the laughter, Clamence suddenly "turns around," a physiological sign of the moral and psychological revolution already taking place within him. He looks in the mirror upon returning home: "It seemed to me that my smile was double" (*TRN*, 1495). Now split, self-conscious, Clamence falls and, at least temporarily, becomes human.

His stated goal, thereafter, is to deconstruct himself, to reenact publicly what had already taken place privately: "To expose to all eyes what he really was, I wanted to split apart the handsome mannequin that I presented everywhere" (*TRN*, 1523). Clamence's inner division is already evident in his ability to speak of himself in the third person, as if he were his own ventriloquist. Clamence's confession appears to be, therefore, the result of a fractured consciousness.

A mannequin's inexpressive face, that place where personality resides, is Camus' satirical version of the inexpressive statues he praised in *Nuptials*. Camus' self-satire, however, is Clamence's desperate tactic. Clamence presents himself as the active agent, the one destroying the wax dummy in the act of a contrite confession. He would turn his fall, his accident, something that happened to him and outside his control, into a calculated, premeditated leap. What the laughter introduced into Clamence's life was another invasive, human perspective. Not only does that perspective function of its own volition, independently of Clamence's control, it undoes Clamence at precisely that point at which he had always assumed he was serenely invulnerable, his sexuality. Laughter after the "cigarette of satisfaction," after coitus, renders Clamence's sex life not only risible but almost obscene, as if he had been watched and studied the entire time by a third party. As a lawyer and former amateur actor, Clamence has no problem with being watched. He lives for it. One of the reasons he did not come to the drowning woman's aid was because there was no one there to watch. Being watched, however, is particularly maddening to Clamence in this instance because he did not give the cue. He cannot locate that laughter, that particular subjective point of view that evaluates him and, as far as he is concerned, diminishes him. Laughter had an entirely different function in Camus' presentation of Don Juan: "For Don Juan, the more they laugh at him, the more imposing he becomes" (*E*, 155). As an adversarial figure who disobeys all moralities that preach any form of sexual restraint, Don Juan grows ever "more imposing" by whatever opposes or mocks him. He feeds on it. The chapter on Don Juan in *Sisyphus* and Clamence's dramatic about-face as he experiences, for the first time, a sense not of sexual grandeur but of emotional worthlessness are meant to reflect each other. Through them we can measure Camus' ongoing and evolving investigations into the questions of love and sexuality.

The novel's dramatic impact resides in Clamence's discovery that the laughter and its judgments come as much from within as from outside himself. He resembles in this the nameless renegade of Camus' short story whose tongueless mouth still speaks with an inner voice despite all his conscious efforts to silence it. Clamence, moreover, cannot bring himself to accept the fact that not being omnipotent might be an enabling factor in his own salvation. His outburst at the end: "Don't laugh!" (*TRN*, 1548) is addressed as much to himself as to his listener. The laughter's judgment inflicts a mortal wound on an impenetrable man and not a healing breach.[28] To evaluate, of course, is not necessarily to wound or diminish except in terms of Clamence's global, imperial, and self-regarding perspective, which would render any other perspective immediately suspect. Hence Camus' choice of the monologue as the mold in which Clamence's life is cast and revealed.

This fear of another person's perspective animates the following passage from Camus' notebook: "What man finds intolerable is being judged. Hence that close attachment to the mother, the blinded lover, also our love for animals" (*C3*, 115). What links all three loving attachments, the mother, the lover, and the animal, is that Camus believes them to be unconditional and safe. Neither one possesses a sufficiently subjective and independent consciousness that would in any way threaten a man's coherent and self-enclosed nature. Camus' notebooks also contain this key passage: "Coupling with animals suppresses consciousness of *the other*. It represents 'freedom'" (C2, 40). Individual liberty becomes synonymous with oppression, the elimination of another's subjectivity, so much so that an animal becomes the ideal lover. If the animal is unselfconscious, then what the unselfconscious lover seeks is a partner indistinguishable from himself, one who is not an "other." What might be considered the goal of love is here its precondition. What Camus is reflecting on is a parody of the union of lovers freely consenting to their union. The parody extends from the animal all the way to the woman.

What is disturbing and most relevant to the questions of love and sexuality in *The Fall* is that, alongside "mother" and "animals," we read "blinded lover" instead of "blind lover." Camus perhaps wished to avoid any ambiguity about the literalness of "blind" as opposed to being figuratively "blinded" by love. No reader, however, would have interpreted "blind" literally any more than we would interpret "dry heart" literally. If anything, it is "blinded" that we react to literally. We understand, therefore, that this is a brutally sadistic act on a woman violated in her eyes—in almost the same way that Camus' eyes were violated by the sunlight in Greece[29]—eyes that are the primary means through which her person and her spirit speak.[30] Relevant to this issue of the woman as an independent "other" are the increasing number of references in Camus' notebooks to erotic meetings with girls.[31] Girls, unlike women, have undeveloped perspectives and are unequipped to judge. Camus' future biographer will no doubt have to address this particular issue, but I bring it up here because it points to a peculiar feature of *The Fall*. The woman who commits suicide is described first as a "young woman" (TRN, 1511) and then, in the novel's conclusion, as a "girl" (TRN, 1551), first as a formed woman and then as an unformed adolescent. This transformation would be consistent with Clamence's ultimate goal: "I finally feel that I am adored" (TRN, 1549). Adoration, as he understands it, requires the other's submission, his or her loss of freedom, the adult ability to judge. It requires the dissolution of identity.

Clamence does not understand that his lovers may have a point of view and a capacity to evaluate. When one woman confides to a third party that Clamence was once impotent, he reacts with astonishment: "I felt deceived somehow; she wasn't so passive after all; she didn't lack judgment" (TRN, 1508). He adds a detail that links this episode to the "cigarette of satisfaction": "I pretended to laugh. In fact I did laugh about it" (TRN, 1508). His second reaction, after being astonished, is to torture her: "I began . . . to humiliate her in every way. . . . In the violent disorder of a powerful and constrained pleasure she paid loud tribute to what was enslaving her" (*TRN*, 1508). Up to this point in the novel Clamence had presented his love affairs in terms similar to those Camus had used for Don Juan, as the robust, healthy experiences of a sexual champion. This episode, however, is sadistic. Clamence is not only causing this woman's humiliation—in itself an insignificant factor if we accept the premise that lovers can hurt each other as no one else can—but, more important, he is able to stand outside her pain, untouched and unmoved. Her perspective and her presence as a suffering woman are never allowed to intrude upon his closed perspective and aloof person.

It is difficult to decide whether Clamence is Camus' redescription of Don Juan. Don Juan had successive erotic encounters, each one involving his "entire being." Clamence summarizes his amorous life: "Sensuality, and nothing else, dominated my life. I searched for objects of pleasure and conquest" (*TRN*, 1505). The connection with Don Juan seems, therefore, clear enough.

Yet Clamence has simultaneous liaisons. Erotic focus blurs into erotic absentmindedness and confusion. It is an open question whether Don Juan is a satyromaniac. Clamence certainly is and indeed refers to himself as a "a salacious monkey" (*TRN*, 1528). He is, however, a redescription to the extent that Camus makes explicit what was only implicit, what Roger Scruton calls Don Juan's "deep anxiety."[32] That anxiety manifests itself in Clamence's persistent concern over sexual performance expressed in his repeated use of the verb "to verify":

I satisfied the love I bore myself by verifying each time my wonderful powers. (*TRN*, 1507)
I attempted to resume relations with them . . . to verify that our ties still held and that I alone had the right to tighten them. (*TRN*, 1507)
The problem is that verifications are never definitive. (*TRN*, 1507)

The anxiety that lies below the surface of these passages, however, cannot be attributed solely to sexual performance. Clamence's erotic urges propel him toward the woman's body, a carnal geography he professes to know as well as the Amsterdam he guides us through. Whereas women in *Nuptials* were beautiful and passive flowers, Camus is now addressing the question of a woman's liberty. Don Juan seduced women into consenting to sex. Whatever else it was, each affair was the private affair of consenting adults. Other issues are mobilized in *The Fall* and, without forgetting the woman's report of Clamence's impotence, they go beyond a woman's right to judge.

There is the question of love itself and what it is a woman, whose body is governed by both her instincts and her character, might bring to a man in the act of love.

Clamence, however, desires a woman's body only, and this lover wishes to "conquer" not only her initial resistance, or modesty, or indecisiveness, but her formidable ability to love as well as to make love. According to the Camusian male, that love, as we saw in chapter 2, comes with too much middle-class moral and psychological baggage. More specifically, it introduces into the erotic act the complex dynamics of reciprocity, exchange, and dialogue. In *The Happy Death* Camus has Mersault say: "The love one bears me in no way obligates me" (*MH*, 74). Such a statement is merely cynical. It is also part of Camus' consistent strategy, up to *The Fall*, to uproot love from middle-class moral economy. He can, therefore, while analyzing Roger Martin du Gard's *Les Thibault*, refer to Antoine's lover Rachel as a "royal gift, one that enriches without obligation" (*E*, 1149).[33] Art itself is "a gift without obligations" (*E*, 1160). Under proper conditions love and aesthetics can raise themselves above the burdensome and petty obligations of everyday life. But this is only part of Camus. Another part of him writes: "It is just that writers answer for what they write" (*E*, 313). Here there is linkage. Camus will work this question of social and personal obligation into the fabric of *The Fall*, into Clamence's views and practice of love, enabling us to evaluate him.

Clamence tries to solve the problem of engaging in social or sexual encounters without suffering the ego-threatening effects of obligation. Each social and erotic scene is shaped around the economy of mutual engagement and Clamence's tactics to avoid entanglement:

> My neighbor whom I always obligated without ever owing him a thing. (*TRN*, 1488)
>
> I've learned to be content with mere sympathy. One finds it more easily and besides it is never binding. (*TRN*, 1491)
>
> Do you know why we are always more honest and more generous toward the dead? The reason is simple. With them we have no obligations. (*TRN*, 1492)

The daily inconveniences of social intercourse become particularly acute when the question is love. The gestures of ordinary good manners become even more profoundly compromising when the language of manners becomes the language of love. "If I were to answer yes," Clamence notes when asked by a woman if he loves her, "I found myself bound beyond my true feelings" (*TRN*, 1526).

Clamence offers four solutions to this dilemma, and each one distinguishes him sharply from Don Juan. The first involves multiple liaisons: "I extended to all the other women the debt I had just contracted toward one of them" (*TRN*, 1510). Concerning his law practice and relationship with clients he admits: "The emotions I spent relieved me . . . of any debt toward them" (*TRN*, 1489). The satirical edge of these passages derives from the fact that Clamence is describing bad law, bad love, and bad finances. Clamence develops his economic system of erotics still further when he concludes: "Women, in the final accounting, cost me dear" (*TRN*, 1516). The ultimate purpose of multiple erotic contacts is to absolve Clamence of the individual focus that love requires, leaving his inner self untouched and intact. Clamence is physically promiscuous and a moral virgin.

Multiple liaisons apparently do not always provide Clamence with the psychological contraception he needs to protect himself from emotions. Clamence goes a step further into debauchery, his second solution: "True debauchery is liberating because it creates no obligations. You only possess yourself, and therefore it remains the preferred occupation of the great lovers of their own person" (*TRN*, 1528). Debauchery appears to guarantee what several scattered lovers could not, the suppression of all consciousness of the other person, now the blurred member of a blurred group. Most of all, it might guarantee the suppression of one's own self-consciousness, one's inner division, "a long sleep" (*TRN*, 1529), as Clamence puts it. This vague lust prevents intimacy and, if Clamence means what he says when he calls debauchery "a long sleep," it suppresses desire itself. The announced goal is to reach the point at which a man could exclaim: "No more emotions!" (*TRN*, 1530). Clamence is always desirous, but he understands that each desire opens him up, whereas he would prefer to remain self-enclosed. In moving from multiple mistresses to debauchery, Clamence is moving closer to death, the longest "sleep" of all, to paraphrase him. He does in fact kill the imperfect and conflicted personality he discovers within himself, and he renames himself Jean-Baptiste Clamence to recapture the lost paradise of absolute oneness.

He also proposes a third solution. He would require of every woman the following oath: "Don't love me and be faithful to me" (*TRN*, 1507). In keeping with the satiric thrust of the novel, Clamence is proposing a parody of the marriage vow. A consensual contract between a man and woman has degenerated into a general system of oppression and a specific injustice against women. Camus is moving beyond satire. Since the marriage vow is an oath of loyalty, we can understand why Camus places Clamence among the concentric canals of Amsterdam and, metaphorically,

in the last circle of hell. Dante, in his *Inferno,* reserved that circle for trai-
tors. Clamence admits: "I talked about loyalty and there isn't . . . one single
person I have loved that I did not end up betraying" (*TRN,* 1519). The vow
of loyalty, that cultural intervention into the body's erotic appetites, constitutes one basis of the morality of love Clamence is unable to practice.

The tragic power of *The Fall* derives from its depiction of the violation
of love as a violation of human justice. It is understandable, therefore, that
Fernande Bartfeld would refer to Clamence's possession of a stolen painting, a Dutch masterpiece depicting judges worshiping Christ, as a "robbery
and rape of justice."[34] Clamence himself is explicit. He begins with a general statement: "I was able to love simultaneously . . . women and justice"
(*TRN,* 1489). Justice is already contaminated, not because it is the object
of the verb "love" but because it is paired with the plural "women." Justice, by this declension, acquires a body. Clamence then concludes: "One
would have thought that justice slept with me every night" (*TRN,* 1484).
His system of similes and metaphors brings into sharp focus a process that
prostitutes both women and justice. "Where judgment is concerned," he
goes on to say, following the same line of reasoning, "we're always ready,
as for fornication" (*TRN,* 1514). Clamence's brilliant and vulgar power is
to subvert the achievements of civilization, Christ's teachings included.
Even more explicitly than Meursault moving all his furniture into his bedroom, he reduces these achievements to the dimensions of a loveless bed.
"My kingdom," he declares, "was the bed" (*TRN,* 1519).[35] "Kingdom" is
more than a rhetorical flourish. It represents a political and psychological
program. Clamence's reign becomes firmly established when he can offer
his fourth and final solution to the question of men, women, and the social
contract:

> I used to say to myself that the final solution would have been the
> death of the person I was interested in. Her death would have defini-
> tively solidified our relationship . . . and . . . removed its compulsion.
> . . . I could only live . . . on the condition that all human beings on
> earth . . . were turned towards me, empty forever, devoid of any inde-
> pendent existence . . . doomed to sterility. . . . In short, for me to live
> happily, it was necessary for the human beings I chose not to live at
> all. (*TRN,* 1510)

Not even Sade justified the destruction of women so elegantly: psychological and moral murder in the imperfect and pluperfect subjunctive moods.[36]
Is Clamence's fourth solution a form of necrophilia, a man loving women
on the condition that they do not respond lest their responses awaken com-

promising and divisive forces in him that he does not wish to acknowledge? In a technical sense, no, because the desired woman is resurrected in each sexual scene and then returned to passivity. Clamence's erotic attention does not summon forth the woman's character, only her living body. He does not individualize them. To do so would be to ask who they are and, finally, who he is. It is in this context that we might comprehend Clamence's bizarre assertion, geographically impossible, that he never crosses a bridge in Amsterdam. It was while he was crossing a bridge in Paris that the woman leaped to her death. Henceforth Clamence will remain disconnected, never crossing over to a woman, never allowing any woman to cross over to him.

The dynamics of love through which lovers discover and exchange each other's identities over periods of time, to the point that one might be indistinguishable from the other, are brought to an abrupt halt by Clamence. He does not wish to be revealed and discovered. "No man," he admits, "is a hypocrite in his pleasures" (*TRN*, 1509). Sex and love go hand in hand with self-disclosure. It is the phenomenon of self-revelation and the flight from it that links Clamence's descriptions of his love affairs with the episode of laughter and with the woman's suicide.

Camus' decision to let her die by drowning was not arbitrary. Her death is consistent with that of other drowned victims in his works, notably Jan in *The Misunderstanding*.[37] We should also include Tarrou's figurative drowning in *The Plague* and Louise's in "Jonas."[38] Swimming and drowning in Camus' works are often metaphors for sexual experience:

> She clung to him like a woman drowning, came up for air . . . sank back into the black and frozen waters that burned her like a multitude of gods. (*MH*, 145)
> She loved being loved and he had drowned her with attention. (*TRN*, 1560)
> The water of the night began to fill Janine. (*TRN*, 1575)
> Victoria: Where are those days when waters rose up in my heart the moment I heard your name? (*TRN*, 259)
> Mi: when she made love she breathed like a swimmer . . . then went to collapse on a warm and humid shore. . . . Water was her natural element and earth that avid place where, like a fish dripping wet, she happily suffocated. (*C3*, 211)

Water provides the fluid medium of exchange in the experience of making love, and it facilitates the dissolution of whatever barriers may impede the physical dialogue of two persons. The drowning woman's cry for help in

*The Fall* is therefore more than a physical act. It is a desperate moral as well as erotic alert. It goes as far back as *The Happy Death,* where Lucienne, making love to Mersault, "clung to him." Clamence's admission in describing his relations, "everything slid off me" (*TRN,* 1501), "people followed me, wanted to cling to me, but there was nothing to cling to" (*TRN,* 1501), underlines his unapproachable consciousness and his moral absence. Clamence, therefore, hearing the woman's cry, does nothing. He does not respond to her call because he wants even his lovemaking to be a monologue. There is sex, but a Camusian male like Clamence always flees from the woman, from the love scene, lest he be discovered. Clamence was discovered once by the woman who reported his inadequacies, and he admits: "I had revealed who I was" (*TRN,* 1509). We can understand, therefore, why Camus was so moved by Martin du Gard's character Antoine and his love for Rachel: "Antoine is now aware of other people's existence and that in love . . . we cannot take our pleasure alone" (*E,* 1149). "Now" suggests clearly that the discovery of others and of himself was a gradual process.

Looking back on his past, Clamence summarizes "that period in my life when I used to ask for everything without giving anything of myself" (*TRN,* 1510). Camus himself, in the realm of politics, had all along insisted that men put their persons and lives in line with their ideas. If in politics, why not in love? *The Rebel,* if nothing else, denounces careless words spoken by armchair radicals that lead to bloody deeds. We read in an editorial: "No person should speak without first committing his life" (*E,* 298); Camus in a speech invokes "men committed to speaking clearly and risking their lives" (*E,* 373). Dora, in *The Just Assassins,* a woman ready to risk her life for her political beliefs, worries: "Others will perhaps come who will act on our authority in order to kill but who will not pay with their lives" (*TRN,* 384). *The Fall* penetrates further still into the inner life by requiring that the questions of love and sexuality also be answered by the entire man and the entire woman.

*The Fall,* in the final analysis, is not really a confession at all. It merely gives the impression of one. While deconstructing the "mannequin," what we initially assumed to be a public and false persona, Clamence is at the same time reconstructing another, even more monolithic identity: "For the statue to be bare," he openly admits, "fine speeches must take flight" (*TRN,* 1511). What stands revealed, however, is not the living man but another, more polished, and even more impenetrable artifact.

The only character in *The Fall* renamed and reinvented himself as Jean-Baptiste Clamence. It was a gesture that dismissed his human and imperfect predecessors because John the Baptist shares with Christ the privilege of immaculate conception.[39] A mother's divine purity guarantees the son's freedom from selfhood and exemption from our collective fall. In his final peroration Clamence demonstrates the political and psychological ramifications of his attempt at transcendence: "I pity without absolving, I understand without forgiving and, above all, I feel at last that I am adored!" (*TRN*, 1549). Adoration codifies inferiority. Love may well encourage that same gift of oneself that religious worship often requires, but it is given freely and is never permanent. If it were and if, as in Clamence, it were accepted as such, it would be both a suicide and a murder.

The Fall was an exorcism for Camus. There was his growing conviction, evident in his meditation on suicide in *The Myth of Sisyphus* and on murder in *The Rebel*, that the so-called higher truth of death to which so many of his characters submitted by killing, being killed, or becoming emotionally dead was not an objective fact but a subjective wish. "What finally became clear to me yesterday," Camus wrote in his travel journal, "is that I wanted to die" (*JV*, 115). He realized that he was taking a step ahead of a natural process and grasped the subjectivity underlying so-called transcendent truths. Once Camus was willing to understand and not only justify himself, then, in opposition to Sartre, he would reaffirm the existence of a human nature whose will and energies, both political and sexual, are revealed and modified in and through social contracts. "Our analysis of revolt," Camus wrote, "leads at least to the possibility that there is a human nature" (*E*, 425). To have a human nature, in contrast to Clamence, is to be "an heir before being a precursor" (*E*, 60). This biological as well as social sequence prepares the way for the reentry of women in Camus' works. He will now set himself the deliberate task of writing love scenes, to abandon, if at all possible, the predatory perspectives of Don Juan and Clamence and to bring a man back into a dialogic relationship with a woman. Camus will set himself the task of entering realms of reciprocal response where self-enclosed monologues become dramatic dialogues threatening self-disclosure.

## CHAPTER 4

# *Love Scenes*

Postwar Europe, Camus felt, was "convulsing" for lack of love. "There was darkness . . . in all our hearts" (*TRN*, 1359), he wrote in *The Plague*, including himself in that harsh assessment. His reflections in that novel on Nazism, war, and the Holocaust, amplified in his analysis of Russian and European nihilism in *The Rebel*, convinced Camus that there would continue to be no lack of hate. "What awaits me in these times," he wrote to Jean Grenier about the war with Germany, "is not the danger of death but the spectacle of hate" (*CG*, 39). He wanted to write love scenes in part for himself, for what he gradually came to view as his personal salvation, in part as an urgent antidote for a discontented and sick civilization.

Camus' attitude toward hatred situates and sheds light on his scenes of love between men and women and the reasons why he wanted to write them. This initial inquiry is necessary because Camus gives the impression at times that both love and hate were entirely alien emotions to him, a "spectacle," as he puts it.[1] This theatrical term suggests that Camus could observe hatred as a member of an audience in no way implicated in the destructive tragedy taking place before his eyes. "I have no taste for hatred," he once observed (*E*, 286). Camus attributes this distance, this inability to hate, to his family and to Algerian culture: "In fact they hated no one," he wrote about his boyhood friends, "which would hinder them when they became adults, in the society where they then had to live" (*PH*, 223). Camus was thinking about his move to France, an alien culture, and he listed as one of his literary projects "Play. A man who *cannot hate*" (*C3*, 60). Camus underlines and paraphrases another writer in French history, Jean-Jacques Rousseau, also an alien in France, who was even more explicit in *Reveries of the Solitary Walker:* "I don't know how to hate."[2]

When Camus refers in an early speech to "a world desiccated by hatred" (*E*, 400), we are tempted to bring this vivid observation in line with the creative writer's "dry" or "closed" heart (*E*, 165) from *The Myth of Sisyphus* and also with Camus' personal lament: "Discouraged by my character, by my desert nature" (*C3*, 204). These three deserts, however, are very different. A writer's "closed heart" is presented to the reader as a necessary requirement for creativity, his ability to distance himself from his subject, the means by which he could successfully enter the subjectivity of others. Nor is Camus' "desert nature" the result of hatred. Quite the contrary, the image is all the more disturbing because it describes the inability to feel any emotions whatsoever. A world "desiccated by hatred," in contrast, points to an active and destructive force that sucks the generative sap from life's roots. Camus describes geographical deserts in many of his works, but the implicit contrast throughout is between nature's deserts, which are natural, shifting, and cyclical, and the political and emotional deserts that occupy a permanent place in society and in the human heart.

The sterilizing power of hatred, therefore, is not the result of temporary eruptions of an emotion that might resemble unpredictable accidents in nature. Camus calls these destructive moments "explosions of rage" (*JV*, 128). The hatred he imagines as a permanent desert is an emotion in the service of premeditated policy. Unlike the hatred born of anger, this hatred aspires to intellectual legitimacy. Hence the judge in *State of Siege* speaks "in the name of the law and hatred" (*TRN*, 256), hoping to endow a subjective and variable passion with the objective consistency of legal doctrine. In *The Just Assassins* Stepan explains his radical politics: "As for me, I love nothing and I hate, you hear me, I hate my fellow man" (*TRN*, 356). His subsequent elaboration, which places hatred almost in a positive light, demonstrates how much his inner nature differs from Camus' "desert nature": "It's better than feeling nothing" (*TRN*, 357). For Stepan, hatred at least mobilizes energy, however destructive. As such it can be and is addressed in the play by other characters. It is discussed and challenged in the belief that this energy could be channeled in other, more positive directions.

Camus' most extreme statement on the ability of private hatred to energize public politics is "The Renegade." The nameless renegade admires the tribal leader because "hatred is his commandment" (*TRN*, 1590). He goes on to express a wish that endorses the brutal practices that he observes: "May hatred reign without mercy over a world of the damned" (*TRN*, 1592). The terror in this perverse prayer is that the wished-for hatred is not psychological, the destructive coincidence of specific, external circumstances with an internal disposition. Even if it were circumstantial, the renegade priest seeks to transcend time-bound and accidental circumstances so that hatred might perpetuate itself as in an arithmetic sequence. Hatred, therefore, as in the renegade's prayer, could be summoned forth as if it were subject to an intellectual decision.

Most relevant to our subject is what the renegade learns about sexual relations in this political desert. He witnesses a ritualized rape:

> The Sorcerer . . . held her by her hair which he kept twisting around his fist; she bent back, her eyes bulging out of their sockets, until she finally fell. Releasing her, the Sorcerer screamed. . . . Behind the square-eyed mask his scream rose to a deafening pitch, and the woman rolled on the ground in a kind of fit and, at last on all fours, her head hidden in her locked arms, she too screamed, but with a muffled sound, and the Sorcerer, still screaming and staring at the Fetish, entered her quickly and viciously, without being able to see the woman's face now buried beneath the heavy folds of her dress. (*TRN*, 1586–87)

This is a hate scene but also a cold-blooded scene organized around a performance with staged rituals and props. There is the mask, the fetish, and also musicians playing percussive music. They have their backs turned, and they face the wall so as to endow this brutality with a dangerous magic and mystery. These elements, taken together, raise hatred to sacramental status. Everything in Camus' description of sadistic sex confers anonymity upon both participants: the mask hiding the man's face, where it is now impossible to read a recognizable human emotion; the geometric eyes dominating the woman's eyes bulging in pain, as if pain, were it strong enough, would itself become abstract geometry; words boiling into screams; and finally the woman's face "buried" under "heavy" clothes, as if to underline in the most perverse way what Camus for so long wanted very much to deny, that sex had something to do with recognition, with self-revelation and self-knowledge. The man looks at the fetish, not at the woman, his quick and nasty possession of her motivated by some sublime—or base—imperative. This transcendent imperative not only transforms eyes into cutout squares but transforms life itself into monolithic geometry. The renegade priest admires "the city of order . . . right angles, square rooms, inflexible men. . . . The reign of malice alone was seamless. . . . Truth is square, heavy, dense, it does not tolerate nuances" (*TRN*, 1589). Organic vitality, the kind Camus praised with lush prose in *Nuptials*, has been redesigned in this story as sterile architecture.

The brutal rape in "The Renegade" does not differ all that much from Clamence's torture of his sexual partner in *The Fall:* "I treated her brutally . . . until the day when, in the violent disorder of a painful and constrained pleasure, she paid loud tribute to what was enslaving her" (*TRN*, 1508). This passage is infinitely more elegant and circumlocutionary, and "loud" is apparently the closest a Parisian woman can come to a primitive scream.

Both women, it seems, are sodomized, and the sadistic reality is essentially the same in both descriptions. *The Rebel* opens with: "There are crimes of passion and crimes of logic" (*E, 413*). Neither of these incidents qualifies as a crime of passion. The hatred is too consistent, too predictable. It is the same personal hatred transformed into objective policy that we witness in such "intellectual" murderers as Martha in *The Misunderstanding* and Caligula.

The sexual violence in "The Renegade" occupies the furthest possible extreme from Camus' celebration of innocent eroticism in *Nuptials*. Both, however, manifest themselves in purely physical terms. Whereas Camus will describe erotic feelings with a passionate lyricism, particularly in "Nuptials in Tipasa," detailed descriptions of specific erotic acts are rare, if not entirely absent.[3] The sorcerer, in contrast, twists the woman's hair, they both scream, her eyes bulge with pain, she rolls convulsively on the ground, he grabs her, and then he enters her. Sadism requires details. Innocence does not. Sadistic and innocent sexuality, however, both seek what Peter Cryle calls "unity of the flesh."[4] The body's multiple and contradictory impulses and needs are unified when they are synchronized, as we saw in *Nuptials,* with a cosmic force in nature. Sadism, as a pathological substitute for transcendence, seeks and finds unity in pain. Describing the practice of torture, Camus wrote: "They searched for the soul through the wounds of the body" (*E, 259*). Pain, upon which the entire body is now focused to the exclusion of all else, simplifies. This unity, in contrast to that achieved between two persons joining in love, is oppositional, the separation of two people, often as master and slave. It is a unity of one self realized not with the cooperation of another person but with the abolition of that other person. It depends too on the victimizer's ability to view the victim completely from the outside, unable to share or in some way enter into that pain, thus framing it as we might an aesthetic object.

"Physical love," Camus wrote, "has always been linked for me to an irresistible feeling of innocence and joy" (*C3, 274*). Innocence is possible in the absence of any motives or predispositions, those subjective and social factors that would intrude and unnecessarily complicate the pleasure of two bodies joining. Positive factors, other than physical pleasure, may be absent in this intercourse, but then so are negative factors.[5] In *Nuptials* Camus sees and experiences nature and enjoys women in nature. Even when engaged in sex, he sees through the woman to the nature she temporarily embodies. She is transparent because she is not truly a subject, thus enabling the man to transfer his love elsewhere. The sorcerer-rapist sees only the "fetish," a human construction. In nature, Camus depicts the lovers as depersonalized, and in the totalitarian scenes of "The Renegade" everyone is dehumanized. The sorcerer does not wish to give pleasure. He wants to inflict pain, and that pain would be all the more obscene if it could be inflicted on those parts of the body and in an act that was meant to give the most pleasure. In a very important sense, the Camusian man, up to *The Fall,* seldom violates a woman's physical nature. Early in his life Camus had noted: "Brute, physical desire is easy. But desire together with tenderness requires time" (*C2,* 62). While "tenderness" is already pointing the aroused male in the direction of love, of a more intense form of intimacy, it is one step only. Its problematic effect is to bring into the sexual act motives other than merely physical ones.

One of Camus' principal dilemmas, therefore, in writing a love scene as opposed to a hate scene, was to decide how far he would bring the male in his erotic discourse with a woman without loss of innocence. As long as he remained a sexual male in nature, that is, a material and biological entity, he was innocent. Caligula can refer to his "satisfied flesh" (*TRN,* 59) or sarcastically to the "imperious desires nature creates in us" (*TRN,* 43). Camus can describe his own sexual arousal: "Women in the street. The hot beast of desire that lives in our loins and moves with a fierce sweetness" (*C1,* 59). He describes himself and his childhood friends awakening to sexual urges even more bluntly in *The First Man,* changing "woman" to "female": "Lipstick—they sniffed it, aroused and confused, like dogs that enter a house where there has been a female in heat" (*PH,* 259). Camus understands that we are rooted in biological instinct and that we are not reducible to it. When Patrice Mersault in *The Happy Death* complains, however, that "love and desire express themselves in the same way" (*MH,* 54), he is quarreling with a complex society and with the end of simple innocence. In love, a male might become a man, that is, politically and socially engendered, a member of a polis that determines above and beyond flesh and biology what men are or should be.

Innocence, however, tied to maleness and not to manhood, became increasingly problematic for Camus. All of *Nuptials* celebrates innocence physically and lyrically. In intellectual terms Camus made this claim about man in *The Myth of Sisyphus:* "I begin with the premise of his innocence" (*E,* 149). In its most provocative formulation, Camus will say of Patrice Mersault: "He had killed Zagreus with an innocent heart" (*MH,* 186). Whatever the body does in no way compromises the heart's innocence. This dualism, for all intents and purposes, is nonexistent in *The Happy*

*Death, Nuptials,* and *The Stranger* because innocence subtracts the inner life from human involvement in the erotic. It also provides Camus with spiritual certainty, and his joyous descriptions of physical sex are almost always suffused with that undiscouraged certainty.

War and the composition of *The Plague* catalyzed a radical change in Camus. Speaking about his second novel to Jean Grenier, Camus confessed to a profound vexation: "I believe less and less that man is innocent. . . . Man is not innocent *and* he is not guilty. How do I solve this riddle?" (*CG*, 141). He had already written in his journal a comment that he reproduced almost verbatim in his portrait of Jean Tarrou. Tarrou traces the curve of his life from an early, naive belief in human innocence to a bleak and uncompromising belief in human culpability. For himself, Camus wrote, "I lived out my youth with the idea of my innocence, that is to say, with no ideas at all. Now . . ." (*C2*, 154).[6] The pause after "now" is expressive, a blank space where Camus will rewrite Camus, requiring a radical revision in how he would ask and answer questions about love and sexuality.

As long as women were passive mediators for the man—and they were mediators precisely because they were passive and transparent—love scenes were not necessary. Nothing had to be constructed through mutually cooperative efforts between a man and a woman. As long as nature was there as an immutable, maternal force, men and women could deconstruct themselves into a state of passive receptivity. The innocence of *Nuptials* and the sadism of *The Fall* and "The Renegade" leave out of consideration the entire middle range of human interaction. Camus gradually bent his efforts toward recapturing and revitalizing a more centered human scene. A specific man's union with a specific woman required him to rethink the erotic, to discover projects of intimacy that were neither innocent nor sadistic. He had to challenge or at least engage more skeptically many of his assumptions about love and sexuality. One assumption concerned the relationship between love and choice. Describing Jacques Cormery, Camus summarizes his love life:

> He had loved his mother and his child, everything that did not require him to choose. And finally . . . he had never loved anything but the inevitable. . . . For the rest, for everything that required choice, he forced himself to love. . . . He had no doubt experienced wonderment, passion, and even moments of tenderness. But each moment gave way to other moments, each person to other persons, so that he ended up not loving anything he had chosen. . . . The heart, the heart

above all is not free. It is the inevitable and recognition of the inevitable. And he, in truth, had never loved anything with his whole heart except the inevitable. (*PH*, 309–10)

The inherited bonds of flesh and blood require the passionate commitments of love and fidelity that transcend free will, that transcend, too, all social contracts that are the negotiated results of free choice. Included in that choice are all women other than the biological mother, all persons other than the biological child. In this physiological and psychological order, Jacques loves his mother and is promiscuous precisely because he loves his mother with absolute devotion. That he loves his dependent child, a product of his flesh, only reinforces this equation of love and necessity. Love scenes, if they exist at all, would be mere "moments," subject to the eroding passage of time. Camus is indirectly addressing a fundamental, ethical dilemma. A man's moral bond of love and loyalty to parent and child is seldom compromised by the "imperious," to use Caligula's term, demands of a body's physiological, sexual urges. A man's bond to a wife or lover is.

A second assumption, constructed on the first, concerns the incommensurability of society and the passion of love. Camus wrote in his journal: "Excess in love, the only worthwhile love, characterizes saints. The only excess societies secrete is hatred" (*C3*, 81). Love appears to be incompatible with the normalizing requirements of societies, here portrayed as organisms expert only in secreting hatred. This question of sacred excess, recapitulating Caligula's pride in loving "too much" (*TRN*, 1375) and Camus' own pride in *Nuptials*, where he loved "without bounds" (*E*, 57), renders the composition of love scenes if not impossible, then certainly difficult.

A third and final assumption is the relationship between love and innocence. Camus describes a person, identified as X, and considers his views on love: "For X (and his family) love is inseparable from suffering, anguish. Loving means suffering from or for. For me love has always been inseparable from a certain state of joyous innocence. Whenever I experienced that suffering or anguish I found myself immersed in guilt and no longer able to truly love" (*C3*, 124). Camus is retreating from the notion that love and suffering may at times go hand in hand. Although we are not given enough information about what X means, there seems to be a fundamental misunderstanding. X says "love." Camus means sex. The underlying factor that provokes Camus' negative reaction is human vulnerability, expressed in the prepositions "from" and "for."

Vulnerability, as an openness that is psychological as well as physical, compromises self-regard and self-control and introduces a moral dimension to erotic relationships.[7] As long as sex exemplifies only "joyous innocence," moral questions and responses are largely irrelevant. Camus, however, may be protesting too much. Few writers knew better than he—how else could he have written *The Plague, The Fall,* and "The Renegade"—the suffering human beings inflict on each other. Sexuality, however, had to remain a refuge for whatever innocence we have left as suffering persons. This view gradually became untenable. On his way to South America for a lecture tour, and years before he considered X's views, Camus wrote this unblinking self-analysis: "Haunted . . . by the pain we inflict on others by merely looking at them. I have to confess that for a long time making others suffer hardly mattered to me. It is love that enlightened me on this point. Now I cannot bear it anymore. In a way it is better to kill someone than to make him suffer. What finally became clear to me yesterday is that I wanted to be dead" (*JV*, 114–15).

This passage demonstrates, if a demonstration is needed, Camus' ability to look within himself without equivocation. That a mere glance could cause harm speaks volumes not only about what we are capable of but also what destructive energies Camus sensed within himself.[8] He portrays himself as indifferent to the human suffering he has caused, as sadistic, so much so that murder becomes an act of mercy. Roger Scruton holds that to be able to idealize a woman in the act of love, a man must be able to idealize himself.[9] In this context, and reversing the terms, Camus, in his eloquent conclusion, understands that a man's destruction of women is one stage in the self-centered project of self-destruction. Self-destruction goes hand in glove with self-loathing. Therefore, when Camus asserts that "no one deserves to be loved—no one who measures up to this priceless gift" (*C3*, 117), the pagan, uncensored author of *Nuptials* is now placing love in the Augustinian-Calvinist context of unmerited grace and concludes that no human being is worthy of this mutually transforming passion.

To write love scenes, therefore, was not merely an aesthetic decision, a chance to try something never tried before. It was also a moral decision. It was all the more remarkable in that Camus felt at times that he was truly incapable of love. It was an inner void he thought he shared with his generation:

They blame us for portraying abstract men. But that's because our human model . . . is incapable of love. (*C2*, 215–16)

Those who do not give do not receive. The greatest misfortune is not to be unloved but not to love. (*C3*, 51)

Most often, however, Camus implicates himself directly in this pessimistic assessment of contemporary man, and *The Fall* is, among many other things, a self-condemnation. A love scene would at least offer the opportunity to test the possibilities of dialogue between a man and a woman, unlike *The Stranger,* where dialogues are rare, or *The Fall,* where they are nonexistent, unlike Don Juan, who is content with "the same sentence." Both the man and the woman would have to be active agents in situations in which even listening would be done freely and willingly. These dialogues with their unpredictability and infinite potential would break the family or maternal circle, what Camus called the chains of "necessity," and replace it with other constructs of love if not superior to, then at least equal to the powerful ties that bind parents and children. The woman would come into her own as the one who is chosen and also as the one who chooses. Summing up Antoine's love for Rachel in Martin du Gard's novel *The Thibault,* Camus evokes a new and very old ideal: "Antoine must admit that other people do exist and . . . he discovers that equality within difference which is the highest ideal of bodies and souls" (*E,* 1148). "Equality within difference" and "soul" are entirely new concepts for Camus. The union of a male and female, or the union of a man with nature, would now have to become the union of a man and woman.

A love scene requires that a couple express love through language, gestures, or both. Their love would go beyond sexual attraction while building on it. What we would see, according to Jean Rousset, is a "couple being formed,"[10] and we would have the impression that each scene is a dramatic "threshold"[11] clearly demarcating the past from the future. The love scene would be a personal and interpersonal construction through which a couple comes into being through love. For this to take place, both the man and the woman are in the process of exchanging or modifying in some definable way an old self for a new self.

The idea of construction offered no problem to Camus in the arena of politics. His postwar employment as editor of *Combat* was devoted almost entirely to building a new future for a more just France. Later, devastated by the war in Algeria, he called for a postcolonial political reconstruction: "Those nine million Arabs with whom we wish . . . to construct the same free and fraternal future" (*CAC6,* 53). These calls to action addressed the public scene and, as the word "fraternal" suggests, the mutual engagement of "like" personalities. The unanswered question, however, central to the conflicts that animate *State of Siege* and *The Just Assassins,* was whether a contract could be negotiated between the political construction of public identities and the private constructions of love and desire.

Camus had written in *The Plague* that love requires "a future" (*TRN*, 1367), that it would come into existence gradually through time. But in that very same novel, immediately before the plague strikes and causes the trapped citizens to rethink their lives, Camus had described their love lives very differently: "The desires of our youth," he wrote, "are violent and brief" (*TRN*, 1220). He then concluded: "Our men and women either devour each other rapidly in what is called 'the act of love' or else settle down to a long period of conjugality. . . . For lack of time or reflection, they love each other without knowing it" (*TRN*, 1220). The reader may be amused by the qualifying phrase "what is called," as if "act of love" were a strange and perhaps too elegant term for what the narrator would prefer to consider mere coupling. He nevertheless goes along with the euphemism. The couples in his description veer between boredom and the pleasurable cannibalism of intense sex. The key phrase is "without knowing it." Love scenes would provide that knowledge.

Camus incorporated into the early pages of *The Plague* the sexual urgency of the Don Juan chapter in *The Myth of Sisyphus* and the descriptions of sex he had published years earlier in "Summer in Algiers." There he wrote: "Life follows the curve of our great passions, quick, demanding, generous. It is not to be constructed, but burned" (*E*, 72). Whether myth or sociology, Camus then refers to the Algerian people in the same essay as a "childlike people" (*E*, 72) and "mindless people" (*E*, 73). This absence of mind or soul explains to Camus' personal satisfaction the open, unguarded quality of a people and culture he loves profoundly. It forms one basis of his equation of sex and "joyous innocence" that lasts from his early works through *The Myth of Sisyphus*. The descriptions of disease in *The Plague* and sadism in *The Fall* and "The Renegade," however, eliminate once and for all Camus' optimism. Years later he himself confessed through Jacques Cormery: "I had . . . burned and consumed other people" (*PH*, 304).[12]

All these passages describe sexual encounters. An encounter differs from a love scene in its brevity and the refusal on the part of both men and women to elaborate on their feelings, to go beyond physical sex. I shall study sexual encounters and love scenes together because both illuminate Camus' evolving views about love and the couple and, most particularly, the role of the woman.

Camus wrote in "Nuptials in Tipasa": "It is enough for me to live with my whole body" (*E*, 59). Clamence develops this same thought, but cynically. Stripping away the early essay's youthful fervor, he confesses to "a congenital inability to see in love anything but the physical act" (*TRN*, 1505). The unredeemable, mere physicalness of desire leads Camus himself to conclude: "Nothing can be built on love: it is flight, anguish, magnificent moments or a quick fall" (*C2*, 120). Each element in this summary rings a variation on the theme of our fundamental, emotional anarchy. Camus, in spite of his protestations that love is essential to any new political order, cannot as yet attach any enduring significance to it. Love may inspire vows of fidelity. Sex does not. If the roots of collective society cannot find nourishment in erotic energy as well as stability in love's required loyalty, neither will the individual man or woman. Camus' contemplation of nature and of love's relationship to nature does not yet provide for any reinvestment in society. His politics and his views on love, protests notwithstanding, still represent irreconcilable categories of human experience.

If, as Roger Quilliot informs us, Camus wanted very much to "succeed in writing a love scene,"[13] his first, immediate, and most basic challenge was the spoken word itself. When Zagreus asks Mersault: "Do you like women?" he replies instantly: "When they're beautiful" (*MH*, 69). Mersault answers the question succinctly and expresses his own values about what he views as a necessary female quality. The discussion, however, ends there. There is no further elaboration. The adjective "beautiful" is neither the beginning nor the end of a process. If it did come at the end of an inner meditation, the reader was never given access to it.

Love and language rarely complement each other in Camus' works. If we are to believe Joseph Grand in *The Plague*, language is a feeble substitute for love, an approximate act, a shadow of desire's reality. Rieux, the novel's narrator, describes Grand's marriage: "[Grand] had less and less to say and had failed to keep alive in his wife the feeling of being loved" (*TRN*, 1286). Grand picks up on this insight, but his own analysis differs in one important respect: "As long as we were in love, we understood each other without words. But people don't love forever. When the time came I should have found the words to make her stay, but I couldn't" (*TRN*, 1286). The pathos of Grand's assessment of his failed marriage is that words exist merely to fill a void left by a love no longer felt or shared. Whereas Rieux presents Grand's love as continuous, Grand's description is divided into two distinct parts: love without words, words without love. Silence, therefore, sustains love's authenticity all the while guaranteeing its gradual decline and demise. "Love is silence," Camus wrote in his journal (*C3*, 63). One of Don Juan's goals was to transform tenderness into a "manly silence" (*E*, 153). Don Juan is a specific example of a more general virtue summed up as "man and his silence" (*E*, 167).

Camus, in deference to his mute mother, wants silence to be constitutive of love and perhaps its most essential property, presumably to facilitate access to the universal. He is expressing both an ideal and a dilemma: "Peace would mean loving in silence. But there is consciousness and the person; one must speak. Love becomes hell" (C2, 239). There is a humorous if not unintentionally farcical element in this lament: the beloved reduced to the status of an irritating babbler. It also has its tragic dimension. Camus would direct love not toward a "person" but toward a voiceless experience of a nonhuman world. Human consciousness, presence, and language are obstacles that threaten that bliss, transforming it into a psychological "hell." In practical, aesthetic terms silence is not difficult to achieve in a novel, and in Camus' novels and short stories dialogues are relatively sparse. Even Clamence's monologue is constructed on his interlocutor's silence. The question that remains is how one achieves silence in a play. To write a love scene, Camus is required to privilege spoken language as the primary means lovers use to express their love. The silent and depersonalized love Camus yearns for must be reconstructed as persons and as drama.

To have a clearer understanding of Camus' dilemma, it would be useful to consider first the straightforward sexual encounters between Meursault and Marie in *The Stranger*. These encounters would help us gauge more accurately the psychological and moral distance Camus had to travel on his way to love scenes. In this first episode Meursault has gone to the beach for a swim:

> In the water I met Marie Cardona, a former typist in my office whom I had a thing for at the time. She did too, I think. . . . I helped her onto the float and at the same time brushed against her breasts. . . . She turned toward me. Her hair was in her eyes and she was laughing. I lifted myself up next to her . . . and as if kidding around I let my head fall back and rest on her stomach. . . . The whole sky filled my eyes and it was blue and gold. Under my neck I felt Marie's pulse beating softly. (*TRN*, 1138)

Afterward they go to a film and have sex later that evening. In one paragraph Meursault meets, seduces, and has intercourse with Marie. Their meeting does not qualify as a first and dramatic encounter between a man and a woman who might awaken in each other new emotions. Meursault and Marie already know each other. They recognize each other. Their eyes are alert. Since they are swimming, they are already undressed, and there is no question of gradually reaching beyond clothes, beyond those layers of cultural fabric where social and class identities take precedence over naked flesh. What distinguishes this second sexual encounter—Meursault desired

Marie when she worked in his office—from a love scene is the absence of mutual interpretation. "I brushed against her breasts" may or may not be deliberate. Meursault placing his head on Marie's stomach most certainly is. In neither instance, however, do we have access to Marie's thoughts. At no time is she allowed to have a point of view. She is there. Meursault pays her erotic attention and seduces her. She responds. Desire is basic, uncomplicated, healthy, and easily fulfilled because there is nothing difficult to fulfill.

This same paragraph, nevertheless, has significant nuances. After Meursault has lifted Marie onto the buoy, he notes: "She turned toward me" (*TRN*, 1138). Her physical gesture in turning toward Meursault balances his physical gestures toward her. An important shift in attention then follows: "The whole sky filled my eyes and it was blue and gold. Under my neck I felt Marie's pulse beating softly" (*TRN*, 1138). Meursault is already "filled" with the blue and gold sky before being sexually fulfilled. Camus also wrote in his journal: "I am fulfilled before desiring" (*C1*, 22). Meursault achieves with and through Marie what Camus had achieved alone in "The Wind in Djémila." There he synchronized "the beating of my heart with the great sonorous poundings of nature's heart everywhere" (*E*, 62). Marie's "pulse" forms the steady and stable background rhythm for Meursault's mute reception of a vast world in which she is merely a sign and never a complex presence. She is not yet the "consciousness" and "person" that transforms sex into love and love into a living "hell." Marie will eventually assert herself when she questions Meursault about love and marriage.[14] She understands intuitively that love requires more attention than sexual desire. Their mismatched expectations come to a head in the episode where Meursault takes his leave: "I said goodbye. She looked at me. 'You don't want to know what I have to do?' I did want to know but I hadn't thought to ask and she seemed to be blaming me" (*TRN*, 1157). Marie wants to exist in her lover's thoughts when she is not physically present. She wants to be more than a desirable body. Sex, for her, is becoming a means, not an end, and she now wants a different kind of intimacy.

Their most erotic encounters, moreover, do not take place in bed but in the ocean, to the extent that Camus gives us detailed descriptions of their swimming together. Extended and repetitive though these episodes may be, however, Camus never goes beyond the most basic, erotic impulses. We can, for example, compare passages from two very different novels that describe the same scene of two lovers entering water. The first is a description of Chactas and Atala by Chateaubriand: "When we came upon a river, we crossed it by raft or by swimming. Atala placed one hand on my shoulder; and like two swans we crossed those deserted waters."[15] Out of modesty as well as necessity (she needs one hand to swim) Atala touches Chactas with only one hand. The comparison with two swans presents the hero and heroine as simultaneously different and identical, an image that foreshadows their tragic relationship as lovers and as brother and sister. In contrast, we have the following three descriptions of Meursault and Marie:

> When the sun got too hot, she dove into the water and I followed.
> . . . I wrapped my hand around her waist and we swam together.
> (*TRN*, 1138–39)
> In the water Marie . . . pressed up against me. She put her mouth on mine. Her tongue cooled my lips and we rolled around in the waves for a while. (*TRN*, 1150)
> Marie wanted us to swim together. I got behind her to hold onto her waist and she moved forward with her arms while I helped her by kicking. (*TRN*, 1162)

Chateaubriand's romantic description brings out what is distinctively modern in Camus, who focuses on different parts of the body underlined by possessive adjectives: "my hand," "her waist," "her mouth," "her tongue," "my lips." The person is stripped down to his or her basic physiological reality and denied any metaphorical complexity, the inner life entirely banished.

It is possible, perhaps, that Meursault and Marie, as they join together in water, achieve as a couple a more androgynous, more complex identity. In a love scene, we may witness first the deconstruction of male and female personality, followed by the reconstruction or reaffirmation of a personality that has been rethought and enriched. It is also possible that Camus is willingly lending himself through these fluid couplings to a spiritual and psychological dynamic that might, even for a moment, call masculine identity into question. Given Camus' macho reputation, however, this seems dubious at best. He did, however, make the following assertion: "I believe in dialogue, in sincerity. I believe they are the means to achieve an unprecedented revolution" (*C2*, 160). Dialogue as a vehicle for revolution would assuredly manifest itself in a love scene. Camus' revolution, however, does not consist of inventing or experimenting with personal identity; it consists of revealing unequivocally what already exists, making known what is unknown. Clamence, in the sexual act, admits: "I had revealed who I was" (*TRN*, 1509). In lieu of dialogues that would challenge or at least address received assumptions about male and female identity, we have the ocean enveloping Meursault and Marie in its own fluid dynamic. The human body and its material nature may, up to a point, be destabilized. Camus, nevertheless, anchors his descriptions of the erotic couple in what he is convinced are unassailable biological truths about the masculine male and the feminine female.

Meursault and Marie satisfy their sexual appetites in almost all their encounters. There is one episode, however, in which the lovers are present to each other but separated. That spatial separation raises two questions: will they be able to abolish that separation, and will that space inspire a verbal or gestural language that would lead them beyond basic, erotic impulses? The episode involves Marie's visit to Meursault in prison: "The room was divided into three parts by two large grates that ran along the entire room. . . . There was a space of eight to ten meters between the two grates. . . . Marie . . . was standing between two visitors: a short, tight-lipped old woman dressed in black and a fat, bareheaded woman who was shouting and making a lot of gestures" (TRN, 1178).

Because of the noise made by the prisoners and visitors, both Marie and the wife have to "shout" to be heard. This ugly distortion of the female voice contrasts sharply with the "tight lips" of the old woman visiting her son.[16] Neither speaks a word until they leave. "Both," Meursault observes, "were looking at each intently" (TRN, 1179). This mother-son couple, because of their silence, stand apart from the vulgarity of the "fat woman" and the clumsy, awkward exchanges between Meursault and Marie. The mother, particularly, whose tightened lips may also express defiance, seems unrelated to her surroundings, disconnected from everything that is not her son.[17] Camus is also inviting us to read these three couples from left to right as we would a sentence: mother-son, two lovers, husband-wife. The mother is "short" and her son too is "short"; Meursault and Marie are young; the wife is "fat" and her husband is "tall" (TRN, 1178). As we move from left to right, Camus wants us to observe both the chronology of love and its decadence. We pass from a mother's silence and its plenitude to words between lovers and spouses that are loud, banal, and devoid of meaning. Of the three couples, the only ones freely "chosen" are the last two, and they are the most inferior.

The wide space separating the prisoners from their visitors means very little to mother and son, who cross that space easily with their mutually silent gaze. Meursault's reaction to the now distant Marie is physical: "I looked at her and I felt like caressing her shoulder through her dress. I felt like touching the thin fabric" (TRN, 1179). With his usual honesty he adds, "I didn't know what else I could hope for" (TRN, 1179). Meursault's gaze is replaced by an imaginary physical gesture, his arm and hand reaching through two sets of bars to minimize if not abolish the frustrating distance separating him from the object of his desire. There are, in contrast, neither words nor gestures between mother and son, and Camus insists on it: "The man next to me and his mother were still looking at each other" (*TRN*, 1179); "The only island of silence was next to me where the short young man and the old woman were looking at each other" (*TRN*, 1179). When the son does finally speak, he utters the verbal equivalent of their mutual gaze: "Au revoir, maman" (*TRN*, 1179), which means "good-bye" but literally, "until we see each other again."

Camus was confronting one of the central problems of his life and his art. Years after the publication of *The Stranger* he wrote that he wanted to place at the center of his work "the admirable silence of a mother and a man's efforts to find again a justice or a love that balances that silence" (*E*, 13). Judging from this sentence, Camus did not consider justice directly relevant to love or love relevant to justice. He nevertheless states in "Return to Tipasa": "The unrelenting demand for justice has exhausted love which nevertheless gave birth to it" (*E*, 873). His aesthetic works from *The Plague* to *Exile and the Kingdom* also explicitly argue their inseparability. The plague grows strong through the separation of lovers; Clamence betrays women and resides in hell; and surely the renegade priest knows what he is saying when, on his knees in adoration of totalitarian rule, he acknowledges: "We must settle love's accounts" (*TRN*, 1582). Justice and love are already inseparable in *The Stranger* because Meursault is condemned to death for not loving his mother. Moreover, in the prison scene just alluded to, a son, a lover, and a husband are prisoners. The mother, lover, and wife are free. Three men are prisoners, and each one has a distinct relationship to the woman facing him. Finally, as the guard informs Meursault, prisons are designed for sexual deprivation and Meursault suffers from that deprivation.

If a mother's silence becomes the essential trait around which Camus would organize his aesthetic endeavors, what is the place on this moral and psychological map for a woman in love? Does a woman expressing herself in a love scene automatically demonstrate her inferiority, as Marie and the married woman do in *The Stranger*? Is a love scene even possible? This basic question of expressivity applies also to the man. "A man," Camus maintains, "is more a man by what he does not say than what he says" (*E*, 164). Early in his career Camus expressed the conviction that "the innocent person is the one who does not explain" (*C1*, 90). Clamence, also addressing the very same question of innocence, wonders: "Who would agree that such an attitude was legitimate in matters of love?" (*TRN*, 1520).

A love scene, in which speech shatters silence and terminates innocence, must function somewhere between these opposing claims. Novels are silent, and a man does not compromise his manhood by writing. The stage is another matter. Through dialogue, each lover would be alternately listening or speaking, active or passive, dominant or submissive, masculine or feminine until the moment of reconciliation, until the coming into being of a new couple and a new order. In trying to write a love scene, Camus is asking himself if he is capable of dramatizing this tension, reciprocity, and equality.

He tried in *The Plague*. One of the novel's principal themes is the separation of lovers, and Camus found the words to express himself eloquently about the carnal and spiritual love that binds men and women. If Camus writes well about love, however, it is because women are absent, because the narrator, Rieux, hardly ever speaks. He listens, writes, and describes. There is little or no dialogue between a man and woman, no exchange, no scenes, no drama. Instead there is a deeply moving dissertation. Jean Gassin concludes: "It is when women are absent that men can become . . . heroes."[18] I would add that, up to this point in Camus' evolution as a writer, his heroes can express love only in the absence of a woman.

In choosing to write a love scene in a play, Camus set himself a daunting challenge. He had asserted in *The Myth of Sisyphus* that silence was the single most valuable masculine trait. He also added: "The heart expresses itself, makes its feelings known only through physical gestures—or else through the voice which comes from the soul as well as the body" (*E*, 160). Through its voice, the body allows the inner spirit to be released and the body to transcend itself. Meursault could look at the sky and feel Marie's pulse as he rested his head on her stomach. She had already "turned" toward him, but when Meursault turned toward her it was with his body only. In a love scene, the entire man must face the entire woman. Words will resound through the voices and bodies of the actors, and silence, the constitutive element of Camus' universe, will disintegrate. The woman is now present before the man. What will they say and how will Camus write their love scene?

Camus evidently understood that there was neither reciprocity nor equality between the lovers in *The Stranger*, *The Plague*, or, for that matter, *The Misunderstanding*. Maria, in Camus' play, protests being abandoned by her husband, Jan. Jan is seeking to reconcile with his mother after a twenty-year absence. Maria speaks strongly against her husband's filial quest and for the rights of love and marriage. Jan's plan is to not identify himself and to spend the night incognito in his mother's inn, where he will be murdered by both his mother and sister, neither of whom recognizes him. Marie wants Jan to speak. He in turn wants his mother to offer him the same gaze of maternal recognition and attention the old woman in *The Stranger* gave her imprisoned son. That wished-for gaze would not abolish physical space but the temporal space of a twenty-year absence. Because of Jan's stubborn and ultimately suicidal fixation, Marie is quickly banished from the stage. In fact, Camus added her scene with Jan just before production, almost as an afterthought.

With *State of Siege*, for the first time in Camus' career, a mother no longer occupies the foreground of a major work of fiction. For the first time, two lovers, Diego and Victoria, are able to face each other and elaborate on the love they feel for each other without explicit references to a maternal force or presence.

Nada the nihilist introduces Diego to the audience with a question that evokes Don Juan: "How's your love life?" (*TRN*, 194). Diego's response is significant: "I'm going to marry the judge's daughter" (*TRN*, 194). Diego is neither Meursault nor Don Juan. His response is an attempt on Camus' part to set Diego apart from these self-regarding figures. It distinguishes the one unique beloved from multiple erotic liaisons, and it distinguishes Diego's social and personal commitment to marriage from Nada's persistent and corrosive cynicism concerning marital fidelity.

Diego's reference to Victoria as "the judge's daughter" may be a matter of social propriety and formality. It also prepares us for one of the more dramatic scenes in the play, the domestic quarrel between Victoria's parents. Until "The Renegade" and *The First Man* there is no precedent in Camus' works for so violent a scene. This quarrel, based on mutual accusations of marital infidelity, amply justifies Nada's pessimistic view of human frailty and ends with the judge calling his wife "Bitch!" in the presence of their children (*TRN*, 257). She does not deny her infidelity, but she places it a dualistic context: "I know . . . that flesh has its faults, whereas the heart has its crimes" (*TRN*, 256). In this assessment, her infidelity was an error whereas her husband's was a crime. She accuses the judge of seducing a young servant girl who had enlisted his aid against her abusive master. His crime was premeditated. Hers was not. Victoria's mother is addressing a basic issue of marital ethics, one that never concerned or gave much pause to Camus, who attributed his own cynical views about marriage and love to his first wife's infidelity.[19] Nada himself moves far beyond cynicism toward a virulent misanthropy: "Lovers, for example! I loathe them! I spit on them when they pass me by. . . . And children, that filthy breed!" (*TRN*, 237). More rationally, the wife understands that the socially sanctioned marital vow of loyal love wars perpetually with the body's instinctive surges of sexual desire. This relationship between marriage and morality was never truly an issue for Camus until his second wife's nervous break-down. Clamence's self-lacerating confessions of betrayal have deep roots in Camus' wife's suffering, although certainly are not reducible to it. This moral tension is dramatized in the ugly confrontation between the judge and his wife, witnessed by their children, Victoria in particular, and by her fiancé Diego. The parents' hatred for each other serves to balance and to bring into sharper focus the love scene between Victoria and Diego.

Their private scene takes place in front of Victoria's barred window. The bars that separated Meursault and Marie now separate these two lovers. We are not in prison, however, and the blocked window, perhaps a visual representation of Victoria's virginity, remains a potential opening.

Meursault, in his imagination, had extended his arm through the prison bars, crossing a wide space to reach Marie. According to the stage directions in *State of Siege*, it is Victoria who in reality passes both arms through the bars to embrace Diego. This gesture is the culminating point of an erotic dialogue that she herself initiated: "I felt rising within me the sound of galloping horses getting nearer, louder, making my entire being tremble. . . . Then I saw love's black horses, still quivering" (*TRN*, 199). Diego responds with the same metaphor of love as horses: "I only heard them pawing the ground softly" (*TRN*, 199).[20] Diego continues Victoria's image but modifies it. They are revealing to each other the emotions they felt when Diego asked the judge for permission to marry his daughter. Victoria also reveals her nervous sexual anticipation. Diego is both aroused and calm. As a man he remains in control of himself and tries to remain in control throughout the play as the plague makes its bloody progress. Victoria, however, becomes increasingly hysterical and is reduced to out-bursts born of sexual frustration and punctuated by a series of desperate commands: "Press me close, close, close"; "Hold me close"; "Kiss me"; "Kiss me, I die of thirst" (*TRN*, 212). Diego, trying to balance public and personal duties, counters with negative commands: "Don't touch me"; "Stay away"; "Let me breathe" (*TRN*, 213). This opposition was already foreshadowed in their love scene, but there the opposition, instead of driv-ing them further apart, only intensified their intimacy:

Victoria: It is the wind of your love that has covered me with flowers in one day.

Diego: The flowers will fall!
Victoria: Their fruits await you!
Diego: Winter will come!
Victoria: But with you. (*TRN*, 200–201)

The profusion of metaphorical replies demonstrates their mutual and entire confidence in each other, a linguistic and erotic contrapuntal effect that underlines their sexual pleasure and their love. Diego goes even further than intimacy, suggesting that he and Victoria are becoming one person, when he exclaims: "Tomorrow we'll leave together and we'll ride on the same saddle" (*TRN*, 179). He thus brings to completion Victoria's initial image of the "black horses of love." Victoria's reaction indicates that, for the first time in Camus' works, language, the body, and love are merging into one seamless discourse. "Speak our language," Victoria adds encouragingly, opening her arms toward an approaching Diego and embracing him. Unlike Meursault and Marie, Victoria and Diego are seducing each other, their sexual urges aroused and mutually satisfied. Their sexuality is also linked to the experience of love, meaning that it is part of a larger project. If their relationship were merely sexual, it would be virtually indistinguishable from any other sexual coupling. Victoria's key reference to "our language" raises a purely sexual encounter to a much more complex level. Victoria and Diego are required to interpret each other until such time that the man's language and the woman's language, like the two lovers on "the same saddle," become, at least for a time, indistinguishable. At that point, one can speak of carnal knowledge.

Irene Finel-Honigman complains with justification that women in Camus' works generally function "outside the realm of independent action or creativity."[21] *State of Siege,* however, is Camus' first sustained attempt to grant a woman the power to inspire love in a man. *The Just Assassins* will go even further. Previously there had been women in love, Marie and Maria particularly, but Meursault and Jan were engaged in other, more self-centered adventures.[22] Their dilemmas as couples were based on mutual misperceptions and mismatched projects.

A dissonant note is also heard in the dialogue between Victoria and Diego, a dissonance that intensifies until the play's tragic ending, Diego's decision to give his life for Victoria's. He says: "How beautiful you are," and she responds, "How strong you are" (*TRN*, 200). Without knowing it, through this pair of adjectives that complement and oppose each other, they have foreseen their definitive separation. The plague will test Diego's "strength," inseparable from his masculine nature ironically recognized and legitimized by Victoria herself. That strength is linked to his altruism, his ability to sacrifice himself for others. Soon Victoria, like Maria before her, will be reduced to a series of solo speeches on the theme of abandonment. When confronted with human suffering, Diego cries out, "I feel pity," but Victoria counters selfishly with "I feel pity for us" (*TRN*, 213). In the play's opening scenes, Diego had stated that happiness required "peace in our cities and in the countryside" (*TRN*, 196). There are, therefore, prior conditions for love to come into being, and in this respect *State of Siege* is closest in spirit to *The Plague*. These conditions are political. Politics and the fraternity of men, so often invoked by Camus and almost always accompanied by the adjective "virile," counterbalance love. In contrast to the novels of André Malraux, they exclude each other.[23]

Rieux in *The Plague* had already described love as "egotistic." Dora will also use the same adjective in *The Just Assassins,* and critics have generally given their approval to this negative judgment. Alan Clayton, for example, analyzes the opposition in Camus' works between male, political fraternities and "feminine values."[24] Raymond Gay-Crosier views the opposition in terms of "egotistical love" and "altruistic duties."[25] Joseph Hermet similarly sees a consistent contrast between women and a man's "desire to serve."[26] English Showalter Jr. concludes more generally that, in Camus' overall scheme of things, words are "feminine" and deeds "masculine."[27] Diego certainly matches these descriptions of male altruism and political commitment. Egotism, however, as a general defining feature of love and more specifically of the emotions Camus' female characters feel, may at times be an appropriate term, but it is insufficient. Love and marriage, proposed by Marie and Victoria, justified by Maria, represent a human emotion and a human event in which the biological, the cultural, and the psychological intersect in ways that are crucial to any living society.

In writing *The Plague* and *State of Siege* and, later, *The Just Assassins* and "The Renegade," Camus would have us understand that the experience of love is no less public and no less private than politics. On this specific point, the way Victoria parries Diego's pessimistic thrusts is significant. Victoria describes herself as a flowering tree, but Diego adds, "The flowers will fall" (*TRN*, 201). He fears that the passage of time may diminish their love. Victoria responds quickly: "Their fruits await you" (*TRN*, 201), promising her lover that their love is inherently generative and will transform an amorous couple into a parental couple, the antonym of egotism. Love, marriage, and procreation are essentially social, no less so than politics. Marriage and politics offer the Camusian hero, however, two different points of entry into society, two different ways to achieve integration. In Camus' summary, the choice was between "justice" or "love."

Camus, while slowly adopting the view that they are ultimately code-pendent, still sees them in this play as contradictory and mutually exclusive.

Camus was sufficiently aware of the irreconcilable dualism between love and politics in his works that he once again attempted to write a love scene in *The Just Assassins.* He created a female character, Dora, who works and lives on an equal footing with a terrorist group dominated by men. "Am I still a woman?" (*TRN,* 392) she asks at a crucial point. She has decided to throw a bomb at a human target and is transformed by this decision from a woman whose job was to prepare the explosive—the woman who traditionally works with basic material—into a woman who will throw the bomb in an act others in the play consider exclusively masculine.

Dora's presence in *The Just Assassins* was dictated by historical reality. Camus, however, takes inspiration from the early years of the Russian Revolution and the life of Dora Brilliant to write a love scene in which the revolutionaries Dora and Kaliayev, equal in their commitment to a political cause, indifferent to the sexual opposition between beauty and strength that divides Diego and Victoria, could finally express and elaborate on their love.

Critics agree that their love scene is marked by a "growing eroticism."[28] This intensity, however, is balanced by a corresponding loss. In the beginning, Kaliayev tells Dora: "You whose heart I know" (*TRN,* 351), and moments later she replies: "You understand everything" (*TRN,* 352). The two lovers understand each other intuitively and do not need words. In fact, their love scene begins where most love scenes end, with a mutual investigation of two lovers into each other's mystery, with a corresponding initiation into knowledge of another person. The scene, however, continues, the lovers speak, and, even as the eroticism intensifies, their initial intuitive union becomes disunion. According to the stage directions, Dora, before uttering a word, "goes towards him and reaches out. But she changes her mind" (*TRN,* 349). Kaliayev has just decided to assassinate the grand duke, and this bloody gesture isolates him. He will, in fact, define himself throughout the love scene by that future act of political justice and, in spite of Dora's entreaties, remains enveloped within it. Dora no doubt fears that her intimate gesture might in some way weaken his resolve. She nevertheless wants Kaliayev to speak about his love for her, to give voice to the emotions contained within him.

Some readers might feel that this is one more example—Marie and Maria come to mind—of what appears to be the Camusian woman's basic weakness: her need to hear and enjoy the language of love. Victoria embraces Diego only after she has heard him speak. One might reply that the need for Don Juan and Clamence to "verify" their sexual powers countless times is no more and no less weak than a woman's desire to have inner thoughts externalized through language. The difference is Camus' own notation that the body speaks for itself but that the human voice speaks for the soul.[29] Camus is unable to synthesize the two, to make the body serve the heart or soul. Literally or figuratively, Camus' female characters are committed to hearing the soul speak. The men are not.

Dora, to this end, asks Kaliayev sixteen questions, and their scene is organized around two of them: "Do you love justice with tenderness?" and "Do you love me with tenderness?" (*TRN*, 352). She is addressing an issue Camus also addressed in his preface to *Right Side and Wrong Side*: whether a man could find a love *or* a form of justice that might in some way correspond to a mother's beatific silence. Dora is telling Kaliayev that she is both a loving woman and a just woman. Her questions are both intellectually abstract and sexually urgent.

Kaliayev offers Dora his own definition of love: "To give everything, sacrifice everything without expecting anything in return" (*TRN*, 351). Dora develops this altruistic definition further and describes love as a "pure and solitary joy" and as a "monologue" (*TRN*, 351). Dora, however, also wishes love to come alive through an expressive dialogue between a man and a woman—hence her sixteen questions. Questions themselves do not necessarily constitute a dialogue. If anything, they might resemble an interrogation, and Kaliayev does at times react as if he were on trial. Dora, nevertheless, clearly wants her questions to be preparations for dialogue, and she is desperate. At one point, she defines herself in a manner that recalls the monologic solitude of selfless love defined by Kaliayev: "Those who love justice have no claims on love. They stand tall as I do, heads raised, eyes fixed" (*TRN*, 351). Dora is sculpting a statue of herself. Immobile, with inexpressive eyes, it is the same statue Camus idealized in *Nuptials* and the same statue Clamence sculpted as his public persona. In each instance, there is no inner life. The public persona, however aesthetically pleasing, remains impenetrable stone.

Dora, however, wants to transform herself in her lover's presence from a statue symbolizing the love of justice into a vital woman of flesh and blood who loves a man. Like Victoria, she meditates on the relationship between love and language: "I ask myself if love . . . could stop being a monologue, if there isn't a response sometimes" (*TRN*, 351). She is referring to her love for the Russian people, who are unaware of her existence. Political reciprocity is impossible because she works in secret. In this scene, however, she is alone with Kaliayev, and both wonder if their love will remain one-sided. Dora takes the first step in initiating an erotic dialogue,[30] and she encourages Kaliayev with the phrase: "Our arms open" (TRN, 351).[31] It is a gesture of preparedness and receptivity, and it calls our attention to a similar passage in "The Growing Stone." The hero, D'Arrast, also de-scribed as "statuesque," is observing with his friend the cook a Macumba dance in South America: "D'Arrast leaned against the wall and crossed his arms. . . . But the chief, cutting through the circle of dancers, came towards [him] and said a few words to the cook. 'Unfold your arms, captain,' the cook said. 'You're embracing yourself, you're preventing the saint's spirit from descending'" (TRN, 1674). The chief opens the circle of dancers to invite D'Arrast to break his own self-embracing circle. By opening his arms, D'Arrast is making a public and spiritual gesture. Dora's invitation is intimate and erotic.

Her anxious questions to Kaliayev are attempts to negotiate her trans-formation from an invulnerable statue into a vulnerable woman in front of a man who keeps pushing her back into abstraction. Dora does not want her transformation to be the negative one we observed in The Stranger: the lineup left to right of the mother, the awkward fiancée, the shouting wife. Meursault hated questions, particularly a woman's questions. So does Kaliayev. I would not go as far as Alan Clayton, who holds that Kaliayev resists Dora's questions and erotic advances to suppress feminine qualities within himself.[32] Each question, however, is a verbal penetration that risks compromising masculine resolve. For his part, Kaliayev admits that he is unable to separate Dora from "the Organization and from justice" (TRN, 352). He prefers that her identity remain entirely political and abstract. She in turn insists on that separation, on her right to relocate her identity away from the collective and the abstract into her living body, and on what a lover owes a beloved, a passion that she identifies as "egotistic." Whatever negative connotations this adjective may have, it also means that Dora is completely there. Kaliayev is there and elsewhere. That Dora can refer to her lover as Kaliayev, Yanek, and "dearest" or "darling" is not insignifi-cant. He is complex, and her relationship with him is nuanced and evolv-ing, depending on the particular moment. For Kaliayev, Dora is always "Dora" and, as much as he loves her, he prefers that she remain an essential and unchanging part of a political organization, a symbol rather than a presence.

One question among the sixteen is the most important. Dora asks: "Would you love me were I unjust?" (TRN, 352). The question goes to the heart of the conflict between love and justice and echoes a celebrated passage from Malraux's *Man's Fate*. Kyo Gisors is trying to sort out what he owes his political party during the Chinese Revolution and what he owes his wife, May: "May was the only person for whom he was not Kyo Gisors, but instead the most intimate complicity. . . . Men are not my equals; it is they who watch me and judge me; my equals are the ones who love me . . . in spite of everything, who love in spite of disgrace, in spite of meanness, in spite of betrayal, who love me and not what I have done or will do."[33]

Kyo is not Kyo Gisors to his wife because he is more to her than his official identity. Politics, based in part on public actions and perceptions, do not have application to their love. He outlines a moral system in which love, rooted in private loyalties, is immune to the vices of external gestures. For this reason, May's infidelity, something she "did," to paraphrase Kyo, has no lasting effect on him. However romantic, Kyo has reconciled love and politics to his own satisfaction. Kaliayev never achieves this resolution with Dora and does not respond to her challenge asking whether he would love her were she unjust. Like Corneille's heroes, Kaliayev's love for Dora is inseparable from esteem and in turn inseparable from her political nature.

The adjective "unjust" leads Dora to use two other astonishing adjectives. They are not strictly logical but belong to an intuitive logic particular to her and to Kaliayev. "Would you love me were I unjust" becomes "Would you love me if I were fickle and easy-going?" (*TRN*, 353). Dora has chosen two adjectives that abolish the stone statue once and for all. Kaliayev still refuses to answer. He fears becoming vulnerable at a time when he needs all his strength for an assassination.

Kaliayev does not answer Dora's questions, but he does react, and his reaction is typical of the Camusian hero. When Marie asked Meursault if he loved her, he answered "no" (*TRN*, 1151); when Rieux, in the opening chapter of *The Plague*, saw his wife's tears, he told her "no" (*TRN*, 1225). In the final pages he saw his mother's tears and ordered her "not to cry" (*TRN*, 1460). Twice Kaliayev commands Dora: "Be quiet!" (*TRN*, 353). Emotions revealed are intolerable, breaching the fortress self. Kaliayev's commands are followed by an admission that compensates somewhat for his male bluntness: "My heart speaks to me only of you" (*TRN*, 353). Kaliayev is not really expressing his love. He is describing it in the form of an inner dialogue. Dora had all along understood that a love scene, particularly in the context of an extreme political crisis, might be egotistical, that it might compromise feelings that were better mobilized and directed toward collective and altruistic ends. It was a matter of either/or. At the same time it is Kaliayev's admission that is truly egotistical because he is speaking to himself. At best, Dora overhears. She instinctively understands Kaliayev's closed, emotional circle and repeatedly tries to intervene and provoke a dramatic, that is, externalized, dialogue. Love would then transform itself from a latent state of mind into a manifest act, from one man speaking to himself into a man and woman speaking to each other. This entire love scene is Dora's attempt to initiate a love scene. Kaliayev repeatedly blocks her efforts. She realizes that she cannot be an object of love for Kaliayev until he confronts her and recognizes her as a vital and independent woman who is willingly giving herself to him.

Catherine, Marie, Maria, Victoria, and now Dora all make profoundly vulnerable and compromising gestures toward Mersault, Meursault, Jan, Diego, and Kaliayev. Dora had reached out to touch Kaliayev and then changed her mind. She already knew he was untouchable. At the end of the scene we read this stage direction: "They will not touch each other" (*TRN*, 354). The prison bars in *The Stranger* and the window bars in *State of Siege* have become in this play inner, invisible barriers and all the more insurmountable. Dora and Kaliayev eventually reunite but only in his death. Camus' original title for the play was *The Rope*, and the rope that hangs Kaliayev becomes their sole, palpable link.[34]

In a sense, Kaliayev was already dead before he died, at least for Dora. Arguing for the flesh and for her presence as a complex woman inhabiting her aroused body, with all the vulnerability that attends such embodiment, she is ultimately arguing for sin and guilt, summed up as "egoism." Kaliayev prefers to speak mystically: "I choose to be innocent," he affirms early in the play (*TRN*, 341), adding that justice "will make our hearts transparent" (*TRN*, 361). Pressing toward innocence and transparency, he defines politics as a radical and necessary redefinition of man "so that the innocent may inhabit the earth" (*TRN*, 322). Kaliayev is basically reiterating, albeit in more poetic and extreme terms, an editorial comment Camus had published in *Combat* in 1944: "Justice for all requires the submission of personality to the collective good" (*E*, 271). To be innocent and transparent means not to be a subjective person. However much Dora and Kaliayev love each other, she can never be a loving subject for him if he cannot be a subject to himself. She states her preference boldly: "Love rather than justice" (*TRN*, 386). Camus himself will be equally bold and years later paraphrase his own character. Verbally attacked by a militant leftist student during the Algerian crisis, he replied: "I believe in justice, but I will defend my mother before justice" (*E*, 1882). Camus was again speaking of love and "necessity" and defending a different kind of love than

Dora. They both understand, however, the value of the real over the abstract.

Dora, moreover, understands Kaliayev not only as a sexual woman and political activist but also maternally. She understands that Kaliayev wants to be a child, an unformed subject, close to innocence and transparency. In the play's most moving scene, she imagines for herself and for the audience her lover's death by hanging, the sound of the trap door opening beneath his feet: "That horrible noise was enough to deliver him back to the joy of childhood" (*TRN*, 392).[35] Shortly afterward, she wonders out loud and with great insight if she is a woman. The tragic pathos is that she is a woman for us but not for Kaliayev or for any other man in the play.

The critical reaction to *The Just Assassins* after the premiere was mixed but not as corrosive as the reaction to *State of Siege*. One particular criticism, however, vexed Camus: "Criticism of *The Just Assassins:* 'No idea of love.' If I had the misfortune not to know love and wanted to put myself in the ridiculous position of seeking instruction, it is not in Paris or the gazettes that I would take my classes" (*C2*, 300). Camus was stung, and he responded privately and sarcastically. Later he wrote, again privately: "I sometimes accuse myself of being incapable of love" (*C3*, 280). Love scenes were therefore more than an aesthetic experiment. It was not only a question, moreover, of the impossibility or inability to love on the part of Camus' major heroes. All the while trying to write a successful love scene, Camus was apparently unaware that he had already succeeded: the fraternal communion of Meursault, who, before D'Arrast opened his arms, opened himself "to the tender indifference of the world" (*TRN*, 1211); Janine's more explicit erotic union with the night sky; the scene of fraternal love between Rieux and Tarrou, who swim in unison off the shore of Oran and do not utter a word, the one indispensable condition of Camus' universe. In each scene Camus gives us detailed descriptions, and in spite of all his efforts in his plays, there is a clear distinction between descriptions in which silence is valued and sustained and dialogues in which silence is broken, almost always tragically.

We should go one step further. It is a risky step given Camus' devotion to the theater, but the root problem in Camus' love scenes in general and dialogue in particular is that he had little or no talent for dramatic art. What I mean by this is the ability of a character, through words, to influence and bring about meaningful change in another character. What chance does Dora have when Kaliayev desires the transparent innocence of childhood? The essential feature of Camus' heroes is "fidelity to the earth,"[36] faithful, in other words, to a mute, maternal power. Dora is therefore "traced over a maternal model."[37] If so, what choice does Dora or any woman have in Camus' works? If Camus' genius is expressed most forcefully in his profound portraits of solitary beings such as Mersault, Meursault, Clamence, Tarrou, Janine, the renegade, Daru, and D'Arrast, does the "other" person truly exist, be it man or woman?

Camus knew this and was torn by it. Love scenes from *The Plague* to *The Just Assassins* demonstrate his attempts to investigate and bring to light a dying civilization and his own "desert nature." Love posed no problem for the young Camus, who made it a matter of transcendent unions with nature on the one hand and basic hygiene on the other. It became an increasingly profound problem when Camus came to view love as a crucial force for Europe's moral and political renaissance. He wrote bluntly in his journal near the end of his life: "For lack of love, concentration camps" (*C3*, 33). Camus continued to formulate projects for love scenes. They would have to be more than Rieux's eloquent dissertations, or Diego's altruism, or Kaliayev's evasions, more than the telegrams separated lovers are forced to send each other in *The Plague*, where the complex emotions of desire and love are reduced to matters of mere health or banal sentiment: "People committed to each other through intellect, the heart, or flesh were reduced to seeking out the signs of their past communion in the capital letters of a ten word telegram. . . . Long lives spent together or painful passions were rapidly summed up in a periodic exchange of trite formulas such as: 'Am well. Thinking of you. Love'" (*TRN*, 1274).

Camus never ceased trying to find a language of love through which character is constructed, revealed, and cherished, not suppressed by silence, banal telegrams, or innocence. "Intellect, the heart and the flesh" are all-inclusive. The human stakes in love's progress or decadence, consequently, will be that much higher. Camus' love scenes up to this moment in his career try to be inclusive but always fail. There is no drama, and there would never be any drama so long as his male characters remained obsessed with innocence and silence. Camus did, however, write one very powerful and successful love scene. It takes place in *The First Man*. It does not involve a man reunited with a maternal nature or childlike men in love with maternal women. It takes place between a boy and his mother.

## CHAPTER 5

# Mothers and Sons

*The First Man* is an incomplete masterpiece, a work in progress fixed in its present form by Camus' early death. The title (Camus was also considering *Adam*)[1] gives some measure of Camus' epic ambition: the story of his childhood played out against the frontier history of French Algeria from its early nineteenth-century settlers to the civil war and against the background of biblical stories and events—Adam and Eve, Cain and Abel, the life of Christ—that also shape our individual and collective lives.

Camus' previous description of his artistic efforts as a "long labor" (*E*, 9) altered significantly during the composition of this novel: "I am going to speak of people I love. And no one else. Profound joy" (*PH*, 312). There remained, no doubt, the tedious and lonely business of writing every day, but Camus sensed that he was tapping into something he had never done before to so great a degree. His evident joy is in writing about himself without restraint, without his customary reserve.[2] Camus complained that his previous artistic achievements were sometimes too tightly structured, his characters perhaps too contained by his private arguments with the world and with people, "that rigidness" (*E*, 12), as he put it. Now he is generous and expansive, and *The First Man* is his most densely populated novel. The "surge of love and detachment" that Germaine Brée astutely observed in *Right Side and Wrong Side*,[3] Camus' earliest collection of personal essays that forms an indispensable backdrop to *The First Man,* is also evident in this last work. It was such a radical departure from almost anything he had written that Camus was willing to exaggerate and affirm: "I was nowhere to be found in what I have said and written" (*PH*, 299). One way to read this remarkable statement is that Camus was Camus in Algeria and not in France. Consequently, whereas the civil war in Algeria, originally planned as the novel's conclusion, was an intellectual exercise for men like Sartre, for Camus it was his very flesh and blood.

*The First Man* is primarily autobiographical. Although he calls himself Jacques Cormery, allowing himself to stand at some aesthetic remove from his principal character, this unfinished work gave Camus the opportunity to achieve what he said in his preface to *Right Side and Wrong Side* he would one day achieve: "That balance . . . between what I am and what I write" (*E*, 12).[4]

"What I am," a simple enough statement, nevertheless required Camus to delve deeply into his own past, into the past of North Africa, and even as far back, if we take the novel's title seriously, as creation itself. Camus wants to know how each human being is shaped by historical and nonhistorical forces such as the French invasion of Algeria, the civil war, and the uncompromising climate. He also examines familial and social structures, including the four other members of Jacques' immediate family and the working-class neighborhood where they lived.

"Each man is the first man," Camus writes, describing each man as a new beginning, but then he cancels his own conclusion by adding, "no one is" (*C3*, 142). Camus is trying to sort out our freedoms from our moral and psychological burdens and from our biological tropisms. Camus is dramatizing, in opposition to the self-regarding heroes of his early works, the identity we constitute for ourselves and the identity other people, things, and places constitute for us. Here is Jacques reflecting on his father's life: "The life of L.C. Never able to exercise his own will, except the will to live and to persist. Orphanage. Farm laborer obliged to marry his wife. His wife goes on despite him—and then the war kills him" (*PH*, 316). We note, and will examine later in greater detail, that Jacques refers to his mother as "his wife," as if he were dealing with two entirely different women. The main point of this grim description is the passivity imposed on his father. His father never had the opportunity to exercise his will, sexually, socially, or politically, in any constructive way. That passivity haunts Camus. He has a mature Jacques stand in front of his father's tomb, in front of his father's passive life. In two powerful movements, he asserts first his willpower, his success in the face of his father's defeat, and then his fear of death and of passivity, which is death in life: "He alone had created himself, he was aware of his strength, his energy, he met life head on and kept control. But . . . that statue that every man molds and hardens in the crucible of experience, into which he then pours himself to await the final return to dust, was rapidly cracking, was already collapsing" (*PH*, 30).

Reminiscent of the idealized, inexpressive statues in *Nuptials*, of Clamence, who had announced, "For the statue to be bare, fine speeches must take flight," this passage reveals a Camus wondering if a man's self-sculpted statue, symbol of a virile and dynamic will, is destined merely to decorate a tomb. He is wondering if, finally, there is no difference between father and son. Only forty years old and trying to comprehend a buried man's meaningless life, Jacques the man-statue "cracks" and experiences an almost literal breakdown. He seems to be dying before his time, suffering in his father's presence a profound, psychic diminution. He nevertheless came from this man. Recognizing this unavoidable and powerful fact of filial continuity within mortal discontinuity, Jacques is able to reclaim himself and reassert his separate but now dependent existence. He does so because he is able to make a father he never knew a major voice in his own life: "Closer to me now than anyone else in the world" (PH, 31). He will investigate his father's life and try to reconstruct it in all its particulars. In so doing, he rethinks his own. Most particularly, he must rethink his relationship with his mother. Camus/Jacques realizes how closely his own life, claustrophobically bound by poverty and an unhappy family, could have retraced itself over his father's absurd life. He comes to understand that he had indeed a predecessor, an understanding that eventually extends to his mother and also his older brother. He realizes that had not this brother been forced to seek employment after finishing elementary school to help put food on the family table, thereby freeing him to pursue advanced studies, there would have been no Camus, willpower or no willpower.

His father's early death haunts Jacques, but even more his mother's fading memory of him. She alone holds the key to understanding a significant portion of his life as fiancé, husband, and the father of two sons. "No one had known him," Camus informs us, "except his mother" (PH, 31). Jacques' many questions to her, several of which she answers vaguely, others not at all, appear simple enough and objective but are in fact anxious attempts to retrieve both father and mother from present and future oblivion:

> His name was Henri, and what else?
> I don't know.
> He didn't have other names?
> I think so, but I don't remember. . . .
> When was he born?
> I don't know.
> And you, in what year were you born?
> I don't know. (PH, 63)

Jacques senses that his father dies one more time with each negative reply. His questions, moreover, objective though they seem, are not entirely altruistic.

Jacques is reflecting on love, marriage, and family. He is convinced that, had his father lived, he would have told his son "the secret of family life" (PH, 181). The word "secret" is never elaborated upon, and the reader is left to wonder what internal and hidden dynamic of family life it could be referring to. Jacques is reflecting, too, on his mother's future death. Will he as her loving son remember her or forget her? Most important, he views his mother's amnesia as a form of infidelity: "He wanted her to become deeply involved in describing a dead man . . . whose life she had shared (and had she truly shared it?) for five years. She couldn't; he couldn't even be sure if she had ever loved that man with passion, and, in any case, he couldn't ask it of her, having become like her mute and infirm; at heart he really did not want to know what there had been between them" (*PH*, 79).

Jacques wants his mother to become "passionate" about describing her husband's life. This son, however, changes the affirmative "shared" into an interrogative and uncertain "shared?" In so doing, he makes the word even more sexually explicit, and he suggests that his father's private life and thoughts may have been completely closed to her. He is not at all sure whether she herself loved him "with passion" and, acquiring his mother's severe handicaps, decides, "mute and infirm," that he does not wish to know any more about their sex life. A son's inquiry into his parents' sexuality results in psychological paralysis. Jacques is therefore close in spirit to Jean Tarrou, who, in *The Plague*, decided that his father had extramarital affairs and, without any evidence, that his parents no longer enjoyed a sexual relationship. His mother, for this reason, looms ever larger in his own emotional life. Reversing a man's usual direction in life, he admits: "It is she I wished to be reunited with" (*TRN*, 1446). Like his predecessors Meursault and Jan, he rejoins his mother in death. It is Jan's sister, Martha, in *The Misunderstanding*, who explicitly summarizes this recurring and incestuous reunion of dead mothers and dead sons: "I leave them to their rediscovered love, to their dark caresses" (*TRN*, 176). She adds, for all those left behind: "They are forever unfaithful to us" (*TRN*, 176).[5] Camus brings into clear light the subjective and incestuous undercurrents in Jacques' objective but urgent questions.

These questions at times resemble an interrogation in the sense that Jacques seeks not only facts but motives. Is his mother merely forgetful or is she unfaithful to her husband's memory? He may conclude that he is perhaps invading his mother's privacy, all the while investigating her sexuality and wondering if his father and mother loved each other as husband and wife. He also knows that he and his brother before him were procreated. Their very existence bespeaks their parents' potent sexuality.

It is a peculiar feature of *The First Man* that Camus does not seem to know what to do with Jacques' brother, who appears and disappears at random in the novel. Nevertheless, inasmuch as each of his heroes, Mer-

sault, Meursault, Jan, Diego, Kaliayev, Rieux, Tarrou, Rambert, Clamence, Jonas, D'Arrast, Daru, is an only child, the presence of two brothers in this last work is a biographical fact as well as conclusive, sexual
evidence. It is the kind of evidence that decisively thwarts the attempt we
see in so many of Camus' unique male characters to view themselves as
self-created, thus denying their fathers' existence.[6] The distinguishing feature of *The First Man,* in contrast, is its inclusiveness. Camus wishes to
leave no possible explanation or motive out of his investigations into
Jacques and his family. Reflecting on his mother's lack of memory, he offers
a sociological reason for her deficiency: "The memories of poor people are
less nourished than those of the rich. . . . Of course, there's always the
heart's memory . . . but the heart wears out with suffering and hard labor,
it forgets sooner under the weight of exhaustion. Only the rich can enjoy
the remembrance of things past" (*PH,* 79). Camus is enjoining the reader
to see the connection between *The First Man* and Marcel Proust's *Remembrance of Things Past* and to note the crucial difference in the class status of
their authors.[7] Once poor, Jacques is now a man of means and can therefore seek out memory's "nourishment." The use of "less nourished" imaginatively links memory with the humble meals of the urban poor. "The
heart wears out" is a general statement that Camus is applying to all human affections among the poor and specifically to his mother's relationship
to her husband.

These sociological arguments are sound, but they are basically intellectual arguments and cannot tell the entire story.[8] They mute Jacques' despair
but cannot dispel it. When Jacques informs his mother that there are flowers on her husband's tomb, she replies: "The French are good people" (*PH,*
73). Jacques reacts to her bland observation: "She said it and believed it,
but without giving another thought to her husband, now forgotten. . . .
And nothing more remained, neither within her or in this house, of that
man devoured by a universal conflagration and of whom there remained a
memory as impalpable as a butterfly wing burned in a forest fire "(*PH,* 73).

The emotions of love and the institution of marriage collapse into utter
meaninglessness. Camus' images of personal loss and universal conflagration, while rooted in his description of the psychological impoverishment
imposed by economic poverty, transcend the sociological to address issues
of psychological disorder and filial sorrow in the context of war and chaos.
"Devoured" puts the entire matter on an epic scale. It contrasts the "less
nourished" of the poor with a personified death's gluttonous and primordial hunger. The human scene in *The First Man* is played against this grim

background that represents the last word in Camus' story: our death and oblivion, to die first in our material body and then in the memories, weakening over time, of those who survive us and who themselves die.

The young Jacques Cormery, like Camus, is an orphan, and he is able to give his entire attention to his mother, his sole surviving parent. What kind of mother and woman she is, therefore, has potentially serious consequences because the child's emotional investment in her is total. A telling episode is Jacques' school registration. He is required to list his mother's profession on an official form, and, unsure of what to write because he had not until now given it much thought, he learns that the proper term is "domestic" (*PH*, 187). His overwhelming "shame at being ashamed" leads him to meditate: "By himself a child is nothing, it is his parents who represent him. It is through them that he defines himself, that he is defined in the eyes of others. It is through them that he feels truly judged, that is to say judged without right of appeal and it is this world's judgment that Jacques had just discovered and, with it, his judgment of his own wretched heart" (*PH*, 187–88).

The young Jacques, discovering something about his mother, discovers something about himself, his "wretched heart," reacting with shame to the news that he and his mother are of low estate. There is no other parent to offer another point of view. Jacques always knew that his family was poor, but now it is true publicly. As he quickly realizes, there is no "appealing" an official document. Discovering his mother's dependency on her employers, who engage her menial services, Jacques discovers his dependency on his parents. He cannot as yet "present" himself; he must be "represented" by his family. This passive situation is already beginning to change through the contrast between the active "defines himself" and the passive "is defined." Jacques has in fact won a scholarship and is entering an institution of higher learning that will separate him still further from his family. The dramatic power of this registration episode derives from the transition, in the space of one paragraph, from a child who is "nothing" to a maturing child's return upon himself as he condemns his "wretched heart." Now divided against himself, both judge and judged, he is no longer nothing.

Although this episode occurs near the end of the manuscript, it highlights the novel's principal story: Jacques' life from birth to adolescence, his separation from his mother, and his periodic returns to her. It dramatizes too the novel's core conflict: an orphan who has no father and who may or may not have a mother. His is a mutilated "representation."

For Jacques, having or not having a mother revolves entirely around the question whether or not she loves him. Perhaps the most chilling episode is the adult Jacques' visit after a prolonged absence. His mother embraces him several times:

> She kissed him . . . and put her arms around him to kiss him one more time. . . . . "My son," she said, "you've been far away." And then, immediately after, having turned away, she went back into her apartment and seated herself in the dining room that faced the street; she didn't seem to be thinking of him anymore nor for that matter of anything else, and sometimes she would look at him with a strange expression, as if he were now . . . an intruder disturbing that narrow, empty, and closed world where she lived alone. (*PH, 58–59*)

Camus describes Jacques' mother, his own mother's ability to withdraw into another world where she is no longer a mother, he no longer a son. Here, too, meaning collapses. It is certainly not a question of personal privacy. Her transformation from mother into stranger is as total as it is sudden, achieved simply by her turning her back.[9] It is a scene that Jacques has observed his entire life. This passage is powerful in part because it raises no questions at all. Jacques has witnessed this scene too often, and he describes his mother's disappearance objectively. It is also powerful because a woman who, as a mother, shares with her son one of the most intimate of human relationships, is the same woman who abandons him utterly to return to a secret world he cannot comprehend. "Narrow" and "closed" put us in mind of the closed coffin of Meursault's mother at the beginning of *The Stranger*. He is invited to "uncover" the coffin and look inside, but he declines. Jacques' mother, though alive, dies to the world and to her son, and her withdrawal exerts a powerful influence on him. Had she been an altogether unloving mother, her disappearance would leave little trace because there would have been nothing there to begin with.

In the final analysis, what Jacques—and Camus—are seeing is themselves, their own capacity to withdraw instantaneously all affect from a human scene, to die to others. Years before writing this description of his mother, Camus described himself during his stay in America and then again during his voyage to South America:

> My curiosity for this country has suddenly come to an end. Like certain people I turn away from without any explanation, having simply lost interest. . . . My heart has simply ceased to speak. (*JV, 42–43*)

The idea of leaving this ship, this narrow cabin, where for days on

end I was able to shelter a heart that had turned away from everything, frightens me a little. (*JV*, 69)

Camus is able to observe his own heart that has "ceased to speak" with the
same understated objectivity he will later use to describe his mother's mute
disappearance. The absence of any explanation argues the absence of subjective motive, of cause and effect. A social mask falls and an alien appears.
It is a phenomenon to be simply noted, not pondered. This sudden demise
of human emotions is recorded as a natural occurrence, "simply."

Camus' cabin, also a coffin, has become his private world, taking its
shape from his closed heart, a cherished prison or shelter from a public stage
that requires displays of emotion and moral accountability. His world is as
closed as his mother's, and they both move about in it "alone." Camus is his
mother because he shares her ascetic, otherworldly nature. He is not his
mother because he went into the world, because he was political, artistic,
and sexual. As the son of a father killed in a war, a deep and abiding sense
of his own manhood required it. Camus, in more formal, intellectual terms,
had already noted this transition from the familiar to the strange in *The
Myth of Sisyphus:* "There are days when, beneath the familiar face of a
woman we had once loved months or years, we perceive a stranger; perhaps
we may even wish for what suddenly leaves us so alone. . . . That denseness
and that strangeness of the world is the absurd" (*E*, 108). Camus' experience with his mother is transferred to the more generic term "woman" and
becomes the basis for generalizing about our absurd relationship to the
world.

If we can assume that love is an attempt by the aroused lover to bring the
beloved into her body, into her material reality, then we can understand
that what Camus is describing is the very opposite, the emotional withdrawal of a beloved—mother or woman—so complete that the body can
reconstitute itself as an incomprehensible thing. The reader may well accept Camus' description of his mother as an objective and biographical
fact. When we read "woman," however, we may also ask who is withdraw-
ing into "thingness," the woman or Camus himself. Are we dealing with
a fact or a tactic? Camus goes so far as to suggest that this strangeness may
even be desirable, that the tactic of withdrawal is part of a larger strategy,
a solitude devoutly to be wished. The phrase "perhaps we may even
wish"—and Camus is now no longer speaking for himself—leaves the entire matter open as to whether Camus is describing a self in a specific,
absurd relationship to the world or projecting instead an image of himself
into the world.

Camus' mother was gone most of the day at work and generally unde-monstrative toward her son. Readers may ask which is worse, a dead father or an absent mother. Reflecting on his father, Camus had admitted bluntly: "No memories, no emotion" (*E*, 29). Without memories, without that nec-essary data with which emotions are constructed, his inner life could never be energized by a dead man he never knew. Camus' relationship with his mother, however, was rooted in another crucial question: his inability to decide whether she loved him and, the same question but in reverse, whether he loved her. In an early essay with the indecisive and pertinent title "Between Yes and No," Camus watches his mother with despair as she disappears once again into her locked world: "This animal silence makes him weep with anguish. He pities his mother, but is this loving her?" (*E*, 25). This crucial question of mutual love and indifference is transposed to *The First Man*, filling the book almost entirely. The stakes are particularly high because Camus is really raising the question whether Jacques himself has an inner life. A dead father and absent mother may have resulted in an ever-expanding inner void. Camus fears, not without reason, that his lifelong praise of "consuming oneself," "emptiness," "oblivion," "being nothing," "indifference," and his early views of love as an unnatural middle-class deformation of sex may have all along been compensatory acts, heroic attempts to reconfigure an anomaly or personal defect into a prescribed way of life.

While Camus reflects on the psychological deprivations experienced in the home, he records Jacques' intense, sensual stimulations outside the home. Not since *Nuptials*, but minus its mystical thrust, has Camus de-scribed with such detail and palpable joy the games, walks, sports, films, streetfights, beaches, girls that Jacques and his friends enjoy. These stimu-lations, however, rarely penetrate beyond the surfaces of the body. Intense as they are, they lack probative power in part because they are so quick in passing, in part because there is no inner voice as yet strong enough to call them in, to slow them down through thought and recollection so as to engage them on a deeper level and to let them make their contributions to the building of a self. Instead they provide the growing Jacques with a magnificent armor of sensation. These pleasures and joys may balance but they cannot compensate for an inner despair or sense of emptiness. Camus, therefore, can refer to Jacques' childhood as "the childhood he had never been cured of" (*PH*, 44). A principal goal of *The First Man* is to expose and analyze that wound or sickness.

Recurrent images throughout the novel link several of the major epi-sodes and serve as regular reminders of Camus' fundamental preoccupation: a boy's relationship with his parents and, through them, with the world. Camus, for example, describes the cemetery where his father is buried as "surrounded by high, grim walls" (*PH,* 27); he presents his working-class neighborhood as a "fortress without a draw-bridge" (*PH,* 138). Both images depict inaccessibility, imprisonment, and isolation from society. Jacques is able with a guard's help to enter the cemetery and gain access to his father's tomb. With Camus as guide, the reader enters Jacques' social milieu and family apartment and further still into the inner dynamics of his evolving character. *The First Man* ultimately tries to cast light on what Camus calls "the dark part of his being" (*PH,* 256). Camus wants to know whether that inner obscurity is a vital one, dense with confused and dimly perceived meanings, or a palpable and potentially destructive void.

The word "dark," metaphorically linked to the "walled" cemetery or "fortress" neighborhood, evokes what is resistant to rational intervention, to understanding, to the light of reason. It binds closely the three places where Camus conducts his investigations into his father's life, his mother's character, and his own: the tomb, the family home, and Jacques' inner self. The novel's suspense is generated by one pervasive uncertainty: will Jacques liberate himself from the ghetto conditions of a childhood circumscribed by poverty, by the intellectual and emotional deprivations such a condition seems to impose? Will he, above all, liberate himself from his mother?

Camus insists throughout his story that he had nothing to work with as a child, no familial or social models to aid him in the transitions from birth to childhood and from childhood to manhood. Negative modifiers highlight most of the novel's episodes. Camus depicts Jacques' youth as "without instruction, without a heritage" (*PH,* 70); "without a past, without morality, without religion" (*PH,* 178); "without a name, without a past" (*PH,* 180); "without a father" (*PH,* 181); "without memories" (*PH,* 307); "without God" (*PH,* 321). We have a litany of negatives, each one reinforcing and sustaining through sheer cumulative power Camus' summary of cultural, familial, and personal deprivation. These same negatives, however, also coexist with a profusion of people, details, and incidents that, taken together, dramatize a boy's rites of passage into manhood and into the world: the first communion, the first scholarship, the first job, the first kiss.

This paradox of manhood and independence achieved out of nothing is not resolved and, because the novel is incomplete, can never be resolved. Camus, however, offers an image early on where this paradox finds its most concrete expression. Jacques was an infant when his father died in

World War I. On his way to the cemetery, Jacques, now in middle age, notices a child near the entrance: "A bright-looking child was sitting in a corner doing his homework on a tombstone not yet inscribed" (*PH*, 27). The novel is rooted in this image. Jacques doing his homework is a recurring image, one means by which he will liberate himself from his family and social class to gain access to other professions, other social classes, what Camus simply calls "the world" (*PH*, 149). Just as the child uses the blank tombstone as support for his written work, so will Camus write and construct his novel on his father's tomb. That this tomb displays an inscribed name is not in itself contradictory. Jacques' inquiries into his father's life and character yield few results. The child's tombstone is "not yet inscribed," untouched and intact, and the father's grave bears a name from which memory and meaningful identity have long since been erased. The father's tomb plays "exit" to the child's "entrance," that final punctuation to human life followed by oblivion and then nothing.

The child is on familiar terms with his desk-tombstone, leans on it, uses it, apparently indifferent to it. Jacques, however, finds as an adult that he has crossed a threshold that divides his past from his future. He learns, to his great shock, that his father died at a younger age than he is now. In a psychologically resonant moment, he calls him a child "unjustly assassinated" (*PH*, 30). Camus depicts his father's death as the unjust assassination of a child, a personal murder of someone singled out as opposed to what he really was, an anonymous victim of a collective butchery. Afterward, inquiring about his father and anxious to learn some specific detail or trait that might nourish his emotions, Jacques asks his mother perhaps the most crucial question of all: "He looked like me?" She replies: "The spitting image" (*PH*, 63). Using a slang expression, the mother validates the assumption that father and son are the same person.

Jacques' question, however, is most unusual. A father, after all, does not resemble his son; it is the son who resembles his father. Camus has transposed into *The First Man* virtually the same dialogue from the early essay "Between Yes and No": "Is it true that I look like my father? Oh, the spitting image" (*E*, 29). The change in *The First Man*, a reversal of pronouns, is both slight and radical. Is this change itself an assassination? The reversal makes Jacques his mother's husband, and she herself agreed they were basically the same person.

The question of incest is set forth in the opening pages and will continue to be explored throughout the novel. That reversal in Jacques' question is both the cause and necessary outcome of his own reaction to his father's early death. Having called him a child, time reverses its course. Caligula, in an exalted state, desired to "change the order of things" (*TRN*, 27). More conservatively, more tragically, Jacques laments: "Something here was out of joint and, in truth, there was no order but only madness and chaos because the son was older than the father" (*PH*, 30).[10] Having summarized his father's life as an example of passive victimization, Jacques pushes him still further into passive childhood. Camus himself informed us that a child "by himself is nothing." Jacques stands over his father's grave, and so does Camus the novelist. They both call forth the procreating father, the former in an act of piety, the latter in the creative and complementary act of writing a novel ostensibly consecrated to his father's memory. But are they calling forth a father or a son? No doubt both. Henri procreated Jacques. As a novelist, however, Camus is the author of a dead and forgotten father. Father and son have become mutually dependent. *The First Man* is simultaneously novel, biography, and autobiography. Camus has set the stage for an Oedipal drama in which the son resurrects his father and symbolically kills him in order to achieve independence, a spiritual rebirth above and beyond his biological birth. This act of murder, distinct from a real war with real victims, takes place in the aesthetic confines of a novel, a fictitious murder compensated by a creative act.

The two tombstones, that of Jacques' father and that of the young boy doing his homework, become the two loci where identity is buried and is resurrected. As Jean Sarocchi points out, the question, "Who is my father?" becomes "Who am I?"[11] "The dark part," however, our inner mystery, makes the question of identity extremely problematic. To name and identify a person is to clarify. To name and identify incorrectly makes identity obscurer still. *The First Man* records Jacques' investigations into his father's past, which in turn becomes the history of Algerian colonization and of his own life. Camus has Jacques visit the tomb at a crucial point in his life: "Forty years old, he realizes that he needs someone to show him the way, a . . . father" (*PH*, 288). The principal "way" for Jacques has essentially two conflicting directions: to continue to move ahead into the world or to return to his mother. Women and erotic encounters, politics and novels, are part of the world. In an early passage, Jacques watches his mother ironing and reflects on social class, sexuality, and a boy's transition into manhood. The description is organized around temporal and spacial separation: "As far back as he could remember, Jacques has always seen her ironing the only pair of pants he and his brother each had, until he left, went off into the world of women who neither wash nor iron" (*PH*, 60). This one mother, this one pair of pants, and this cramped apartment balance a vague and vast world of leisured and anonymous women.

As a son also doing his "duty" and visiting the grave at his mother's request, Jacques wants his father's biography to be accurate and precise. The novel records the many moving episodes when his investigations into his father's character receive either blank stares or vague replies. He learns that his father was an orphan, that he was taciturn and, according to several accounts, "hard, bitter" (PH, 67), that he was also very intelligent and had evidently passed his intelligence on to his second son. With so little to work with, Camus sketches this initial portrait of his father riding a horse-driven wagon: "A Frenchman about thirty, with a blank expression on his face, was looking at the rumps moving rhythmically in front of him" (PH, 12). His blank face prevents Camus from reading his father's expressions and from interpreting the life that might have been revealed there. From one perspective, Jacques finds value in his dependency on an unknown father. It requires him to compose and construct, to think in historical terms, to be active and willful. It requires him to seek evidence and go where the evidence leads. As a rebellious son, however, Jacques reverses chronology, rewrites his father's identity, and transforms him into a son. Now joined to his mother, Jacques becomes passive, silent, and inarticulate. Setting in motion an incestuous and potentially tragic conflict, Jacques is working for and against his father, to whom he owes his very existence, working for and against himself.

The conflict and interaction between the procreative and the creative is very much in evidence throughout the novel. Camus describes the generations that came into being in Algeria as a "journey through the night of years in the land of oblivion where each man was the first man" (PH, 180–81). This passage transports us to a prehistoric era. The emphasis on blindness and oblivion makes the story of Algeria and Camus' ancestors nomadic and precultural, with human lives deprived of light and reason, as well as continuity and structure. Each fatherless birth is merely a senseless repetition, a biological treadmill. Yet each birth is the first. Since each man is first, without predecessors who might limit, define, or in some way condition his identity, he was created in the literal sense, ex nihilo, something out of nothing.

Camus describes his own birth as a miracle. Like the God of the Old Testament, he summons clouds forming thousands of miles away to sweep in over the Atlantic and then over North Africa to break in a fecundating rain over a pregnant and insignificant woman in labor and about to give birth, his mother-to-be. This miracle coexists with more mundane matters of the earth: the rain and mud, the horses pulling the wagon and occasionally defecating, the mother's labor pains, the anxious search for the home and village where the father is reporting for work, the child's birth, the blood lost. The entire episode, with its transcendental and primitive components, seems to be traced over the story of Mary and Joseph seeking shelter to prepare for the birth of Christ.[12]

A doctor, secular representative of scientific skill and knowledge, is summoned but arrives too late. "No more need of you, doctor," he is informed, "it happened by itself" (*PH*, 22). In fact, Jacques' birth is attended to entirely by women, and he is named after the principal one, Madame Jacques. Later on, Jacques will observe that he spent his entire youth "lost among women" (*PH*, 163). This feminine presence is one key to understanding the novel insofar as Jacques, in his early years, is under the tutelage of women. The doctor's only anxious question upon arriving late concerns the umbilical cord. He learns to his relief that it has not been touched, and he cuts it, a banal and significant gesture meant to separate Jacques from his mother. Later in the boy's life, Monsieur Bernard will perform a similar function when he convinces the family to let Jacques apply for a scholarship.[13] Jacques wins and finds himself increasingly cut off from his illiterate mother. Until then, Jacques' birth and early life are organized around his mother and grandmother and around his unrelieved sense of his own solitude, repeatedly underscored throughout the novel not only by the negative preposition "without" but also by the adjective "alone." Ironically, the same adjective that endows the infant with the miraculous privilege of coming into the world alone and unaided by a doctor becomes a crushing burden for a boy trying to become a man: "He had to learn alone, grow up alone . . . find alone his own morality and truth, at last to be born as a man and then, in an even more difficult birth, to be born to others, to women" (*PH*, 181). With each rebirth the responsibility weighs that much more heavily on Jacques' shoulders and, given the economic and psychological circumstances of his family, each stage of his development is in danger of being aborted.

Jacques' early years are recorded in everyday scenes of family life. As a novelist Camus also understood that it was not enough to follow Jacques Cormery's chronological life, that the presence of another son who had already lived through similar circumstances, Uncle Ernest, would help the reader evaluate and understand Jacques that much more. There are scenes between uncle and nephew, such as the beach excursion and the hunt, where the uncle plays exceedingly well the role of surrogate father. These two sons, separately and together, also act out harrowing scenes of family confrontations. They act out the domestic drama of incest where Camus brings to light not so much the sexual circumstances and tensions that obtain between a parent and child but rather the all-important difference between family bonds and human bondage.

In a note that illuminates a key part of this conflict, Camus writes about Jacques' mother: "His mother *is* Christ" (*PH*, 283). Her Christ-like nature, underlined by Camus and amply documented throughout the novel, derives not only from her stoic suffering and sweet nature but also from her unwillingness to judge or punish. That function devolves entirely upon Jacques' grandmother. As aggressive and stern as her daughter is passive and kind, she rules the family as absolute matriarch. When Jacques is late for dinner one evening, his mother says: "You know very well . . ." (*PH*, 56). She is about to scold him, but her words are preceded by a "beautiful, soft look" (*PH*, 56), an expression of love already softening what was going to be a mild reprimand. She is not, however, allowed to complete her sentence. The grandmother intervenes decisively: "Erect in her black dress, her mouth set hard, her eyes clear and stern, his grandmother, whose back he was looking at, cut off her daughter: 'Where were you?' she asked" (*PH*, 56). It does not seem to matter that the child can see only the grandmother's back, one of the most inexpressive parts of the body. Her voice seems that much more disembodied and frightening. Her question, moreover, is purely rhetorical, is in fact an accusation. This confrontation, performed many times before, develops into a scene in which the child sees only the back but the novelist describes the front. "Erect," "set hard," "clear," "stern," each adjective, most of them monosyllables that underline the blunt simplicity of her power, reinforces the grandmother's function as high priestess of inflexible dogma, one that requires a child's absolute obedience. Unlike her Christ-like daughter, whom she chronologically precedes, she stands "erect" for the harsher law of the Old Testament. Representative of an unloving theodicy, she tolerates neither questions, evasions, nor interpretations, and her system of justice is founded on the presumption of guilt. Camus does describe her face, but her features and her posture remain hard and inaccessible. Her moment of redemption in the novel comes when she allows Jacques to prepare for the scholarship exam and her subsequent pride in her grandson's success. Until then, one seldom finds in her facial expression that complexity or occasional uncertainty that would soften her moral posture and encourage plain negotiation. There is nothing in that face that an adult, much less a child, can appeal to. It can only be confronted. The grandmother is "erect," immune to the yielding curves of love or affection. The only bodily contact she knows regarding Jacques is physical punishment, and she beats him until he bleeds.

Jacques' physical suffering intensifies the bond he feels with his mother, whose manual labor and physical handicaps also leave her broken. If she accepts her suffering as consonant with the general human condition and her own personal lot in life, her son does not. She is barely able to speak or hear, and her face becomes the focus of the boy's attention. It is unlike the grandmother's face, simultaneously closed and transparent. Jacques can at least try to read his mute mother, even at the considerable risk of reading into her. Most times, she too has her back turned, lost in her own impenetrable world. When she does face her son, her principal expression is her smile.

We are told that when she gave birth to Jacques, "a marvelous smile transfigured the beautiful, exhausted face" (*PH,* 22), and later: "Her smile . . . had filled and transfigured the hovel" (*PH,* 23). Her smile transforms a child's birth into a celestial event. In a passage that Camus planned to include, a mature Jacques, racked by guilt for having left Algeria and abandoned his mother and trying to make his novel an explanation of why he had to leave, writes: "I am speaking to you, I am writing to you, to you alone, and when I'm finished, I will beg forgiveness and you will smile on me" (*PH,* 319). The appearance yet again of "alone" is psychologically troubling when a grown man wishes to focus entirely on his mother, sole source of his loving attention and exclusive source of forgiveness. All his communicative skills of speaking and writing are directed toward a mother who barely speaks, hardly hears, and cannot read. He dedicates the novel to an illiterate widow. For Camus, that is the point. She intuits her son beyond what is spoken or written, beyond culture and all the pros and cons of interpreted evidence. The mother's smile, reminiscent of Dante's Beatrice, makes palpably real the absence of judgment and the promise of absolute forgiveness. Jacque's need for that forgiveness is an essential component of Camus' own existential dilemma, his incurable nostalgia for innocence.

Camus began the novel with a description of Jacques' birth. There are in fact two beginnings. The second chapter, "forty years later" (*PH,* 25), introduces the adult Jacques boarding a train for Saint-Brieuc, where his father lies buried.

Both chapters are written to invite comparison. The parents travel in a wagon pulled by horses. Jacques is on a train. They travel by night and in the rain. He travels on a clear, spring afternoon. They are poor. He is rich. The mother is in labor, trying to control her tears and her screams on the way to the village. Jacques, "still slender in his raincoat . . . gave an impression of competence and vitality" (*PH,* 25). They do not eat. He dines with his friend Malan on leg of lamb. The horses defecate. Jacques is fastidious and washes his hands several times because of the soot in the train station. The wagon is cluttered, filled with luggage and furniture. Jacques "easily lifted his valise out of the overhead rack" (PH, 26). The father is reporting for a new job as overseer of vineyards. Jacques offers Malan his entire wealth. The mother gives birth. The son she gave birth to, now a man in middle age and in the middle of the journey of his own life, to paraphrase Dante, is on his way to visit his father's tomb.

Camus was not entirely satisfied with this initial presentation of his alter ego. In a footnote we read: "From the beginning, should emphasize what is monstrous in Jacques" (PH, 25).[14] The reader is nevertheless intrigued enough to wonder how such a prince came from such a family. The most marked contrast between the two chapters takes place after the child's birth when the mother's "marvelous smile" transforms a shabby room into Bethlehem. For the adult Jacques we read instead: "A rather elegant young woman passed by the window. . . . She noticed the traveler. He looked at her and smiled and she could not help smiling also. The man lowered the window but the train was already leaving. 'Too bad,' he said. The young woman was still smiling at him" (PH, 25). Camus is sketching an erotic, charming, but trivial attraction between two strangers. "Too bad" settles the matter simply enough. It is appropriate that this brief encounter take place at a railroad station. Jacques is designated as a "traveler," and this woman is merely an erotic stopover. His beauty and charm were apparently so evident and so seductive that the young woman "could not help" but smile. The mother's voyage, existentially dense and complex (one need only compare the smiles), was a voyage toward a new child and what both parents planned as a new life. In Jacques' encounter, like most encounters in Camus' works, a man and woman meet and connect in passing.

His brief voyage cannot compete with the story of Mary and Joseph that informs the entire first chapter. It is a central and determining factor in Camus' approach to the questions of love and sexuality that the luminous, divine aura that haloes the mother never becomes an enabling factor in the Camusian male's relationship with a woman. It is a disabling factor. The biblical underpinnings of Jacques' birth never enrich his understanding of women. They trivialize it. Camus evokes this special moment with his mother during her visit to France: "Mother and I are watching this exquisite night with the same beating heart. But she is going to leave and I always fear I will not see her again " (C3, 190). The mother, too, is leaving, but there is no trivial "too bad," only a profound fear of permanent loss. We hear echoes in this poetic passage of Meursault's solitary communion with the night, as well as Janine's in "The Adulterous Woman." Camus, however, shares this vision with his mother, who is virtually indistinguishable from her son. They have become one and watch the night with "with the same beating heart."

Jacques' sacred and secular relationship with his mother is given its fullest expression during Jacques' preparation for his first communion. Indifferent to dull dogma, Jacques responds sensually to the church, whose dark recesses and tactile mysteries, also synonymous with "the dark part" of his being, inspire this revery: "Dreaming darker, deeper dreams with sacerdotal objects and vestments all lustrous gold in the shadows, meeting at last the mystery . . . that was simply an extension of the bare world he lived in; the warm, inner, and vague mystery in which he was bathed only deepened the everyday mystery of his mother's silence and her discreet smile" (*PH*, 159). The vocabulary of darkness and mystery that described Jacques' "fortress" neighborhood and his father's tomb is reinvested in a church that Camus considers the symbolic extension of his home. Just as sexuality is sublimated in the sacred precincts of a church, so is the mother's smile "discreet." Jacques even notes that he cannot remember ever hearing his mother laugh (*PH*, 61). It is as if laughter, distorting the smile, might somehow be too animal, too erotic. The mother's smile harmonizes with the metaphor of home and church. It elevates the mother to the status of Madonna within whose body the young child "bathes," an image of death or suspended animation, of blissful, amniotic unconsciousness, an image too of potential birth and liberation.[15]

The intimacy of mother and son is reenacted in any number of episodes, such as this first communion. The sacrament of the Catholic church is also ironic in Jacques' particular circumstance. It does not, as intended, prepare the child for his formal initiation into the church and into the world. It allows him to withdraw even further into the protective precincts of a mother.

Their closeness also becomes a structuring device within the narrative itself. Chapter 4, entitled "The Child's Games," depicts how Jacques is forced each day to nap with his grandmother, his exuberant, outdoor play afterward with his friends, and his late return home, when he is first questioned by his grandmother and then beaten. Waiting for the siesta, the boy, walking around the kitchen table again and again, repeats to himself: "Je m'ennuie! Je m'ennuie!" (*PH*, 43), "I'm bored, I'm bored." At the chapter's conclusion, Jacques, beaten but trying as powerfully as he can not to let his tears show, hears his mother whisper: "Mange ta soupe. . . . C'est fini. C'est fini" (PH, 56), "Finish your soup. . . . It's all over, it's all over." Her whisper echoes her son's lament. The two moments are superficially unrelated. Jacques was alone when he chanted his refrain, his mother at work. The two moments are nevertheless intimate. Instinctively, mother and son share a common language. In the original French they rhyme.

It is perplexing at first that this mother could be identified as both Mary and Christ, both mother and child. What Camus is pondering in his description of a boy dreaming of his fluid containment within his mother's sacred body is the situation of a child as yet unable to feel himself as a distinct and separate person.[16] Confined within her, he feels unconfined, full, and limitless, part of an inseparable amalgam, and all the disquiets of self dispelled. The vital question becomes whether this exalted moment will be a phase or a permanent state of being. In a note appended to the manuscript Camus wrote: "We have to choose the second we are born, and we are born separate—except from the mother" (PH, 311). This radical exception controls the narratives of many of Camus' early works up to and including The Plague. Camus describes his containment within the church of the Santissima Annunziata and within a maternal nature in Nuptials; The Stranger begins with the announcement of a mother's death; Jan wishes to rejoin his mother in The Misunderstanding; Rieux's wife in The Plague leaves Oran and is replaced by his mother. Camus, deciding to keep a private journal, begins first with some reflections on a mother and son: "The strange feeling a son has for his mother constitutes his entire sensibility. The manifestations of that sensibility in all realms of experience can be sufficiently explained by the latent, physical memory of his childhood" (C1, 15). In Camus' case, the mother was the only parent. There was no other authority, such as a father's, to intervene and modify the son's "sensibility," a word Camus underlines. The choices that mark a son's gradual independence, according to Camus, engage everyone except the mother. The key issue is whether that private covenant by which Mary and Jesus, mother and son, remain indistinguishable one from the other will or will not translate into a social contract. That contract, "to be born to others," "to women," would transform the divine but imprisoned child into a fully independent and individualized man, a person no longer in bondage.

The son's visit to his unknown father's tomb becomes, therefore, much more than a conventional gesture, even though it began as one. Another man, the father, is making his presence felt in the novel, even though it is a confused and conflicted son who is putting him there. The father's intervention in The First Man has many consequences, among them the fact that Jacques is required to reconsider his mother's sexuality.

Jacques has no sooner rediscovered his father when he learns that he was "obliged to marry his wife" (*PH,* 316). Jacques does not refer to his mother directly but instead keeps his distance by giving her entirely to his father, a gesture that is protective of her identity as Mary and Christ. Pregnant with her first child, Jacques' brother, she belongs to her husband; she is "his wife." The most disturbing discovery for Jacques is that his mother was pregnant before the wedding: "At 45 years of age, comparing dates he discovers that his brother was born after two months of marriage? But his uncle who had just described the wedding ceremony for him talks about a long, slender dress" (*PH,* 289). The question mark after the first declarative sentence makes little sense as grammar but a great deal of sense as denial because the official documents are unlikely to be mistaken. Jacques is required to understand that his mother was sexual. He is reserved about this illicit business but will then describe his own birth with the licit and transcendent force of both the Old and New Testaments.

Some measure of the psychological power as well as the psychological perversion unleashed by Camus' idealization of his mother, the very emblem of innocence, can be gleaned from this wrenching confession appended to the manuscript: "Lovers: he wanted all of them to be virgins, no past, no men. . . . He wanted women to be what he himself was not. And what he was got him involved with women who were just like him and whom he loved and seized with rage and passion" (*PH,* 315). If Camus had not put "loved" before "seized" he might well have been describing rape. These women are guilty of not being Camus' mother, of possessing their own distinctive character. Without "men" and without a "past" they would not be persons at all. Much of *The Fall* was already grounded in this confession. Given the inescapable fact that his mother was seven months pregnant when she married, however, these women may resemble Jacques' mother more than he is willing to admit. Camus' rage at these women may also be directed at his mother, unfaithful to his private image of her.

It is also a direct consequence of his rage against himself. He too is sexual and promiscuous and must consequently recognize and assume his fallen human condition:

> No, I'm not a good son: a good son stays home. . . . I've cheated on
> her with trivialities, fame, a hundred women
> But you loved only her?
> Ah! I loved only her? (*PH,* 317).

Camus uses the image of a husband cheating on his wife to describe a son unfaithful to his mother. In broader terms, Jacques is also unfaithful to an image of himself, the "good" son, an image simultaneously banal, if we mean Jacques, and transcendent, if we mean Christ. The paradox of reading his mother as the Madonna is that Camus can transform her from a real and resistant person into a divine but empty vessel into which he could pour his most profound self-image. The last sentence in the passage also contains a significant nuance. It is an ambiguous response to a direct question whether he loves only his mother. His response is both answer and question. The matter, therefore, remains open. In other passages, the matter is forcefully closed and Camus makes a series of preemptive statements:

> His mother as she was would always remain what he loved most in this world. (*PH*, 116)
> His love, his only love would remain forever mute. (*PH*, 292)
> I gave her my whole heart. (*PH*, 319)

Consonant with these statements are references to the mother as "never conquered" (*PH*, 60) and to her life "without a man" (*PH*, 61). The latter in particular inspires one of the novel's most memorable scenes. A suitor, Antoine, visits Jacques' mother regularly, and she comes back to life in his presence as a sexual woman. Contravening the strict codes of her class, she cuts her hair short. The grandmother is furious at this erotic transformation because only "loose" women cut their hair, and she calls her "a whore" in Jacques' presence (*PH*, 116). Hearing herself called a whore, her first reaction is to meet "her son's steady gaze" (*PH*, 116). "Steady" is ambiguous, perhaps an accusation, perhaps an attempt to comprehend, and she withdraws in tears. Shortly thereafter her brother, Jacques' uncle Ernest, beats Antoine and throws him down the stairs.

This confrontation is particularly brutal because the mother is victimized twice. She is not a whore, but neither is she a Madonna. No one, son included, will allow her to move within the limits of her all too human self. The grandmother is perhaps less guilty than Jacques. She reacted spontaneously and ignorantly to one of her daughter's meager attempts at independence. Jacques, however, is consistent in his poetic praise, and his exalted image of his mother damages both of them more than the grandmother's obscene one. Jacques follows his mother into the bedroom to comfort her: "'Mom, Mom,' Jacques said, touching her timidly with his hand, 'you are very beautiful with your hair like that'" (*PH*, 116). She gestures for him to leave. It was not a son's compliment that she desired. The adverb "timidly" works wonderfully well because it can mean so many things: the gesture of a confused child, the fear of contact with a sexual or divine woman. That timidity is still very much alive in the grown man. This same conversation is repeated many years later, and its resonance clearly echoes in Jacques' mind. He has just arrived from France for a visit: "'You've been to the hairdresser,' Jacques said. She smiled with her look of a little girl caught misbehaving. . . . She had always been coquettish in her own barely visible way. . . . He was going to say: 'You're very beautiful' but stopped himself" (*PH*, 60–61).

He stops because they already had this conversation in cruel circumstances. He stops perhaps not to recall his grandmother's obscene comment and perhaps not to violate a tacit pact which he tries to understand: "It would have meant crossing the invisible barrier behind which . . . she had always been protected—gentle, polite, agreeable, even passive—and yet never conquered by anything or anyone. . . . Beautiful certainly but virtually inaccessible and never more so than when she smiled and when his heart most went out to her" (*PH*, 60). Ironically, we never hear the mother's opinion as to who drew that unbreachable line. Camus describes it in the passive mode, leaving the matter unresolved. This "barrier" is redrawn, as we saw, in the prison bars separating Meursault from Marie in *The Stranger*, the barred window between Diego and Victoria in *State of Siege*, and the invisible barriers in *The Just Assassins* that prevent Kaliayev and Dora from ever touching each other. Camus' description of his mother's divine inaccessibility and of his heart ready to go out to her all the more ardently is both moving and troubling. It portrays filial love but also an illegitimate wish to sterilize the beloved, just as Clamence wished to sterilize his many lovers to keep them in thrall to him.

The father's presence has the salutary effect of moving a domestic scene of a mother and son away from the tragic "rage and passion" toward a more negotiable, more centered human scene. It is his love that made her a mother and his death that allowed the suitor, Antoine, to enter this "fortress" apartment, that allowed Catherine Cormery to be a desiring and desirable woman again. It is, however, the uncle who throws him out, and it is a willfully blind Jacques who, knowing this love story firsthand, knowing his mother had two children, one of them conceived out of wedlock, can, as an adult, still refer to her as "inaccessible."

The difference between a son's bond of love with his mother and filial bondage is imprecise, unclear, and potentially tragic. It is a question of whose will is at work and to what end. The situation of Uncle Ernest becomes a primary means through which Jacques can witness that crucial difference between bonds and bondage in the everyday life of another man, another son.

Ernest, like his sister, is partially deaf and mute. These same handicaps which lead Jacques to reflect upon his mother's divinity lead, in Ernest's case, in the opposite direction. His intelligence is described as "instinctive" (*PH*, 95). His virile power and vitality "exploded in his physical life and its sensations" (*PH*, 96).[17] This life of physiological sensation derives primarily from the pleasures of eating and excreting, so much so that Camus can describe Ernest as a child whose mind never developed beyond the confines of his body and its basic needs. The total absence of intellection permits Camus to press beyond Ernest's human character and view him first as a "prehistoric beast" (*PH*, 96) and afterward as the embodiment of "Adam-like innocence" (*PH*, 98). Ernest has a dog named Brillant. We are not surprised when Camus, who is portraying Jacques as indistinguishable from his mother, considers Ernest indistinguishable from the beast to the extent that, during a hunt, it is easy to confuse "Ernest's yelping . . . with his dog's" (*PH*, 105).[18]

Jacques' mother and uncle are both mindlessly innocent. Their innocence, however, is radically different and affects those around them differently. The mother's Christ-like innocence is that of the eternal victim. She was victimized by a childhood illness that left her deaf and dumb, by a war that killed her husband, by unrelenting work and poverty, by her brother and mother who expelled her suitor, perhaps by a son who places her on a pedestal. What characterizes her life is a virtue that Camus admires but cannot emulate, her stoic passivity: "The truth is, despite all my love, I could never live that life of blind patience, without words, without plans. I could never live her life of ignorance" (*PH*, 304). Given Camus' frame of reference, her innocence is too passive, too feminine, and too maternal. It lacks that active sense of self shaped and catalyzed by willpower and intelligence, making "plans" possible.

Ernest's innocence is aggressive and at times savage, a "natural phenomenon" (*PH*, 108). His sudden and unpremeditated rages are beyond the capacity of reason to intervene, understand, or change. It is Ernest who beats Antoine. In an even more harrowing scene, one that puts Camus in mind of Cain and Abel, he attacks his brother Joséphin. Ernest's mother forcefully intervenes, physically placing herself between her two sons. Ernest threatens to strike her: "You, you," she screams, grabbing him by the hair, "you would strike your mother?" Ernest collapses in tears and moans: "No, no, not you, you're the good Lord to me!" (*PH*, 115). Maternal power alone could check a son's blind rage and prevent a fratricide, if not a matricide. There is morality and conscience here but only one step ahead of the bestial.

Ernest's "almost animal attachment" (*PH*, 118) to his mother is a primitive attachment that, as far removed as it may be from Jacques' exalted vision, has substantially the same effect. It elevates her and abases him. Jacques maintains that he too is "nothing . . . compared to his mother" (*PH*, 256), thus doing violence to himself. Jacques and Ernest both look up to their mothers as divine beings. Only Jacques, however, still young and in the process of maturing, has the mind to wonder whether he too will end up imprisoned within an inarticulate self, not to be dead and eternally mute like his father but imprisoned in a living tomb, be it Ernest the "prehistoric beast" or the mother-church that Jacques enters or constructs around himself. Jacques called his father's life "a life without will" (*PH*, 316). It is true that human will seems helpless in the face of overwhelming physical and moral handicaps and a grinding economic necessity that enslaves both body and spirit. It is also helpless against a maternal love elevated to a divine imperative. Whether the grandmother represents the harsh God of the Old Testament, her son Ernest both Adam and prehistoric beast, whether Jacques' mother is the Christ and church of the New Testament and her son unable to forge a distinct and free identity, in each case the theological prayer or command remains the same: Thy will be done.

Through Ernest and Jacques Camus is exploring the range of mother-son relationships from the primitive to the transcendent, which, we are finally given to understand, is the primitive in its most exalted form. One major difference, however, is that Ernest's love for his mother goes unquestioned. This constancy provides the background that throws into sharp relief Jacques' shifting, contradictory, and evolving relationship with his mother. She may be a Madonna but she is also alien to Jacques' intellectual life. She is alien to the very idea of meaning, and her own meaninglessness will always exercise upon Jacques, upon Camus, the most profound and at times irresistible attraction.

As a student of uncommon intelligence and sensitivity, Jacques comes to the attention of his teacher Monsieur Bernard.[19] The doctor who cut the infant's umbilical cord thought mistakenly that he was separating mother and child. It is Monsieur Bernard who successfully performs this psychological operation. He intervenes in the Cormery family with all the considerable male authority and charm he can muster, and confronts the recalcitrant grandmother, who finally agrees to let her grandson apply for a scholarship. The gap between Jacques and his mother thereafter grows ever wider. The shifting range of emotions between them is already suggested in the episode where Jacques is doing his homework. His mother touches his book, a foreign object to her: "She passed her wrinkled and swollen fingers over the page . . . as if she were trying to understand what a book was . . . a book where her son found . . . a life that was unfamiliar to her and from which he would return, gazing upon her as if she were a stranger" (*PH*, 229).[20] Standing alone at some point beyond culture, by her otherworldliness and by Jacques' deepest, private need to see her there, she becomes increasingly a stranger to her son whose brilliant progress through the French educational system would eventually make him Albert Camus.

The growing distance between them does not follow a clear and uninterrupted line of development. In this passage Camus uses a formal "gaze" to convey their estrangement but also to convey the psychological delicacy of his gesture. Jacques sees something in her beyond the "swollen fingers," a fragility that requires him to be, in this instance, visually discreet and as timid as the time he put his hand on her body "timidly." Mother and son look at each other throughout the novel, rarely at the same time:

> His mother . . . looked at him with her beautiful, gentle look. (*PH*, 56)
> Decades of hard labor had spared the young woman in her that Cormery admired with greedy eyes. (*PH*, 58)
> His mother asked him nothing . . . looked at him with her soft eyes. (*PH*, 208)
> Jacques looked at her greedily. (*PH*, 216)
> "You have done a good job," she said . . . looking at him. He looked at her too. (*PH*, 235)
> Her sad eyes for one moment caressed her child. (*PH*, 252)

The words "soft" and "caressed" respect the codes of maternal and filial love. "Greedily," however, appearing twice, is crossing over into the erotic, as if a son's gaze would not suffice for such a woman. Her maternal nature collapses under the weight of so many hungry eyes. If their eyes seldom meet, it is in order to respect their proper relationship as much as possible.

The pathos is that Jacques does not truly know if his mother loves him, and the boy is almost forced to transgress into the erotic, into the abnormal, to catch a glimpse of the normal. Knowledge of her love does finally take place. It occurs the day Jacques and his brother entertain the family with songs learned especially for the occasion. The situation is banal enough, a grandmother showing off her performing grandsons. The romantic lyrics Jacques sings include "It is really you my man, you whom I loved so much" (*PH*, 89). He has just finished his song:

> Catherine Cormery alone had remained in a corner without saying a word. And Jacques still remembered that Sunday afternoon when, about to leave with his music, he heard his mother say, in reply to a compliment his aunt had paid him: "Yes, it was nice. He's intelligent.

. . ." But when he turned around . . . his mother's eyes were already fixed upon him with such a trembling, sweet, and feverish expression that he stepped back, hesitated, and fled. "She loves me, she really loves me," he said to himself on the staircase, and he understood at the same time that he too loved her desperately, that he craved her love with his entire being, and that until that moment he was never sure. (*PH*, 89–90)

"In a corner" puts the mother out of the way on a family occasion when she would normally take center stage as a proud parent. On this as on every other occasion she abdicates her legitimate authority in deference to her own mother. At the same time, her self-effacement heightens the impact of the revelation of her love. That impact is already suggested when Camus calls her by her full name, "Catherine Cormery." The sheer volume of her given and married names brings her forcefully to the reader's attention, even if no one else has paid her any heed.

With "Jacques remembered," Camus changes the time sequence from a description in the present to the memory of a past scene. This change underlines the scene's enduring power as a revelatory moment that divides Jacques' life with as much force as the day he visited his father's tomb. Jacques is able to remove himself temporally from the scene's powerful emotion just as the child's instinctive decision to "flee" outside removes him in space. "When he turned around" is more than a physiological gesture, even if it begins that way. It traces a revolution that takes place between Jacques and his mother and also within himself. His mother's loving gaze, moreover, was already "fixed," already on him when his back was still turned and, though still discreet, was probably all the more direct and uncensored because his back was turned. Jacques' about-face begins as a vain, banal gesture—he heard a compliment—and becomes a revelation. The three adjectives that describe the mother's look, "trembling, sweet, feverish," encompass without explicitly describing a wide range of emotions. The mother seems as fearful, "trembling," as her son who once touched her "timidly." "Sweet" and "feverish" suggest maternal and erotic emotions, combining a mother's pride with the heat of passion already initiated by Jacques' romantic ballad. The power of this look of love, now shared by both mother and son, is such that Camus needs three verbs to describe Jacques' initially confused reaction: "stepped back, hesitated, and fled." That recoil, hesitation, and flight may be a reaction to something totally unexpected—a mother's expression of love—or a reaction to a love perceived as illicit. What is certain is that they allow the child, even in his state of exaltation, to obtain the necessary distance, solitude, and presence of mind to understand that his mother loves him and that he loves her. "At the same time" restates and strengthens their communion. Their shared glance, however, remains somewhat out of sync because we never see Jacques' glance. Nevertheless, unlike Jacques' dreamy reveries of his sacramental containment within the mother-church, his developing personality here remains separate, distinct, and free. He takes action and is becoming a man.

Camus has written a love scene. He ends where most writers begin. Mother and son, who have always been together, now form a couple. Both have knowledge of each other, but it is not a carnal knowledge. It is true that in this as in any love scene, the man and woman, in this instance a mother and boy, begin to summon each other and themselves into their bodies. "Trembling" and "feverish" signal this difficult passage of inner character into the body, this embodiment. "He too loved her desperately" confirms it. Without the word "mother," this entire scene would have been a dramatic encounter between a man and a woman who discover their love for each other. The language of maternal and filial love and erotic passion once again exhibits its particular isomorphism. It cannot be stressed enough, however, that the revelation for Jacques is not that his mother loves him incestuously, though clearly there are incestuous elements from which the boy "steps back." The revelation is that this mother, almost always located somewhere beyond human history as "Christ" or else in society's lower depths as a servant, has, during a family gathering, entered a human scene to tell her son with her eyes that she loves him. Jacques' confusion about the love he now shares with his mother and the contradictory dynamics of filial and erotic bonds are never resolved. *The First Man* is, in equal parts, the story of a boy's liberation from his mother and the story of a man's return to her.

What matters most to Jacques is the knowledge of this love, the sheer clarity of it, summarized simply enough in the brief phrase "he understood." That clear understanding is superior to confused feelings about dimly perceived mysteries. With this knowledge, Jacques develops and strengthens his will and is able to do something his uncle Ernest could never do or even want to do, which is to rebel and depose his grandmother: "One day, he who until then had patiently accepted being beaten by his grandmother, tore the leather strap out of her hands, suddenly crazy with rage and ready to strike that white head whose clear, cold eyes were driving him mad that the grandmother understood, stepped back . . . moaning . . . that she had raised unnatural children" (PH, 253).

This confrontation is the reverse side of the love scene but shares a similar vocabulary. The grandmother "understands" her grandson's independence with the same clarity that Jacques "understood" his mother's love. The grandmother, like Jacques, also "steps back." Camus' harrowing description establishes the similarities between an adolescent's one moment of madness and his uncle's many inexplicable rages.[21] "Patiently" describes how much Jacques once resembled his mother, but no more. He lists three reasons why he is able and ready to strike his grandmother, Ernest's "good lord": he worked the entire summer to bring home a salary; he became goalie on a soccer team. Like all lists, the most important reason comes last: "This adolescent . . . in a swoon had for the first time tasted a girl's lips" (*PH,* 253). Each reason takes Jacques further out of his home and maternal church, out of the fortress neighborhood and fortress self, and further into the outside world. His sacred covenant with his mother has become, through work, play, and sex, through intelligence and the exercise of willpower, a social contract.

The unnamed girl possesses the principal virtue of existing outside the family circle. As an independent person, she represents another human, subjective perspective that enables Jacques' erotic desires to be satisfied outside the two theodocies of his family. The grandmother calls him "unnatural." Given her former omnipotence, she does so with good reason. Jacques broke God's chain of blind obedience, the family chain, and he will eventually break the chain of poverty. Jacques reaches out beyond bondage and wins the right to strike back and to experience licit love. He wins for himself the right to transform theological commands into a liberated, secular discourse and secular contract where there will never again be a first man.

The hypnotic pull, however, back toward the mother, toward stasis and suspended animation, is always there. *The Stranger* begins with a mother in a coffin and ends with her son in prison. In *Nuptials* mother and nature contain the son whose narrative contains the mother. Jan in *The Misunderstanding* returns to his mother, who murders him. Tarrou thinks about his mother and admits: "It is she I always wanted to be reunited with" (*TRN,* 1446). Tarrou dies, but then, having wished to be a saint and to return to his mother, he was already dead. "Fight" (*TRN,* 1453), his friend Rieux commands him, but Tarrou's disease is not the bacillus.[22] He had long since given up the battle of a son's liberation from his mother. In *The First Man* Camus speaks like Tarrou: "O mother, O tender, beloved child, greater than my times, greater than history that forced you into submission, truer than all that I have loved in this world, O mother, forgive your son for having fled from the night of your truth" (*PH*, 273). This is Camus' Gethsemane. The language of this lyrical prayer is magnificent, and the feelings it conveys are tragic, the feelings of a man willing to deny everything he has achieved and everything he is to return to his mother, to the night of her living death, and to his own oblivion. He does not want the cup to pass from him. Even here, there is perhaps a self-protective gesture. He calls her a child, just as he called his father a child, to hold on to some kind of authority in the face of his own self-willed destruction. Yet calling her a child may inspire pity and only intensify his moves toward her.

Camus, writing this prayer, had already presented the adolescent Jacques as lost in an intoxicating "swoon," taking sexual nourishment from a girl's mouth. Between these two opposite poles, mutually reflective, lies a central and unresolved drama of Camus' work and life. He had expressed the desire "to find again a justice or love" that would reflect and balance his mother and her enigmatic silence. To find again means something was lost, something good worth finding again. Camus taps deeply into an obscure well of confused feelings. The questions of love and sexuality are organized around the question whether to remain hypnotized in and by that dark region—the mother's night, the wish to die—or else bring it to light through art and the will and intelligence that art mobilizes and society demands. Should a man's inner self be furnished, open, populated, or should it be transcendent and perhaps hollow? Should filial love remain private in a self-constructed prison or made to serve more public goals, perhaps as elementary and as revolutionary as a man's ability to love another woman? The man, Camus reminds us, who refuses to love is the man who wants to die. Camus was talking about himself, and he was not talking about loving one's mother but the ability to love a woman. In an appended note to *The First Man* he sums up this profound conflict as "energy and nada" (*PH*, 284), the call to life and the call to death.

Love *or* justice, Camus wrote, perhaps pessimistically, or simply out of modesty. But if his works, both fiction and nonfiction, demonstrate anything about the questions he asked about love and sexuality, it is that love and justice, our private passions and public laws, engage and condition each other. Camus' mother, appearing in various guises throughout his works and in her own person in *The First Man*, is almost always portrayed as innocent, kind, polite, conciliatory, passive, victimized. She demonstrates the power of powerlessness, the irresistible attraction of meaninglessness. Camus was always drawn to her and always struggled, in his art and in his life, to come to terms with her and move on, to be reborn, in his own words, "to others" and "to women." He died too young to find out if ever there would be or indeed could be a resolution.

Sisyphus, pushing his rock up the mountain only to watch it roll back into the dark valley below where the self is mute or dead, was one of Camus' most cherished mythological figures. For himself, Camus knew that with each step he took away from his mother into the populated world where the self speaks and loves, he had only to turn around to see himself turning back.

# Notes

## Chapter 1

1. Donald Lazere writes: "His portrayals of marriage, family life, and women are especially restricted" (*Unique Creation of Albert Camus,* pp. 195–96). Jean Gassin also underlines this aspect of Camus' works: "None of his heroes has a family life" (*L'Univers symbolique d'Albert Camus,* p. 92). He adds: "None of his great heroes is a father" (p. 182); "Compared to a mother's love, conjugal love is a paltry thing in Camus' works" (p. 212).

2. Roger Quilliot is convinced that "the essay form seeks a consensus" (*La Mer et les prisons,* p. 102). The idea of Camus' essays negotiating a point of view with the reader is perhaps better applied to *The Rebel.* Germaine Brée even considers the overall tone of *The Myth of Sisyphus* to be "dictatorial" (*Camus,* p. 194).

3. Jean Bloch-Michel, Camus' friend, felt that Camus, more than most of his contemporaries, was able to make the intimate connection between thought and action that would be a sign of existential authenticity: "How many writers are there who resemble their works, how many for whom honesty is not only to mean what you say but to live according to what you say?" ("Albert Camus et la tentation de l'innocence," p. 375). Bloch-Michel, however, presents as a given what Camus presents as a goal to be achieved. Simone de Beauvoir takes the opposite view: "In Camus' case, there was a profound gap between his life and his art" (*La Force des choses,* p. 65). Olivier Todd, in his excellent biography, quotes Camus, who was completing *The Stranger:* "At this moment there is no distance between my life and my work" (*Albert Camus,* p. 241).

4. Pierre Van Den Heuvel is sensitive to the phenomenon of writing as Camus' attempt to speak silently: "Camus' written word is . . . his 'spoken silence'" ("Parole, mot et silence," p. 65). Alain Costes, studying Camus' theatrical adaptations of the works of Faulkner, Dostoyevsky, and Larivey, sees in them an elaborate attempt to be "silent and speaking simultaneously" (*Albert Camus ou la parole manquante,* p. 211).

5. S. Benyon John explains that "*Nuptials* is directed away from the human world to a larger, non-human collectivity" ("Albert Camus," in *Camus,* ed. Brée, p. 87). Picking up on this point, Alan Clayton states that love in Camus is "the sign of a larger and more basic impulse" ("Camus ou l'impossibilité d'aimer," p. 10).

6. In Camus' summary: "I do not believe in God *and* I am not an atheist" (*C3,* p. 128).

7. Pierre V. Zima's assessment of Meursault is relevant here since Camus' protagonist shares the same impulse as the narrator in *Nuptials*. By "obeying" nature, Meursault submits to "a blind power that accepts no coherence and no subjectivity" ("Indifférence et structures narratives dans *L'Etranger*," in *Albert Camus*, ed. Smets, p. 92). It seems clear, however, that coherence and subjectivity are not synonymous terms for Camus and that coherence is achieved against subjectivity. Laurent Mailhot also writes, "Man 'released from the human' is released first of all from women, sex, and love" (*Albert Camus ou l'imagination du désert*, p. 273).

8. It is necessary to point out that, in celebrating naked bodies on the beaches, Camus had in mind the minority European component of the Algerian population. As he surely knew, Muslim women never disrobed on a public beach. David Sprintzen also summarizes Camus' intellectual and emotional roots: "Algeria was the bodily source. . . . Europe was the mental horizon" (*Camus*, p. 275).

9. Marcia Weis understands the situation in her study of "Nuptials in Tipasa" when she writes: "Life here is one-dimensional, of the senses only, and lived entirely in the present" (*Lyrical Essays of Albert Camus*, p. 132).

10. José Barchilon offers a psychoanalytical interpretation of Camus' revolt against procreation: "The total absence of procreation . . . indicates . . . a level of pregenital fixation" ("Profondeur et limite de la psychologie de l'inconscient chez Camus," in *Albert Camus*, ed. Gay-Crosier and Lévi-Valensi, p. 21). Another striking example of the capacity to escape restrictive forms of love is the last scene in "The Adulterous Woman." Even more striking is that Camus ascribes this capacity exceptionally to a woman, Janine, who feels the same yearning for transcendent unity.

11. Jean Sarocchi interprets the suppression of personality as "the dionysian wish to abolish distinctions" (*Albert Camus et la recherche du père*, p. 102). Frantz Favre also stresses Camus' desire in *Nuptials* "to break with the idea of the individual" ("Camus et la poétique des ruines," p. 114).

12. The Camusian actor, Patrick McCarthy observes, "feels no emotions but mimes them all" (*The Stranger*, p. 85).

13. Examples include Hutcheon, "'Le Renégat ou un esprit confus' comme nouveau récit," pp. 67–87; Mellon, "An Archetypal Analysis of Albert Camus's 'La Pierre qui pousse,'" pp. 934–43; Lynch, "L'Image du colon dans 'La Femme adultère,'" pp. 139–52; Mistacco, "Nomadic Meanings," in *Albert Camus' L'Exil et le royaume: The Third Decade*, ed. Rizzuto, pp. 71–84, and "Mama's Boy," pp. 152–69; Clarke and Makward, "Camus, Faulkner, Dead Mothers," pp. 194–208; Horowitz, "Of Women and Arabs," pp. 54–61; Barberto, "Perception and Ideology," pp. 34–38.

14. Jean Bloch-Michel points out: "Innocence is linked to sensual happiness, to youth . . . the pleasure of bodies," adding this equally important factor: "The innocence of the world is joined to the innocence of man" ("Albert Camus et la tentation de l'innocence," p. 376).

15. Jean Gassin comments on the "stupid" women in Camus' works in *L'Uni-*

*vers symbolique d'Albert Camus,* p. 180, as does Maurice Weyembergh in "Une Lecture nietzchéenne de *La Mort heureuse*" in *Albert Camus,* ed. Smets, p. 44.

16. Identifying nature in Camus' works as the "good mother," the psychoanalyst Alain Costes offers the following interpretation of this containment: "The absolute and everlasting fusion with the good object represents a return to a unified, narcissistic universe whose paradigm is the pre-natal state where . . . all distinctions between Self and Other are abolished" (*Albert Camus et la parole manquante,* p. 64).

17. "Santissima Annunziata" refers simultaneously to the Annunciation and the Virgin Mary who receives the announcement.

18. José Barchilon reminds us that John the Baptist and Christ alone are "of immaculate conception," and we can conclude that Camus, for all his revolt against family and procreation, feels at home in this virgin church ("Profondeur et limite de la psychologie de l'inconscient chez Camus," in *Albert Camus,* ed. Gay-Crosier and Lévi-Valensi, p. 23). Jean Sarocchi also feels that Camus named the hero of *The First Man* Jacques Cormery because his initials, J.C., are also those of Jesus Christ (*Albert Camus et la recherche du père,* p. 188). Olivier Todd also notes that Camus named his twin children Jean and Catherine and that their initials are, once again, the initials of Jesus Christ (*Albert Camus,* p. 741).

19. Jean Sarocchi interprets the transition to tragedy as follows: "Camus will reduce in his fictional works the role . . . of nature and the royal privilege of nudity. . . . Dionysius will be replaced by Oedipus" (*Albert Camus et la recherche du père,* p. 107); similarly Hiroshi Mino: "Becoming God, an easy metamorphosis . . . in *Nuptials,* becomes a bloody business . . . in *Caligula*" (*Le Silence dans l'oeuvre d'Albert Camus,* p. 75).

## Chapter 2

1. Sarocchi offers this insight: "Camus' fictions bear the scar of disappointed love which his Donjaunism conceals and compensates for" (*Albert Camus et la recherche du père,* p. 61). According to Camus' first biographer, Herbert R. Lottman, Camus informed Francine, his second wife, that "he believed in a kind of marriage in which husband and wife would each keep his freedom" (*Albert Camus,* p. 184). Olivier Todd confirms this view: "He gives in and agrees to marry Francine but without promising to be faithful" (*Albert Camus,* p. 226). Again according to Todd, Camus had already spoken "furiously" against marriage, against "that unnatural institution" (ibid., p. 67).

2. "She murmured that I was strange and that was why she probably loved me but that one day I might disgust her for the same reason" (*TRN,* 1156). In an otherwise excellent translation, Matthew Ward renders the last part of that sentence incorrectly as "one day I might hate her for the same reason" (*The Stranger,* p. 42). Only one male character in Camus' works, Marcel in "La Femme adultère," laughs like Marie: "Marcel . . . laughed nervously, like a woman who wants to please a man and is not sure of herself" (*TRN,* 1567).

3. McCarthy, *The Stranger,* p. 50.

4. Ghani Mérad expresses the opinion that the relationship between Meursault and Marie is "a little unusual, if not improbable." He is referring specifically to the importance of female virginity in Mediterranean cultures. This was no doubt true in villages and perhaps still is to this day, but without a complete sociological study it is difficult to assess Mérad's opinion about women in Algiers, a cosmopolitan city (*"L'Etranger* de Camus vu sous un angle psychosociologique," p. 65). Todd observes that in the Algerian middle class, "virginity represents insurance" (*Albert Camus,* p. 60).

5. What Camus described in *Nuptials* is what Avital Talmor identifies as cosmic marriages, orgasmic unions of man and nature that anticipate Janine's transcendent experience in "The Adulterous Woman" ("Beyond 'Wedlock' and 'Hierogamy,'" p. 79). In both his notebooks and later fiction Camus adopted counterpositions to this totalization.

6. Camus is using imagery he had already used for Meursault's confrontation with the Arab in *The Stranger.* Loraine Day's remarks about Janine in "The Adulterous Woman" also apply to Camus in the passage just quoted: "The invasion of her being is experienced not as a violation, but as a sacrament" ("Theme of Death," p. 71).

7. This is no doubt the reason Raymond Gay-Crosier can refer to Meursault as the prototype of an "unselfconscious Donjuanism" ("Camus et le Don Juanisme," p. 818).

8. See p. 15.

9. Sarocchi, *Albert Camus et la recherche du père,* p. 67.

10. Clayton, "Camus ou l'impossibilité d'aimer," p. 17.

11. Sarocchi, "Genèse de *La Mort heureuse,*" in *La Mort heureuse, Cahiers Albert Camus,* 1, pp. 12, 13.

12. In contrast, there is the salesman Marcel in "The Adulterous Woman." Loraine Day examines "his obsession with money and material security" in her article "The Theme of Death."

13. Camus distinguishes himself from his contemporaries in this regard: "As a writer . . . I began by admiring other writers" (*E,* 8).

14. Lottman, *Albert Camus,* p. 619. According to Todd, Camus' friend Pascal Pia wrote to André Malraux about obtaining a stipend for Camus, whose first novel, *The Stranger,* was about to be published: "I know him and he will never ask for anything by himself" (*Albert Camus,* p. 304).

15. Lottman, *Albert Camus,* p. 408.

16. Excrement, in contrast, figures positively in this description of a visit to friends in Italy: "Afterwards we leave in a damp carriage that smells of leather and dung. Male friendship always tastes good" (*C3,* 142).

17. See p. 4.

18. Vicki Mistacco in an important article analyzes Meursault in *The Stranger,* particularly his relationship to women and patriarchy. Her views could also be applied to Patrice Mersault, "Mama's Boy," esp. pp. 161–63.

19. In Ghani Mérad's analysis, Camus had to achieve manhood in a North African society firmly grounded in the "pater familias" (*"L'Etranger de Camus,"* p. 63). As Camus, however, makes abundantly clear in *The First Man,* there were many orphans in Algeria whose fathers were killed in World War I.

20. Several scholars have commented on Camus' "aristocracy": Arnold, *La Poétique du premier Caligula,* in *Caligula version de 1941,* p. 127; Sarocchi, *Albert Camus et la recherche du père,* pp. 54, 133, 272; Gay-Crosier, "Camus et le Donjuanisme," p. 818.

21. Vertone, "La Tentation nihiliste et hédoniste du jeune Camus," p. 78.

22. Quilliot, "Clamence et son masque," p. 90.

23. Several scholars have noted the element of play in Camus' representation of sexuality: Stoltzfus, "Caligula's Mirrors," p. 81; Bartfeld, *L'Effet tragique,* p. 131; Gay-Crosier, "Camus et Sade," p. 167.

24. Meursault's incarceration, in contrast, is unnatural. The guard in *The Stranger* explains the loss of sexual liberty to a Meursault tormented by desire. His enforced abstinence is punitive, as it is for most of the main characters in *The Plague,* particularly Rambert.

25. The relationship between sexuality and asceticism has attracted the attention of scholars: Gay-Crosier, "Camus et le Donjuanisme," p. 827; Meunier, "Approches de l'art camusien," p. 13; Arnold, *La Poétique du premier Caligula,* in *Caligula version de 1941,* p. 15; Viallaneix, *Le Premier Camus,* in *Ecrits de jeunesse,* p. 15.

26. Camus writes further on: "Wisterias. . . . They've been more alive, more present in my life than many individuals . . . except the one who right now is ill next to me and whose silence has never ceased speaking to me for half my life" (*C3,* 263).

## Chapter 3

1. Walter, "Le Complexe d'Abélard ou le célibat des gens de lettres," p. 143.

2. Esposito insults his boss: "Esposito went wild with anger and told him he wasn't a man" (*TRN,* 1600).

3. See p. 47.

4. Camus wrote to Jean Grenier in 1933: "I have only one ambition. To be a man as simply as possible" (*CG,* 16). Marrying Francine Faure, Camus noted, according to Todd: "I consented to try . . . to be like other men" (*Albert Camus,* p. 222).

5. Alan Clayton writes: "No doubt the most serious objection to love is that it conflicts with a certain conception of manliness and heroism" ("Camus ou l'impossibilité d'aimer," p. 15).

6. See pp. 9–12.

7. *E,* 1929.

8. Camus wrote to Grenier: "Ivan suited me, being an intellect without God and without love" (*CG,* 30).

9. Gay-Crosier, "Camus et le Donjuanisme," pp. 818, 826, 825.

10. Scruton, *Sexual Desire,* pp. 82, 106, 111, 121–22.

11. Camus observes a seduction and notes: "I feel an inner pang as I watch her follow him so submissively. They're all submissive at that moment" (*C3*, 270).

12. The word "nothing" controls the opening scene of *Caligula:* "Still nothing"; "Nothing in the morning, nothing in the evening"; "Nothing for three days"; "There's nothing to be done" (*TRN*, 8–9).

13. "To be nothing" appears for the last time in *The First Man*. Camus notes Jacques' "yearning to be nothing" (*PH*, 257). In this instance, however, Camus is looking back on his youth.

14. Carl Viggiani holds the view that fraternity is Camus' "fundamental preoccupation" ("Malraux and Camus," p. 81).

15. Sarocchi, *Albert Camus et la recherche du père*, pp. 99–101.

16. Gay-Crosier, "Camus et le Donjuanisme," p. 827. In his biography, Todd quotes one of Camus' letters in which he compares marriage and friendship: "Chains in marriage and freedom in friendship" (*Albert Camus*, p. 155).

17. Gay-Crosier, "Camus et le Donjuanisme," p. 829.

18. Camus writes: "Disgust, nauseating disgust for that dispersal in other people" (*C2*, 135).

19. Eric Walter asks: "Celibacy and castration: could these be the attributes of a literature that seeks legitimacy in social sterility and, assuming authority through a doctrinaire anti-utilitarianism, postulates its own sterility as a prerequisite for creation?" ("Le Complexe d'Abélard," p. 130). Jean Gassin also writes: "Classically, biological fertility is transposed into the intellectual domain" (*L'Univers symbolique d'Albert Camus*, p. 21).

20. See p. 59.

21. Clamence wonders about himself on this very issue: "I love life, that's my real weakness.... There is something low class about such avidity, don't you agree? Aristocracy is unimaginable without some distance with regards to itself—even to one's own life" (*TRN*, 1514).

22. Lazere, *The Unique Creation of Albert Camus*, p. 208.

23. Similarly we have Camus' view of his novel *The Plague:* "It's a world without women and therefore suffocating" (*JV*, 59).

24. Anderson, *Making Americans*, p. 106.

25. Kaliayev states: "Have you every looked at children? That serious look that they sometimes have. I could never bear that look" (*TRN*, 332).

26. Evelyn H. Zepp summarizes Clamence: "He wants to be total, fixed, complete" ("Self and Other," p. 52).

27. See p. 63.

28. Scholars are divided on this point. Jean Gassin considers the Camusian hero "easily penetrable" ("A Propos de la femme automate," in *Albert Camus,* ed. Gay-Crosier and Lévi-Valensi, p. 83); "Meursault," writes M. G. Barrier, "remains self-enclosed" (*L'Art du récit,* p. 62). Like Gassin, Alain Costes analyzes in Camus' works what he calls the "permeability of the self" (*Albert Camus ou la parole manquante*, p. 75).

29. See p. 28.

30. Camus expresses this view about modern painting: "The Ancients and the classics feminize nature. They entered it. Our painters make her masculine. It is she who enters our eyes, to the point of slashing them" (*C3*, 40). He is describing modern painting exactly the same way Meursault describes the Arab and his knife.

31. *C3*, 33, 56, 170.

32. Scruton, *Sexual Desire*, p. 169.

33. The same vocabulary applies to Don Juan's love: "He must repeat that gift" (*E*, 97).

34. Bartfeld, *L'Effet tragique*, p. 134.

35. George J. Makari offers this insight: "Meursault has withdrawn from the communal rooms and set up a self-sufficient world in the bedroom of his self" ("The Last Four Shots," p. 362).

36. An initial version of Clamence's wish appears in *The Plague*. Describing Rambert's longing for his lover, Camus concludes: "The great desire of an anxious heart is to possess the beloved forever or to be able to plunge this human being, when the time of separation occurs, into a dreamless sleep that would continue unbroken till they meet again" (*TRN*, 1309). The woman is not even to be granted the meager freedom of a private dream. During his lecture tour in South America, Camus wrote to his lover, the actress Maria Casarès: "The man who has not dreamed of a perpetual prison for the woman he loves . . . has not loved" (Todd, *Albert Camus*, p. 500).

37. Sarocchi, *Albert Camus et la recherche du père*, p. 155.

38. Camus describes Tarrou's death: "The human form . . . slowly sank . . . into the floods of the plague" (*TRN*, 1457); Jonas looks at his wife, who has learned of his infidelity: "His heart broken, he saw that Louise had the look of a drowned woman, the look that comes from shock and too much pain" (*TRN*, 1650). Lottman also informs us that Camus in his youth admired a sculpture of "a beautiful girl drowning in the Seine" (*Albert Camus*, p. 111).

39. José Barchilon calls our attention to this fact in "Profondeur et limite de la psychologie de l'inconscient chez Camus: les jeux du narcissime," in *Albert Camus*, ed. Gay-Crosier and Lévi-Valensi, p. 23.

## Chapter 4

1. Todd quotes Camus: "I have no capacity for either love or suffering" (*Albert Camus*, p. 589).

2. Rousseau, *Les Rêveries*, p. 114.

3. Jean Gassin writes about the sexual episodes in Camus' works: "The most detailed descriptions are those where sexuality is usually evoked in the emotional terms of a child at a mother's breast, while genital relationships are only indicated in the most elliptical way" ("Le Sadisme," p. 125).

4. Cryle, *The Thematics of Commitment*, p. 257.

5. This, no doubt, is what Roger Quilliot means when, assessing Camus' views on love, he writes: "Not to love too much in order not to hate too much" (*La Mer et les prisons*, p. 111).

6. Tarrou says: "When I was young, I lived with the idea of my innocence, that is to say, with no ideas at all" (*TRN*, 1420).

7. As Edouard Morot-Sir points out, love is "an opening" ("L'Esthétique d'Albert Camus: logique de la limite, mesure de la mystique," in *Albert Camus*, ed. Gay-Crosier and Lévi-Valensi, p. 94).

8. Tarrou speaks in a similar vein: "I realized that . . . we could not make a single move in this world without running the risk of killing someone" (*TRN*, 1425).

9. Scruton, *Sexual Desire*, p. 237.

10. Rousset, *Leurs Yeux se rencontrèrent*, p. 56.

11. Ibid., p. 77.

12. Camus reportedly told Simone de Beauvoir apropos of love: "We must choose: either it lasts or it consumes; the dilemma is that it cannot last and consume at the same time!" (*La Force des choses*, p. 65).

13. *TRN*, p. 1823.

14. Pierre Van Den Heuvel writes: "Communicating with Marie, physical contact is far more preferable to conventional language where words like *love* and *marry* are problematic" ("Parole, mot et silence," p. 70).

15. Chateaubriand, *Atala*, p. 79.

16. Carina Gadourek calls our attention to the biographical elements in this scene: "The mother's silence . . . takes on a positive value in contrast to the shouts and vulgar expressions of the grandmother" (*Les Innocents et les coupables*, p. 19).

17. Jean Sarocchi summarizes this scene: "Meursault prattling with his lover appears ridiculous next to their harmonious silence and gaze" (*Albert Camus et la recherche du père*, p. 72); Jacqueline Lévi-Valensi speaks of this filial and maternal harmony as a "mute and absolute harmony" ("*La Chute* ou la parole en procès," p. 39).

18. Gassin, "Le Sadisme dans l'oeuvre de Camus," p. 135.

19. See p. 26.

20. This is the second time that Camus employs what we might call an echo dialogue. The first one took place between Caligula and Scipion, identified by A. James Arnold as a "love duet," in *La Poétique du premier Caligula*, in *Caligula version de 1941*, p. 151.

21. Finel-Honigman, "The Orpheus and Euridyce Myth in Camus' *The Plague*," p. 211.

22. In Jean Gassin's opinion: "In Camus' works it is always the woman who loves" ("Compte-rendu," p. 214).

23. Robert W. Greene has written an insightful analysis of love and political fraternity in Malraux's *La Condition humaine*, in "Women and Words in *La Condition humaine*," esp. p. 172.

24. Clayton, "Camus ou l'impossibilité d'aimer," p. 21.

25. Gay-Crosier, "Le Jeu dans le jeu," p. 7.

26. Hermet, *A la rencontre d'Albert Camus*, p. 140.

27. Showalter, *The Stranger*, p. 38.

28. Gay-Crosier, "Le Jeu dans le jeu," p. 53.

29. See p. 98.

30. Alain Costes stresses this point in *Albert Camus ou la parole manquante*, p. 160.

31. Peter Cryle considers this specific gesture essential to our understanding of Camus ("Bodily Positions and Moral Attitudes in *L'Exil et le royaume*," in *Albert Camus' L'Exil et le royaume*, ed. Rizzuto, p. 37).

32. Clayton, "Camus ou l'impossibilité d'aimer," p. 23.

33. *La Condition humaine*, pp. 67–68. Camus quotes this passage in his journal but without commentary: *C1*, 184. In *The First Man*, however, Camus has Jacques Cormery paraphrase Kyo Gisors: "The ones I love, nothing I myself could do, above all nothing they could do would make me not love them" (*PH*, 38).

34. Raymond Gay-Crosier has written an important analysis of this relationship between love and death: "Le Jeu dans le jeu," esp. pp. 51, 53–55.

35. Kaliayev himself had said: "I smile, you see, and I go back to sleep like a child" (*TRN*, 323).

36. Werner, *De La violence au totalitarisme*, p. 31.

37. Costes, *Albert Camus ou la parole manquante*, p. 159.

## Chapter 5

1. Lottman, *Albert Camus*, p. 8.

2. Jean Sarocchi writes: "That reserve, which never concerned him much in life, is at the core of his writing" (*Albert Camus et la recherche du père*, p. 203). A letter from Louis Germain, Camus' elementary school teacher, to Camus, is included in *The First Man*. In it Germain refers to his former pupil's "instinctive reserve" (*PH*, 328).

3. Brée, *Camus*, p. 79.

4. See p. 7.

5. Alain Costes, employing the technical vocabulary of psychoanalysis, interprets this central story of mothers and sons who separate and then reunite: "How to live separated from the original object and how not to die by wishing to return to it" (*Albert Camus ou la parole manquante*, p. 96).

6. I analyze this theme in *Camus' Imperial Vision*.

7. Camus expresses great admiration for Proust's novel, calling it "a heroic and virile work of art" (*C2*, 43).

8. Camus made this statistical observation after World War II: "80% divorce rate among repatriated prisoners. 80% of human loves collapse after five years of separation" (*C2*, 158).

9. Todd quotes from a letter Camus wrote to his lover Yvonne: "I have an intense desire to kiss you, and an intense desire to turn away" (*Albert Camus*, p. 243). In another letter to Mamaine, Arthur Koestler's wife, we read: "Turn a little towards me" (ibid., p. 425).

10. This passage recalls *The Fall*, where Clamence states: "There are no more fathers, no more rules!" (*TRN*, 1545).

11. Sarocchi, *Albert Camus et la recherche du père*, p. 181.

12. Jean Sarocchi also thinks that Camus had Moses in mind in describing Jacques' birth during a rainstorm (ibid., p. 188).

13. Camus writes: "It was he who had sent Jacques into the world" (*PH*, 149).

14. Camus will state again but more emphatically: "He is a monster—and that is what I am" (*PH*, 284).

15. Donald Lazere observes a similar phenomenon in "Between Yes and No" where Camus lies down in bed next to his sleeping mother. She had been assaulted, and he is taking care of her. Lazere talks about the "simultaneous breathing of mother and fetus" *(Unique Creation of Albert Camus*, pp. 77–78).

16. Developing the theme of separation in *La Peste*, Camus refers to a "mother amputated from her son" (*TRN*, 1458), as if the son were an essential part of a maternal body.

17. Jean Sarocchi refers to the mother and father in *The First Man* as revealing "the most unambiguous traits of masculinity and femininity" (*Albert Camus et la recherche du père*, p. 182). Uncle Ernest also embodies virility but in a primitive form.

18. Ernest and his dog form an intimate couple: "Ernest and his dog were inseparable and their mutual understanding was perfect. You could not help thinking of them as a couple. . . . They spoke in onomatopoeia and enjoyed each other's smells" (*PH*, 100–101).

19. Monsieur Bernard is based on Camus' teacher Louis Germain, to whom he dedicated the "Discours de Suède."

20. Camus is writing his own variation of Flaubert's "A Simple Heart" in which the illiterate servant girl Félicité thinks she can find her beloved nephew's house on a map of the Caribbean: "She leaned over the map; the crisscrossing network of colored lines tired her eyesight. . . . She asked [Bourais] to show her the house where Victor lived" (p. 37).

21. In a note appended to the manuscript we also read: "The son who makes his mother respected and strikes his uncle" (*PH*, 273).

22. Tarrou, according to Sarocchi, "belongs to the secret succession of Camus' heroes, more than Rieux" (*Albert Camus et la recherche du père*, p. 139).

# Bibliography

## Works by Camus

*Carnets 1*, mai 1935–février 1942. Paris: Gallimard, 1962.

*Théâtre, Récits, Nouvelles.* Edited by Roger Quilliot. Bruges: Gallimard, 1962, 1967 printing.

*Carnets 2*, janvier 1942–mars 1951. Paris: Gallimard, 1964.

*Essais.* Edited by Roger Quilliot and L. Faucon. Bruges: Gallimard, 1965, 1993 printing.

*La Mort heureuse, Cahiers Albert Camus, 1.* Edited by Jean Sarocchi. Paris: Gallimard, 1971.

*Ecrits de jeunesse d'Albert Camus* in *Le Premier Camus.* Edited by Paul Viallaneix. *Cahiers Albert Camus, 2.* Mayenne: Gallimard, 1973.

*Journaux de voyages.* Edited by Roger Quilliot. Mayenne: Gallimard, 1978.

*Fragments d'un combat, Cahiers Albert Camus, 3.* Edited by Jacqueline Lévi-Valensi and André Abbou. Paris: Gallimard, 1978.

*Correspondance Albert Camus–Jean Grenier 1932–1960.* Edited by Marguerite Dobrenn. Mayenne: Gallimard, 1981.

*Caligula version de 1941 suivi de La Poétique du premier Caligula.* Edited by A. James Arnold. *Cahiers Albert Camus, 4.* Paris: Gallimard, 1984.

*Albert Camus, Editorialiste à L'Express, Cahiers Albert Camus, 6.* Edited by Paul F. Smets. Paris: Gallimard, 1987.

*Carnets 3*, mars 1951–décembre 1959. Paris: Gallimard, 1989.

*Le Premier homme, Cahiers Albert Camus, 7.* Paris: Gallimard, 1994.

## Works Consulted

Abbou, André. "Les Paradoxes du discours dans *L'Etranger:* De la parole directe à l'écriture inverse." *Revue des Lettres Modernes,* nos. 212–16 (1969): 35–76.

Amiot, Anne-Marie. "*La Chute,* ou, de la prison au labyrinth." *Annales de la Faculté des Lettres et Sciences Humaines,* no. 2 (1967): 121–30.

Anderson, Quentin. *The Imperial Self.* New York: Knopf, 1971.

———. *Making Americans: An Essay on Individualism and Money.* New York: Harcourt Brace Jovanovich, 1992.

Archambault, Paul. *Camus' Hellenic Sources.* Chapel Hill: University of North Carolina Press, 1972.

Barberto, Patricia. "Perception and Ideology: Camus as 'Colonizer' in 'The Adulterous Woman.'" *Celfan Review* 7, no. 3 (1988): 34–38.

Barchilon, José. "A Study of Camus' Mythopoeic Tale *The Fall.*" *Journal of the American Psychoanalytic Association* 19 (April 1971): 193–240.

Barnes, Hazel E. *The Literature of Possibility: A Study in Humanistic Existentialism.* London: Tavistock, 1961.

Barrier, Maurice George. *L'Art du récit dans "L'Etranger" d'Albert Camus.* Paris: Nizet, 1966.

Bartfeld, Fernande. "Deux exilés de Camus: Clamence et le renégat." *Revue des Lettres Modernes,* nos. 360–65 (1973): 89–112.

———. *L'Effet tragique: Essai sur le tragique dans l'oeuvre de Camus.* Paris-Geneva: Champion-Slatkine, 1988.

———. "Le Monologue séducteur de *La Chute.*" *Revue des Lettres Modernes,* nos. 904–10 (1989): 119–28.

Barthes, Roland. "*L'Etranger,* roman solaire." *Club (Bulletin du Club du Meilleur Livre),* no. 12 (April 1954): 7.

Beauvoir, Simone de. *La Force des choses.* Paris: Gallimard, 1963.

Bernard, Jacqueline. "The Background of *The Plague:* Albert Camus' Experience in the French Resistance." *Kentucky Romance Quarterly,* no. 2 (1967): 165–73.

Bersani, Leo. "The Stranger's Secrets." *Novel 3,* no. 3 (Spring 1970): 212–24.

Bespaloff, Rachel. "Le Monde du condamné à mort." *Esprit,* no. 163 (January 1950): 1–26.

Bloch-Michel, Jean. "Albert Camus et la tentation de l'innocence." In *Preuves,* 374–84. Paris: Julliard, 1989.

Blythe, Hal, and Charlie Sweet. "Speaking in Tongues: Psychosis in 'The Renegade.'" *Studies in Short Fiction* 25 (Spring 1988): 129–34.

Bonnier, Henry. *Albert Camus ou la force d'être.* Lyon-Paris: Vitte, 1959.

Brady, Patrick. "Manifestations of Eros and Thanatos in *L'Etranger.*" *Twentieth Century Literature* 20 (July 1974): 183–88.

Braun, Lev. *Witness of Decline: Albert Camus, Moralist of the Absurd.* Rutherford, N.J.: Fairleigh Dickinson University Press, 1974.

Brearley, Katherine. "The Theme of Isolation in Camus." *Kentucky French Language Quarterly* 9 (1962): 117–22.

Brée, Germaine. *Albert Camus.* New York: Columbia University Press, 1964.

———. *Camus.* Rev. ed. New Brunswick: Rutgers University Press, 1972.

———. *Camus and Sartre: Crisis and Commitment.* New York: Delacorte Press, 1972.

———, ed. *Camus: A Collection of Critical Essays.* Englewood Cliffs: Prentice-Hall, 1962.

Brisville, Jean-Claude. *Camus.* Paris: Gallimard, 1959.

Brombert, Victor. *The Intellectual Hero.* Philadelphia: Lippincott, 1961.

Burton, Arthur. "Schizophrenia and Existence." *Psychology: Journal for the Study of Interpersonal Processes* 23 (November 1960): 385–94.

Bychowski, Gustav. "The Archaic Object and Alienation." *International Journal of Psycho-Analysis* 43 (1967): 384–93.

Carruth, Hayden. *After the Stranger: Imaginary Dialogue with Camus.* New York: Macmillan, 1965.

Casarès, Maria. *Résidente privilégiée.* Paris: Fayard, 1980.

Castex, Pierre-George. *Albert Camus et "L'Etranger."* Paris: Corti, 1965.

Chaitin, Gilbert D. "Narrative Desire in *L'Etranger.*" In *Camus' "L'Etranger": Fifty Years On,* edited by Adele King, 125–38. New York: St. Martin's Press, 1992.

Champigny, Robert. "Camus' Fictional Works: The Plight of Innocence." *American Society of the Legion of Honor Magazine* 28 (1957): 173–82.

———. *Sur un héros païen.* Paris: Gallimard, 1959.

———. *Humanism and Human Racism: A Critical Study of Essays by Sartre and Camus.* The Hague: Mouton, 1972.

Chateaubriand, Francois-René de. *Atala.* Paris: Garnier-Flammarion, 1964.

Chavanes, Francois. *Albert Camus: "Il Faut Vivre Maintenant."* Paris: Les Editions du Cerf, 1990.

Cielens, Isabelle. *Trois Fonctions de l'exil dans les oeuvres d'Albert Camus: Initiation, révolte, conflit d'identité.* Uppsala: Almquist and Wiksell International, 1985.

Clarke, Deborah, and Christiane P. Makward. "Camus, Faulkner, Dead Mothers: A Dialogue." In *Camus' "L'Etranger": Fifty Years On,* edited by Adele King, 194–208. New York: St. Martin's Press, 1992.

Clayton, Alan J. *Etapes d'un itinéraire spirituel, Albert Camus de 1937 à 1944.* Paris: Lettres Modernes, 1971.

———. "Camus ou l'impossibilité d'aimer." *Revue des Lettres Modernes,* nos. 419–24 (1975): 9–34.

Cohn, Lionel. "La Signification d'autrui chez Camus et chez Kafka, tentative de lecture de Camus et de Kafka d'après la philosophie d'Emmanuel Levinas." *Revue des Lettres Modernes,* nos. 565–69 (1979): 101–30.

Cohn, Robert Greer. "The True Camus." *French Review* 60 (October 1986): 30–38.

Comte-Sponville, Andre, Laurent Bove, and Patrick Renou. *Camus: De L'Absurde à l'amour.* Contains four previously unpublished letters of Camus. Paris: Editions Paroles d'Aube, 1996.

Conroy, Peter V., Jr. "La Vision schizophrène chez Meursault." *Revue des Lettres Modernes,* nos. 479–83 (1976): 129–43.

Coombs, Ilona. *Camus, homme de théâtre.* Paris: Nizet, 1968.

Costes, Alain. *Albert Camus ou la parole manquante; étude psychanalytique.* Paris: Payot, 1973.

———. "Etudes psychanalytiques francophones." *Revue des Lettres Modernes,* nos. 985–92 (1991): 179–92.

Courrière, Yves. *Le Temps des léopards, La Guerre d'Algérie,* vol. 2. Paris: Fayard, 1969. Contains five previously unpublished letters of Camus to Charles Poncet in Algeria.

Crochet, Monique. *Les Mythes dans l'oeuvre de Camus.* Paris: Editions Universitaires, 1973.

Cruickshank, John. "Camus' Technique in *L'Etranger.*" *French Studies* 10 (July 1956): 241–53.

———. "The Art of Allegory in *La Peste.*" *Symposium* 1 (Spring 1957): 61–74.

———. *Albert Camus and the Literature of Revolt.* London: Oxford University Press, 1960.

Cryle, Peter M. "Diversité et symbole dans *L'Exil et le royaume.*" *Revue des Lettres Modernes,* nos. 360–65 (1973): 7–19.

———. "*L'Exil et le royaume*" *d'Albert Camus.* Paris: Lettres Modernes, 1973.

———. "Sur 'Le Renégat' et 'El Hadj ou le traité du faux prophète' d'André Gide." *Revue des Lettres Modernes,* nos. 360–65 (1973): 113–18.

———. *The Thematics of Commitment: The Tower and the Plain.* Princeton: Princeton University Press, 1985.

———. "Espace et éthique dans *La Peste.*" *Roman,* no. 2 (December 1986): 47–56.

Curtis, Jerry L. "Meursault or the Leap of Death." *Rice University Studies* 2 (1971): 41–48.

———. "Camus' Vision of Greatness." *Orbis Literarum* 29 (1974): 338–54.

———. *The Hero Incarceratus in Camus, Beckett, and Desvignes.* Knoxville: New Paradigm Press, 1995.

Day, Loraine. "The Theme of Death in Camus' 'La Femme adultère' and 'Retour à Tipasa.'" *Essays in French Literature,* no. 20 (November 1983): 67–94.

Dennis, William D. "Jean-Baptiste Clamence—A Resurrected Meursault?" *College Language Association Journal* 8 (1964): 81–87.

De Rycke, Robert M. "*La Chute:* The Sterility of Guilt." *Romance Notes* 10 (Spring 1969): 197–203.

Dong-Nai, Ton That. "L'Héroisme moderne de Camus: Une étude de trois femmes." *Chimères* 14 (1981): 73–82.

Doubrovsky, Serge. "La Morale d'Albert Camus." *Preuves,* no. 116 (October 1960): 39–49.

Dubois, Lionel. "*Le Premier homme:* Le roman inachevé de Camus." *French Review* 69 (March 1996): 556–65.

East, Bernard. *Albert Camus ou L'Homme à la recherche d'une morale.* Montreal: Editions Bellarmin, 1984.

Ellison, David R. "The Rhetoric of Dizziness: *La Chute.*" *Contemporary Literature* 24 (Fall 1983): 322–48.

Engleberg, Edward. *The Unknown Distance: From Consciousness to Conscience, Goethe to Camus.* Cambridge, Mass.: Harvard University Press, 1972.

Erkoreka, Yon. "Le Donjuanism." In *Albert Camus: Tout Savoir ou Rien,* 134–36. Montreal: Editions Paulines et Mediaspaul, 1987.

Falk, Eugene H. *Types of Thematic Structure: The Nature and Function of Motifs in Gide, Camus, and Sartre.* Chicago: University of Chicago Press, 1972.

Favre, Frantz. "Camus et la poétique des ruines." *Revue des Lettres Modernes,* nos. 904–10 (1989): 105–16.

Finel-Honigman, Irene. "The Orpheus and Eurydice Myth in Camus' *The Plague.*" *Classical and Modern Literature* 1 (Spring 1981): 207–18.

Fitch, Brian T. "Aesthetic Distance and Inner Space in the Novels of Camus." *Modern Fiction Studies* 10 (Autumn 1964): 279–92.

———. *Le Sentiment d'étrangeté chez Malraux, Sartre, Camus, et S. de Beauvoir.* Paris: Minard, 1964.

———. *Narrateur et narration dans "L'Etranger" d'Albert Camus.* Paris: Lettres Modernes, 1970.

———. "Le Statut précaire du personnage et de l'univers romanesques chez Camus." *Symposium* 24 (Fall 1970): 218–28.

———. *"L'Etranger" d'Albert Camus: Un texte, ses lecteurs, leurs lectures.* Paris: Librairie Larousse, 1972.

———. "Narcisse interprète: *La Chute* comme modèle herméneutique." *Revue des Lettres Modernes,* nos. 632–36 (1982): 89–108.

———. *The Narcissistic Text: A Reading of Camus' Fiction.* Toronto: University of Toronto Press, 1982.

Flaubert, Gustave. "Un Coeur simple." In *Trois Contes.* Paris: Garnier, 1956.

Fletcher, John. "Interpreting *L'Etranger.*" *French Review* 43 (Winter 1970): 158–67.

———. "Meursault's Rhetoric." *Critical Quarterly* 13 (Summer 1971): 125–36.

Fortier, Paul A. *Une Lecture de Camus: La Valeur des éléments descriptifs dans l'oeuvre romanesque.* Paris: Edition Klincksieck, 1977.

Foucault, Michel. *Histoire de la sexualité.* 3 vols. Paris: Gallimard, 1976, 1984.

Fouchet, Max-Pol. "Camus, Mémoire parlée." *Magazine Littéraire* 8 (June 1967): 4–7.

Freeman, Edward. *The Theatre of Albert Camus: A Critical Study.* London: Methuen, 1971.

Frohock, W. M. "Image, Influence, and Sensibility." In *Style and Temper: Studies in French Fiction,* 103–15. Cambridge, Mass.: Harvard University Press, 1967.

Gadourek, Carina. *Les Innocents et les coupables: Essai d'exegèse de l'oeuvre d'Albert Camus.* The Hague: Mouton, 1963.

Gagnebin, Laurent. *Albert Camus dans sa lumière: Essai sur l'évolution de sa pensée.* Lausanne: Cahiers de la Renaissance Vaudoise, 1964.

Gaillard, Pol. *Albert Camus.* Paris: Bordas, 1973.

Galpin, Alfred. "Italian Echoes in Albert Camus: Two Notes on *La Chute.*" *Symposium* 12 (Spring–Fall 1958): 65–79.

Gassin, Jean. "Fils et mère chez Camus: Aux origines d'un lien exceptionnel." *Revue des Lettres Modernes,* nos. 315–22 (1972): 271–73.

———."Le Sadisme dans l'oeuvre de Camus." *Revue des Lettres Modernes,* nos. 360–65 (1973): 121–44.

———. "Compte-rendu: Alain Costes, *Albert Camus ou la parole manquante.*" *Revue des Lettres Modernes,* nos. 360–65 (1973): 199–223.

———. "De Tarrou à Camus: Le Symbolisme de la guillotine." *Revue des Lettres Modernes,* nos. 479–83 (1976): 73–102.

———. "Les Facteurs homosexuels de la création littéraire: Le Cas d'Albert Camus." *Australian Journal of French Studies* 17 (May–August 1980): 181–93.

———. *L'Univers symbolique d'Albert Camus.* Abbeville: Minard, 1981.

Gay-Crosier, Raymond. *Les Envers d'un échec: Etude sur le théâtre d'Albert Camus.* Paris: Minard, 1967.

———. "Camus et le Donjuanisme." *French Review* 41 (May 1968): 818–30.

———. "L'Anarchisme mesuré de Camus." *Symposium* 24 (Fall 1970): 243–53.

———. "L'Absurde hypostasié au dépens de l'espérance." *Revue des Lettres Modernes,* nos. 315–22 (1972): 189–94.

———. "Le Jeu dans le jeu ou la tragi-comédie des *Justes.*" *Revue des Lettres Modernes,* nos. 419–24 (1975): 45–70.

———. "Camus et Sade: Une relation ambigue." *Zeitschrift für Französische Sprache und Literatur,* no. 2 (1988): 166–73.

———. "La Navette entre l'exil et le royaume comme apprentissage du désenchantment chez Albert Camus." *Lendemains* 81 (1996): 70–85.

———, ed. *Albert Camus 1980.* Gainesville: University Presses of Florida, 1980.

Gay-Crosier, Raymond, and Jacqueline Lévi-Valensi, eds. *Albert Camus, oeuvre fermée, oeuvre ouverte?* Paris: Gallimard, 1984.

Geerts, W. "Sur le 'soleil' dans *L'Etranger:* Psychocritique et analyse formelle." *Revue Romane,* no. 8 (1973): 406–7.

Geha, Richard, Jr. "Albert Camus: Another Will for Death." *Psychoanalytic Review* 54 (Winter 1967): 106–22.

Gélinas, Germain Paul. *La Liberté dans la pensée d'Albert Camus.* Fribourg: Editions Universitaires, 1965.

Gharghoury, Marie. *L'Erotique méditerranéenne dans le roman français contemporain (1920–1965).* Sherbrooke: Editions Naaman, 1979.

Gilead, Amihud. "Plato's Eros, Camus' Sisyphus and the Impossibility of Philosophical Satisfaction." *Clio* 17 (Summer 1988): 323–44.

Ginestier, René. *La Pensée de Camus.* Paris: Bordas, 1964.

Girard, René. "Camus' Stranger Retried." *PMLA* 79 (December 1964): 519–33.

Goedert, Georges. *Albert Camus et la question du bonheur.* Luxembourg: Edi-Centre, 1969.

Greene, Robert W. "Fluency, Muteness and Commitment in Camus' *La Peste.*" *French Studies* 34 (October 1980): 421–33.

———. "Women and Words in *La Condition humaine.*" *Modern Language Quarterly* 46 (June 1985): 162–77.

Grenier, Jean. *Albert Camus, souvenirs.* Paris: Gallimard, 1968.

Grenier, Roger. *Albert Camus: Soleil et ombre.* Paris: Gallimard, 1987.

Guérin, Jeanyves. *Albert Camus: Portrait de l'artiste en citoyen.* Paris: Editions Francois Bourin, 1993.

———, ed. *Camus et la politique.* Paris: Edition l'Harmatton, 1986.

Hanna, Thomas. *The Thought and Art of Albert Camus.* Chicago: Regnery, 1958.

———. *The Lyrical Existentialists.* New York: Atheneum, 1962.

Hardstock, Mildred. "Camus' *The Fall*: Dialogue of One." *Modern Fiction Studies* 7 (1961): 357–64.

Hart, Elizabeth. "Le Féminin et l'éthique dans l'oeuvre de Camus." In *Les Trois Guerres d'Albert Camus,* edited by Lionel Dubois, 233–49. Poitiers: Les Editions du Pont-Neuf, 1995.

Hermet, Joseph. *A la rencontre d'Albert Camus.* Paris: Beauchesnes, 1990.

Hewitt, Nicholas. "*La Chute* and *Les Temps Modernes.*" *Essays in French Literature,* no. 10 (1973): 64–81.

*Hommage à Albert Camus.* Paris: Gallimard, 1967.

Horowitz, Louise K. "Of Women and Arabs: Sexual and Racial Polarization in Camus." *Modern Language Studies* 17 (Summer 1987): 54–61.

Hughes, Edward J. *Le Premier homme; La Peste.* Glasgow: University of Glasgow French and German Publications, 1995.

Hutcheon, Linda. "'Le Renégat ou un esprit confus' comme nouveau récit." *Revue des Lettres Modernes,* nos. 360–65 (1973): 67–87.

Imada, Harutoshi. "*Le Premier homme,* roman ou autobiographie." *Etudes Camusiennes* 2: 81–95.

Ionescu, Rica. "Paysage et psychologie dans l'oeuvre de Camus." *Revue des Sciences Humaines* 34 (April–June 1969): 317–30.

Jacobi, Finn. "La Métamorphose de Meursault: Une Interprétation du premier chapitre de *L'Etranger* de Camus." *Revue Romane* 4 (1969): 138–47.

Jeanson, Francis. "Albert Camus ou l'âme révoltée." *Les Temps Modernes,* no. 79 (May 1952): 2070–90.

———. "Pour tout vous dire." *Les Temps Modernes,* no. 83 (August 1952): 354–83.

Johnson, Patricia J. "An Impossible Search for Identity: Theme and Imagery in Camus' 'Le Renégat.'" *Research Studies* 37 (September 1969): 171–82.

———. "A Further Source for Camus' *L'Etranger.*" *Romance Notes* 2 (1970): 465–68.

Johnson, Robert B. "Camus' *La Chute* ou Montherlant s'éloigne." *French Review* 44 (May 1971): 1026–32.

Joiner, Laurence D. "Camus' 'Le Renégat': A Quest for Sexual Identity." *Research Studies* 45 (1977): 171–76.

Kaplan, Donald M. "Homosexuality and American Theater." *Tulane Drama Review* 9 (Spring 1965): 25–55.

Keefe, Terence. "Camus's *La Chute*: Some Outstanding Problems of Interpretation Concerning Clamence's Past." *Modern Language Review* 69 (July 1974): 541–55.

———. "More on Clamence's Interlocutor in Albert Camus' *La Chute.*" *Romance Notes* 16 (Spring 1975): 552–58.

———. "Marriage in the Later Fiction of Camus and Simone de Beauvoir." *Orbis Litterarum* 33 (1978): 69–86.

———. "Clamence and Women in Albert Camus' *La Chute.*" *Modern Fiction Studies* 25 (Winter 1979–80): 646–51.

———. "'Heroes of Our Time' in Three of the Stories of Camus and Simone de Beauvoir." *Forum for Modern Language Studies* 17 (January 1981): 39–54.

Kellogg, Jean Defrees. *Dark Prophets of Hope—Dostoevsky, Sartre, Camus, Faulkner.* Chicago: Loyola University Press, 1975.

King, Adele. *Camus.* Edinburgh: Oliver and Boyd, 1964.

Kirk, Irina. *Dostoevsky and Camus.* Munich: Fink, 1974.

Kirk, Russell. *Enemies of the Permanent Things: Observations of Abnormality in Literature and Politics.* New Rochelle: Arlington House, 1969.

Knapp, Bettina L., ed. *Critical Essays on Albert Camus.* Boston: G. K. Hall, 1980.

Knoff, William F. "A Psychiatrist Reads Camus' *The Stranger.*" *Psychiatric Opinion* (1969): 19–21, 24.

Lazere, Donald. *The Unique Creation of Albert Camus.* New Haven: Yale University Press, 1973.

Lebesque, Morvan. *Camus par lui-même.* Paris: Editions du Seuil, 1965.

Leclerq, P. R. *Rencontres avec Camus.* Paris: L'Ecole, 1970.

Leparulo, William E. "Albert Camus and Italian Renaissance Figurative Arts." *Italian Culture,* no. 4 (1983): 83–91.

Lévi-Valensi, Jacqueline. "*La Chute* ou la parole en procès." *Revue des Lettres Modernes,* nos. 238–44 (1970): 33–57.

———. "*La Peste*" *d'Albert Camus.* Paris: Gallimard, 1991.

———, ed. *Les Critiques de notre temps et Camus.* Paris: Garnier, 1970.

Longstaff, Moya. "A Happy Life and a Happy Death: The Quest of Camus' *L'Etranger.*" *French Review* 64 (October 1990): 54–68.

Lottman, Herbert R. *Albert Camus.* Garden City: Doubleday, 1979.

Luppé, Robert de. *Albert Camus.* Paris: Editions Universitaires, 1952.

Lynch, Martha. "L'Image du colon dans 'La Femme adultère.'" *Revue des Lettres Modernes,* nos. 985–92 (1991): 139–52.

Mailhot, Laurent. *Albert Camus ou L'Imagination du désert.* Montreal: Presses de l'Université de Montréal, 1973.

Majault, Joseph. *Camus, révolte et liberté.* Paris: Editions du Centurion, 1965.

Makari, George J., M.D. "The Last Four Shots: Problems of Intention and Camus' *The Stranger.*" *American Imago* 45 (Winter 1988): 359–74.

Malraux, André. *La Condition humaine.* Paris: Gallimard, 1946.

Manly, William M. "Journey to Consciousness: The Symbolic Pattern of Camus' *L'Etranger.*" *PMLA* 79 (June 1964): 321–28.

Maquet, Albert. *Albert Camus ou L'Invincible été.* Paris: Nouvelles Editions Debresse, 1956.

Massey, Irving. *The Uncreating Word: Romanticism and the Object.* Bloomington: Indiana University Press, 1970.

Masters, Brian. *Camus, a Study.* Totowa: Rowman and Littlefield, 1974.

McCarthy, Patrick. *Camus.* New York: Random House, 1982.

———. *The Stranger.* Cambridge: Cambridge University Press, 1988.

McDowell, Robert E. "Tirso, Byron, and the Don Juan Tradition." *Arlington Quarterly* 1 (Autumn 1969): 52–68.

Mellon, Linda Forge. "An Archetypal Analysis of Albert Camus' 'La Pierre qui pousse': The Quest as Process of Individuation." *French Review* 64 (May 1991): 934–43.

Mérad, Ghani. *L'Etranger* de Camus vu sous un angle psychosociologique." *Revue Romane* 11 (1975): 51–91.

Merton, Thomas. *Albert Camus' "The Plague."* New York: Seabury Press, 1968.

Meunier, André. "Approches de l'art camusien." *Revue des Lettres Modernes,* nos. 212–16 (1969): 9–33.

Miller, Owen J. "L'Image du miroir dans l'oeuvre romanesque de Camus." *Revue des Lettres Modernes,* nos. 212–16 (1969): 129–50.

Mino, Hiroshi. *Le Silence dans l'oeuvre d'Albert Camus.* Mayenne: Corti, 1987.

Mistacco, Vicki. "Mama's Boy: Reading Woman in *L'Etranger.*" In *Camus' L'Etranger: Fifty Years On,* edited by Adele King, 152–69. New York: St. Martin's Press, 1992.

Nguyen Van-Huy, Pierre. *La Métaphysique du bonheur chez Albert Camus.* Neuchâtel: La Baconnière, 1962.

———. "Camus et le problème de la dualité." *University of South Florida Language Quarterly* 8 (Fall–Winter 1969): 9–15.

———. "Camus et le problème de la dualité II." *University of South Florida Language Quarterly* 8 (Spring–Summer 1970): 37–47.

Nguyen Van-Huy, Pierre, and Mai Phan Thi Ngoc, with the collaboration of Jean-René Peltier. *"La Chute" de Camus; ou, Le Dernier testament: Etude du message camusien de responsabilité et d'authenticité selon "La Chute."* Neuchâtel: La Baconnière, 1974.

Nicolas, André. *Une Philosophie de l'existence: Albert Camus.* Paris: Presses Universitaires de France, 1964.

———. *Albert Camus ou Le Vrai Prométhée.* Paris: Seghers, 1966.

Nuttal, A. D. "Did Meursault Mean to Kill the Arab? The Intentional Fallacy Fallacy." *Critical Quarterly* 10 (Spring–Summer 1968): 96–106.

O'Brien, Conor Cruise. *Albert Camus of Europe and Africa.* New York: Viking Press, 1970.

O'Hanlon, Redmond. "The Rite of Friendship: An Analysis of the Bathing Scene in *La Peste.*" *Modern Languages* 61 (September 1980): 120–25.

Onimus, Jean. *Camus.* 3d ed. Paris: Desclée de Brouwer, 1966.

Palmer, William J. "Abelard's Fate: Sexual Politics in Stendhal, Faulkner and Camus." *Mosaic* 7 (1974): 29–41.

Parker, Emmett. *Albert Camus: The Artist in the Arena*. Madison: University of Wisconsin Press, 1965.

Patri, A. "Note sur un sentiment d'étrangeté." *L'Arche* 2 (August–September 1944): 115–17.

Petrey, Sandy. "Speech, Society and Nature in Camus' 'Les Muets.'" *Romance Notes* 22 (Winter 1981): 161–66.

Pichon-Rivière, Arminda A. de, and Willy Baranger. "Répression du deuil et intensification des mécanismes et des angoisses schizo-paranoïdes (notes sur *L'Etranger* de Camus)." *Revue Française de Psychanalyse* 23 (May–June 1959): 409–20.

Pinnoy, M. *Albert Camus*. Paris: Desclée de Brouwer, 1961.

Quilliot, Roger. *La Mer et les prisons: Essai sur Albert Camus*. Paris: Gallimard, 1956.

———. "Camus—*L'Exil et le royaume*." *La Revue Socialiste*, no. 109 (July 1957): 217–18.

———. "Un Monde ambigu." *Preuves*, no. 110 (April 1960): 28–38.

———. *L'Univers théâtral et romanesque d'Albert Camus*. Rodez: Subervie, 1964.

———. "Albert Camus ou les difficultés du langage." *Revue des Lettres Modernes*, nos. 212–16 (1969): 77–102.

———. "Clamence et son masque." *Revue des Lettres Modernes*, nos. 238–44 (1970): 81–100.

Redfern, W. D. "The Prisoners of Stendhal and Camus." *French Review* 41 (April 1968): 649–59.

Reichelberg, Ruth. *Albert Camus: Une Approche du sacré*. Paris: Nizet, 1983.

Rey, Pierre-Louis. *Camus: La Chute*. Paris: Hatier, 1970.

———. *Camus: L'Etranger*. Paris: Hatier, 1970.

Rhein, Phillip. *Albert Camus*. New York: Twayne, 1969.

Richmond, Hugh M. "Personal Identity and Literary Personae." *PMLA* 90 (March 1975): 209–21.

Rizzuto, Anthony. *Camus' Imperial Vision*. Carbondale: Southern Illinois University Press, 1981.

———. "Camus and a Society Without Women." *Modern Language Studies* 13 (Winter, 1983): 3–14.

———. "La Scène d'amour chez Camus." In *Albert Camus: Les Extrèmes et l'équilibre*, edited by David Walker, 211–25. Amsterdam: Rodopi, 1994.

———. "Albert Camus' Don Juan: Class and Sexuality." *MIFLC Review* 5 (October 1995): 29–37.

———. ed. *Albert Camus' "L'Exil et le royaume": The Third Decade*. Toronto: Les Editions Paratexte, 1988.

Roblès, Emmanuel. *Camus: Frère de soleil*. Paris: Editions du Seuil, 1995.

Roeming, Robert F. "The Concept of the Judge-Penitent of Albert Camus." *Transcript of the Wisconsin Academy of Science, Arts, and Letters* 48 (1960): 143–49.

Ross, Stephen. *Literature and Philosophy: An Analysis of the Philosophical Novel*. New York: Appleton-Century-Crofts, 1969.

Rossi, Louis R. "Albert Camus: The Plague of Absurdity." *Kenyon Review* 20 (Summer 1958): 399–422.

Rougemont, Denis de. *L'Amour et l'occident*. Paris: Plon, 1939.

Rousseau, Jean-Jacques. *Les Rêveries du promeneur solitaire*. Paris: Garnier-Flammarion, 1964.

Rousset, Jean. *Leurs Yeux se rencontrèrent*. Paris: Corti, 1981.

Rysten, Felix. *False Prophets in the Fiction of Camus, Dostoevsky, Melville, and Others*. Coral Gables: University of Miami Press, 1972.

Sarocchi, Jean. *Camus*. Paris: Presses Universitaires de Paris, 1968.

———. *Albert Camus et la recherche du père*. Services de Reproduction des Thèses, Université de Lille III, 1979.

———. *Le Dernier Camus ou "Le Premier homme."* Paris: Nizet, 1995.

Sartre, Jean-Paul. "Explication de *L'Etranger*." *Situations*, 1. Paris: Gallimard, 1947.

———. "Réponse à Albert Camus." *Situations*, 4. Paris: Gallimard, 1964.

Scott, Nathan A. *Albert Camus*. New York: Hillary House, 1962.

Scruton, Roger. *Sexual Desire: A Moral Philosophy of the Erotic*. New York: Free Press, 1986.

Seidenberg, Robert. "Fidelity and Jealousy: Socio-Cultural Considerations. *Psychoanalytic Review* 54 (Winter 1967): 27–52.

Shattuck, Roger. "Two Inside Narratives: 'Billy Budd' and '*L'Etranger*.'" *Texas Studies in Literature and Language* 4 (1962): 314–20.

———. *Forbidden Knowledge: From Prometheus to Pornography*. New York: St. Martin's Press, 1996.

Showalter, English, Jr. *Exiles and Strangers: A Reading of Camus's "Exile and the Kingdom."* Columbus: Ohio State University Press, 1984.

———. *The Stranger: Humanity and the Absurd*. Boston: Twayne, 1989.

Simon, Pierre-Henri. *Présence de Camus*. Brussels: Renaissance du Livre, 1961.

———. *L'Homme en procès: Malraux, Sartre, Camus, Saint-Exupéry*. Paris: Petite Bibliothèque Payot, 1965.

Sjursen, Nina. "Meursault un rescapé de la normalisation ou *L'Etranger* 'lu par Foucault.'" *Revue des Lettres Modernes*, nos. 904–10 (1989): 95–104.

Slochower, Harry. "Camus' *The Stranger*: The Silent Society and the Ecstasy of Rage." *American Imago* 26 (Fall 1969): 291–94.

Smets, Paul F., ed. *Albert Camus*. Bruylant-Brussels: Editions de l'Université de Bruxelles, 1985.

Smith, Albert B. "Eden as Symbol in Camus' *L'Etranger*." *Romance Notes* 9 (Autumn 1967): 1–5.

Sperber, Michael A. "Camus' *The Fall*: The Icarus Complex." *American Imago* 26 (Fall 1969): 269–80.

———. "Symptoms and Structures of Borderline Personality Organization." *Literature and Psychology* 23 (1973): 102–13.

Sprintzen, David. *Camus: A Critical Examination*. Philadelphia: Temple University Press, 1988.

St. Aubain, F. C. "Albert Camus: Dialogue or Monologue." *Books Abroad* 31 (Spring 1957): 122–25.

Stamm, Julian L. "Camus' Stranger: His Act of Violence." *American Imago* 26 (Fall 1969): 281–90.

Stephenson, Katherine. "The Signifying Decor in Camus' 'The Wind at Djémila.'" In *Semiotics 1985*, edited by John Deely, 357–65. New York: University Press of America, 1986.

———. "Camus' 'Le Renégat': The Interior Monologue as Psycho-Babble." In *Semiotics 1986*, edited by John Deely and Jonathan Evans, 108–14. New York: University Press of America, 1987.

Sterling, Elwyn F. "Albert Camus: The Psychology of the Body and the Stranger." *USF Language Quarterly* 25, nos. 3–4 (Spring–Summer 1987): 11–20.

Stokle, Norman. *Le Combat d'Albert Camus.* Quebec: Presses de l'Université Laval, 1970.

Stoltzfus, B. F. "Caligula's Mirrors: Camus' Reflexive Dramatization of Play." *French Forum* 8 (January 1983): 75–86.

Storzer, Gerald H. "The Concept of 'Dénuement' in Camus' Prose Fiction." In *Twentieth Century Fiction: Essays for Germaine Brée*, 102–22. New Brunswick: Rutgers University Press, 1975.

Sugden, Leonard W. "Meursault, an Oriental Sage." *French Review* 6 (1974): 196–207.

Sypher, Wylie. *Loss of Self in Modern Literature and Art.* New York: Vintage, 1962.

Takatsuka, Hiroyuki. "L'Amour pour l'inaccessible—écriture comme moyen de 're-garder' la mère." *Etudes Camusiennes*, 2: 53–55.

Talmor, Avital. "Beyond 'Wedlock' and 'Hierogamy': Non-Marriage in Modern Fiction." *Durham University Journal* 77 (December 1984): 79–85.

Tarrow, Susan. *Exile from the Kingdom: A Political Rereading of Albert Camus.* Tuscaloosa: University of Alabama Press, 1985.

Thody, Phillip. *Albert Camus: A Study of His Work.* London: H. Hamilton, 1957.

———. "Meursault et la critique." *Revue des Lettres Modernes* 8 (Autumn 1961): 11–23.

———. *Albert Camus, 1913–1960.* New York: Macmillan, 1962.

Todd, Olivier. *Albert Camus: Une Vie.* Paris: Gallimard, 1996.

Treil, Claude. *L'Indifférence dans l'oeuvre d'Albert Camus.* Sherbrooke: Editions Cosmos, 1971.

Tremblay, V. L. "La Structure mytho-rituelle de l'imaginaire camusienne." *French Review* 62 (April 1989): 783–92.

Tucker, Warren. "*La Chute*: Voie du salut terrestre." *French Review* 43 (April 1970): 737–44.

Van Den Heuvel, Pierre. "Parole, mot et silence: Les Avatars de l'énonciation dans *L'Etranger* d'Albert Camus." *Revue des Lettres Modernes*, nos. 632–36 (1982): 53–88.

Vertone, Téodisio. "La Tentation nihiliste et hédoniste du jeune Camus." *Cahiers d'Etudes Romanes,* no. 6 (1980): 69–82.

Viallaneix, Paul. "Le Testament du *Premier homme.*" *Equinoxe* 13 (1996): 95–99.

Viggiani, Carl A. "Camus' *L'Etranger.*" *PMLA* 71 (1956): 865–87.

———. "Camus and the Fall from Innocence." *Yale French Studies,* no. 25 (Spring 1960): 65–71.

———. "Malraux and Camus, 1935–1960: Master and Disciple?" In *Witnessing Andre Malraux,* edited by Brian Thompson and Carl A. Viggiani, 73–88. Middleton: Wesleyan University Press, 1984.

Vilhena, Maria Da Conceiçáo. "*L'Etranger* de Camus: Parole et silence." *Arquipelago,* no. 2 (1980): 297–315.

Wagner, Robert C. "The Silence of *The Stranger.*" *Modern Fiction Studies* 16 (Spring 1970): 27–40.

Walker, David H. "De *L'Exil et le royaume* au *Premier homme.*" Equinoxe 13 (1996): 83–93.

———, ed. *Albert Camus: Les Extrèmes et l'équilibre. Actes du Colloque de Keele, 25–27 Mars 1993.* Amsterdam: Rodopi, 1994.

Walter, Eric. "Le Complexe d'Abélard ou le célibat des gens de lettres." In *Dix-Huitième Siècle, Représentations de la vie sexuelle,* 127–52. Paris: Garnier, 1980.

Ward, Matthew, trans. *The Stranger.* New York: Vintage, 1988.

Wasserton, William. "In Gertrude's Closet." *Yale Review* 48 (1958): 245–65.

Weis, Marcia. *The Lyrical Essays of Albert Camus.* Sherbrooke: Editions Naaman de Sherbrooke, 1976.

Werner, Eric. *De la violence au totalitarisme: Essai sur la pensée de Camus et de Sartre.* Paris: Calmann-Lévy, 1972.

Willhoite, Fred H. *Beyond Nihilism: Albert Camus' Contribution to Political Thought.* Baton Rouge: Louisiana State University Press, 1968.

Woefel, James W. *Camus: A Theological Perspective.* Nashville: Abingdon Press, 1975.

———. *Albert Camus on the Sacred and the Secular.* Lanham: University Press of America, 1987.

Zants, Emily. "Camus' Deserts and Their Allies, Kingdoms of the Stranger." *Symposium* 17 (1963): 30–41.

Zepp, Evelyn H. "Dialogizing the Monologue: The Creation of the 'Double-Voiced' World in Camus' *La Chute.*" *Symposium* 35 (Winter 1981–82): 357–71.

———. "The Generic Ambiguity of Albert Camus' *La Chute.*" *French Forum* 7 (September 1982): 252–59.

———. "Self and Other: Identity as Dialogical Confrontation in *La Chute.*" *Perspectives on Contemporary Literature* 12 (1986): 51–56.

# Index

Anthony Rizzuto is an associate professor of French at the State University of New York at Stony Brook. He is a specialist in nineteenth- and twentieth-century literatures. In addition to numerous articles on Musset, Reverdy, Sartre, and Camus, he has published *Style and Theme in Pierre Reverdy's "Les Ardoises du toit"* (1971) and *Camus' Imperial Vision* (1981) and is the editor of *Albert Camus' "L'Exil et le royaume": The Third Decade* (1988). He is the recipient of a Fulbright fellowship and a National Endowment for the Humanities summer grant.